Bird Boxes and Feeders for the Garden

Bird Boxes and Feeders for the Garden

Dave Mackenzie

GUILD OF MASTER CRAFTSMAN PUBLICATIONS LTD

First published 1997 by
Guild of Master Craftsman Publications Ltd,
166 High Street, Lewes,
East Sussex, BN7 1XU

Reprinted 1998

ISBN 1 86108 065 4

Photographs by Dave Mackenzie, except: photos of wildlife on pages *vi*, 29, 41, 44, 47, 55, 65, 77, 99, 112, 151, and 165 courtesy of Windrush Photographic Agency; photos of boxes and feeders on pages 29, 30, 35, 41, 46, 52, 55, 56, 61, 67, 73, 77, 78, 82, 88, 95, 99, 100, 109, 116, 121, 122, 128, 144, 151, 152, and 157 by Dennis Bunn.

Line drawings by Dave Mackenzie, except decorative birds by John Yates

Designed by Ian Hunt Design

Typefaces: Palatino and Cygnet

Originated and printed in Singapore under the supervision of MRM Graphics

Contents

Introduction

The countryside is in a constant state of change. When you look across acres of green fields with animals grazing or rows of crops with the odd area of woodland, it looks timeless, but this is not so. At one time most of the countryside was covered with forests, except where the conditions were not good for trees. These have, to a large part, been cleared to enable arable and livestock farming. In the last 45 years the pace of change has accelerated, and large tracts of open land are disappearing due to urban development and road building.

Farming methods are also changing, hedgerows are disappearing, ponds and wetlands are being drained, and cropping is denser. All of this puts a strain on wildlife survival and emphasizes the importance of creating gardens as a life-saving environment.

KESTREL

In the centre of a city, gardens and open spaces are the service stations that give wildlife the facilities they require to survive. This applies particularly to birds who migrate through inhospitable parts to get to green areas rich in food. However, other wildlife also penetrate the inhospitable areas, via the urban waterways and the overgrown banks of the railways, to 'commute' to the city centres.

Given that gardens are vital to the wellbeing of many birds and small animals, how can they be made a more attractive place for them? The basic requirements for all living creatures are food, water and shelter, so if these are provided then the wildlife will follow. Putting out kitchen scraps in a suitable feeder will instantly attract many birds and if a wide variety of food, together with a container of water, is presented, this will attract a greater number of species. Feeding birds is now so popular, it is almost a national pastime. Organizations such as the Royal Society for the Protection of Birds (RSPB) has millions of members, most of whom first became interested in wildlife by feeding the common garden birds.

Many people find that an enthusiasm for wildlife goes hand in hand with an affection for other animals as pets and companions. Because these also require care and accommodation some of the projects presented are for them.

NOTE ON MEASUREMENTS

True and accurate measurements are given in imperial: the metric measurements given are only conversions from these. Throughout the book instances will be found where an imperial measurement has slightly differing metric equivalents as these have been rounded up or down in each case.

1

MATERIALS

Wood for nest boxes does not have to be of the highest quality. Given a choice, it is better to get it with a rough, sawn finish because the surface has more grip, which will help the chicks climb out of the box. Ensure, wherever possible, that the wood is seasoned timber to avoid problems with cracking as it dries out. Cracks in a nest box will let in a draught and nest boxes should be as warm and snug as possible for the birds to successfully raise a family.

SOLID TIMBER

Solid timber can be obtained new from DIY stores and timber merchants, or acquired from second-hand sources and recycled. It is categorized into two types, hardwood and softwood, and both are suitable for our purposes. In general hardwood is more expensive, but the finished project will be more durable. Softwood is easier to obtain: most DIY outlets stock it in standard sizes, either planed or with a sawn finish.

All woods resist rotting to a certain degree. In general, hardwoods are more resistant than softwoods, although there are exceptions. For example, Canadian redwood is a softwood, but is very water-resistant. Of the British hardwoods, elm is the most waterproof, and oak is also very good.

HARDWOODS

Most hardwoods are suitable for the projects in this book, although I avoid rainforest timbers because of the environmental concerns associated with them. In any case, they are generally too expensive to use for this type of project. Oak, elm or beech, if they can be obtained for a reasonable price, are eminently suitable as they will last for many years. Elm in particular is naturally water-resistant and is used for garden furniture, lock gates and coffins. Unfortunately, supplies of home-grown elm have dwindled due to Dutch elm disease. Oak is probably the easiest suitable hardwood to obtain.

SOFTWOODS

Pine, fir, larch and spruce are all softwoods sold under the collective name of pine at timber merchants and DIY stores. Most of them are not as durable as hardwood, but, treated with a water-resistant finish, will last for 10 or 15 years, which is probably long enough. Redwood, from North America, is naturally resistant to water and will last as long as hardwoods. Tongue-and-groove pine floorboards are one of the cheapest ways of getting new pine boards that are suitable for making nest boxes and feeders.

SECOND-HAND

Both hardwood and softwood can be obtained second-hand for much lower prices or even free of charge. Builders' merchants and demolition companies sell second-hand softwood floorboards and roof joists, all of which can be used.

The place to look for free timber is in skips or at the houses of friends and neighbours who are spring cleaning. People throw away large amounts of timber that is suitable for our purposes, or burn it as rubbish. Old fencing, furniture, packing cases and pallets can all

provide useful pieces of timber and the birds do not care if their 'des. res.' started life as a packing case. If you obtain second-hand material there is extra work involved in making it ready for use. Most importantly, all nails, staples, and tacks must be found and extracted because of the damage they will do to saws and chisels.

RUSTIC

A couple of the projects use logs and timber with the bark still attached. This can be obtained from saw mills and timber contractors – this timber is from the part of the tree that is usually thrown on the scrap pile. Most saw mills will let you take wood from the scrap pile for a small charge or for nothing and neighbours cutting down a tree are usually very happy to let you dispose of any logs they have lying around. That is how I obtained the log to make the rustic nesting box for blue tits. The type of tree is not important.

Man-made Boards

PLYWOOD

Plywood is made up from three or more layers of wood veneers laid orthogonally to each other and bonded together. It comes in a variety of thicknesses and different types for different applications. For the projects described, boards with good quality veneers on the surface, and ply that is not water-resistant are not suitable.

Water-resistant plywood is subdivided into 'exterior quality' and 'marine' plywood. How weather-resistant the plywood is depends on the type of resin used to bond the layers. Marine plywood is of the very best

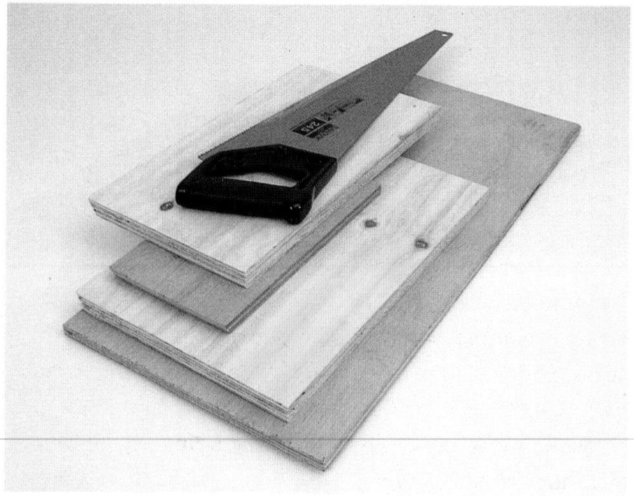

Fig 1.2
Various thicknesses of exterior quality plywood.

quality. It is available from specialist dealers such as boat building suppliers. Exterior quality plywood is water-resistant and comparatively inexpensive: it is the grade I have used for most of the projects given here.

CHIPBOARD AND FIBREBOARD

These boards are both made from small wood chips and fibres that are bonded under pressure. They are available in thicknesses varying from $^{3}/_{16}$–1in (4–25mm). Many of them are not water-resistant and if untreated, will quickly revert back to the small particles they were originally made from. Others have a limited water-resistance and if treated with wood preserver will last for several years. However, they are not much cheaper than plywood and do not appear to have any other advantages for these projects, so in general I have used plywood.

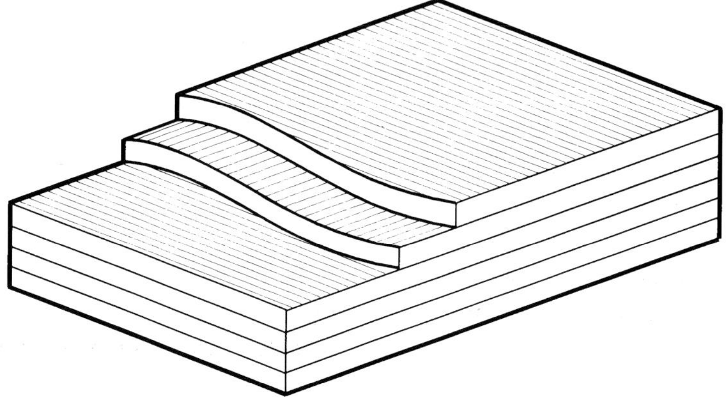

Fig 1.1
Plywood construction.

ADHESIVES

All the projects are glued using waterproof, PVA (polyvinyl acetate), white wood glue. I use PVA because it is an excellent general purpose glue: it is very effective, convenient to use, has a long shelf life and is the cheapest of the waterproof glues.

There are several other waterproof glues available. One of the most effective is urea-formaldehyde adhesive. This comes as a powder and has to be mixed with water before use. It is quite expensive, but I use it occasionally because it has good gap filling properties (for those wobbly joints).

Fig 1.3
PVA exterior adhesive.

WOODSCREWS, NAILS AND STAPLES

Woodscrews have a countersunk head so that they can be fitted flush with the surface of the wood. I have used several sizes, ranging from ½–1½in (12–38mm) long. The diameter of the shank is given as a gauge size which does not vary with the length. For example, a ½in (12mm) No. 8 screw is the same diameter as a 1½in (38mm) No. 8.

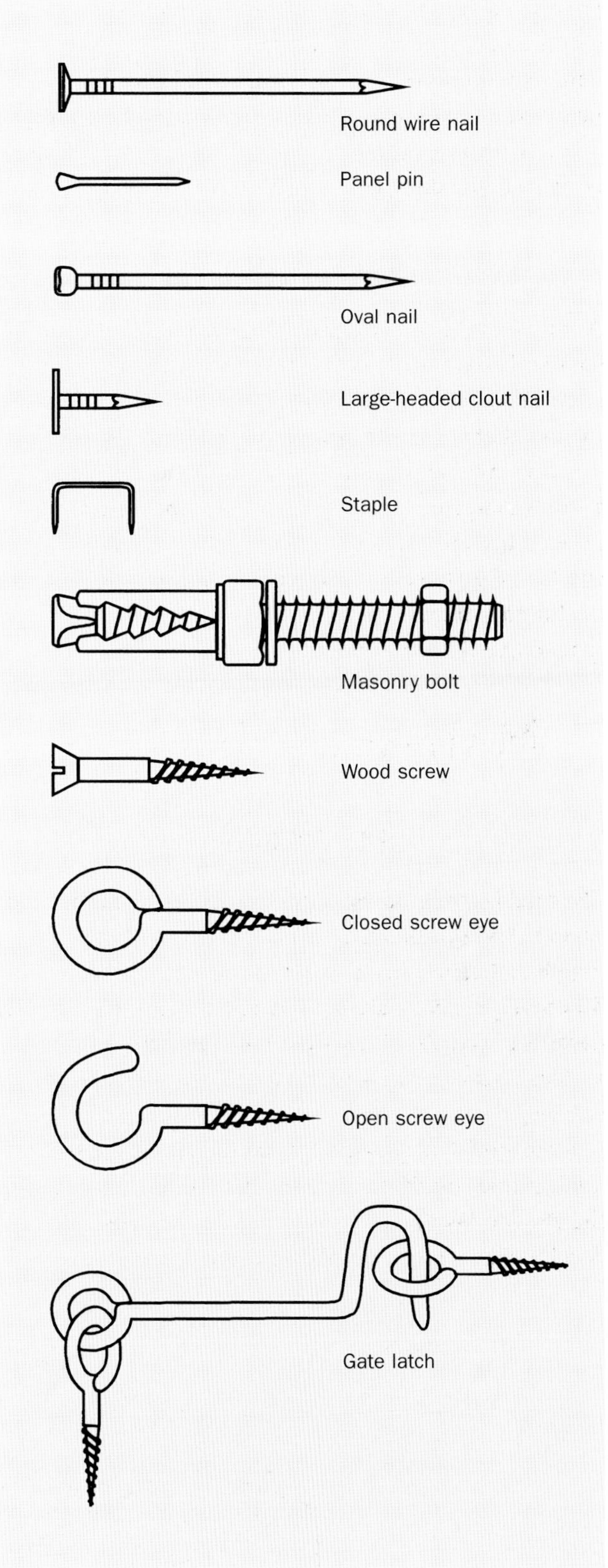

Fig 1.4
Nails, screws and other hardware used in the projects.

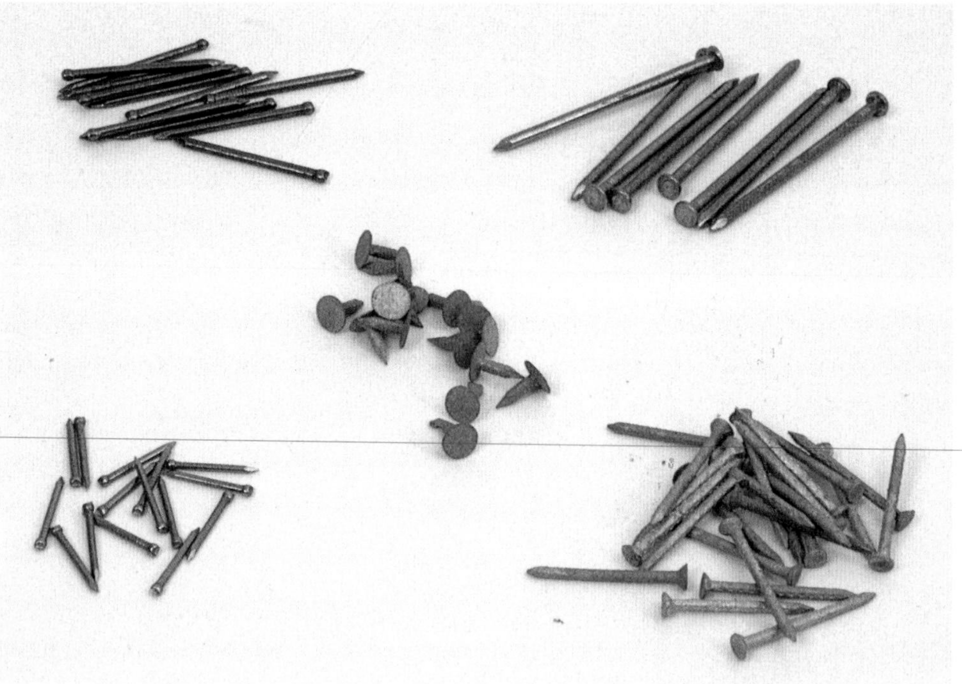

Fig 1.5
Some of the types of nails used in the projects.

Nails are specified by length and shape, for example, 1in (25mm) oval nails. They are available in a variety of different metals; iron, copper and aluminium are the most common. For exterior use, some iron nails can be obtained with a zinc coating (galvanized) to prevent them from rusting.

The staples specified for a number of the projects have a ½in (12mm) crown with a ½in (12mm) leg length and are fixed with a stapler. A heavy duty stapler that uses staples with a longer leg length would be an advantage for the aviary as less staples would then be required.

Various other pieces of hardware, such as bolts and latches, are also used. These vary according to their task, and are specified in the individual projects.

Artists' Paints

For the two projects that require a multi-coloured finish I have used artists' paints. Many different types of paints could be used to achieve the required effect – the two I have tried are acrylic and oil paints. Both can be applied thickly so that the brush strokes, if applied in the correct direction, can help to give the illusion of a feathery surface, and both are available in a huge selection of colours. However, acrylic paint dries darker than when it's first mixed. What you see when the paints are wet is not what you get after drying, so care must be taken to mix the colour to a slightly lighter shade than required. The main disadvantage of oil paints is the length of time they take to dry.

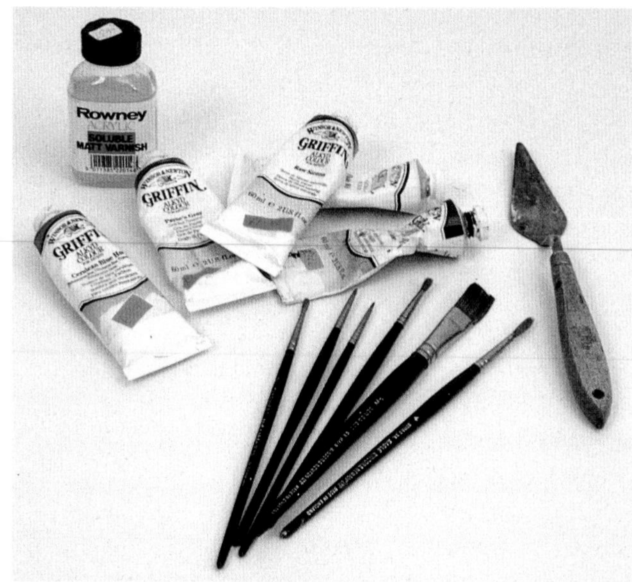

Fig 1.6
Artists' paints.

Fig 1.7
Paint for wrought-iron work.

ACRYLICS

I use the Rowney Cryla range of acrylic polymer paints, commonly called acrylics. These come as a thick paint, in tubes, and as a liquid, in jars. They take only about two hours to dry. There are variations in the quality of the paints available, but in general it is better to buy artists' rather than students' colours, because of their smoothness and resistance to fading when exposed to daylight.

Acrylics are available in a large range of traditional colours and hues, and some additional colours that are not available as oils or watercolours. They can be applied in a number of different ways. They have very good covering ability when applied thickly and, straight from the tube, are ideal for impasto effects. When acrylics are diluted with water and applied thinly, they get progressively lighter and more transparent, and a similar effect to painting with watercolours can be achieved.

OILS

Oil paints also come in a large range of colours. Unlike acrylic paints, they take a long time to dry, although there are some types available that dry a lot quicker including the Griffin Alkyd range.

Oil paints can be used thinned with artists' turpentine and this will affect their drying time. If a lot of turps is used they will dry in a few days, but straight from the tube, without any turps, they can take several weeks to dry. If too much turps is used, the paint gets a bit thin and does not have such good covering properties, but, particularly for early applications, thinning can work well. It is better to build up a colour with several thin coats rather than one thick one.

If you use oil paint straight from the tube you get an impasto effect in which a raised surface texture is left by the bristles of the brush. This is an effect exploited by artists who apply the paint with a palette knife. It can be useful to apply the paint thickly when painting a bird model because the brush strokes can be used to suggest the texture of the feathers.

FINISHES

When the paints are dry they will be water-resistant, but to protect them, it is usual to apply two or three coats of either gloss or matt, clear varnish. There are varnishes available from artists' suppliers that are formulated for this purpose. They give a clear finish, without a colour bias, and do not degrade the colours of the paint.

MIXING COLOURS

I use a sheet of glass laid on a white board background to mix my colours. Other palettes are made from wood, metal and ceramics. Plastic palettes should be avoided as the paint might stain them permanently.

Correcting mistakes is easy. If the paint is still wet, simply wipe it off with a rag and if it has dried, cover it with another layer of paint: this can be white if you want to start again from scratch. If the layers of paint are too thick, you can thin them with glasspaper until the surface is smooth, and this provides an excellent ground for applying the new layers of paint.

Acrylic paints are often used under oils. The two forms of paint work well together as long as the acrylic

is applied first and allowed to dry. I paint some of my carvings in this way.

BRUSHES

Sable brushes are ideal for painting small carvings. Use a No. 0 or No. 1 for fine detail and a No. 6 for blocking in larger areas of colour.

When working with acrylic paints, all brushes should be cleaned immediately after use with water. If the paint is allowed to dry on the brush it will be ruined for ever.

Fig 1.9
Various wood finishes and brush cleaner.

Household Paints

GLOSS

Where gloss paint is specified it means exterior quality household paint. This is readily available from any DIY store, as is the wood primer and undercoat. Black paint for wrought iron work is used on the hoops of the duck barrel.

VARNISHES

Two different varnishes are used on the projects. Matt polyurethane is used where a clear, tough, water-resistant finish is required, and a wood preserver with a stain incorporated is used where a water-resistant colour finish is required.

Fig 1.8
Clear, matt varnish.

OTHER WOOD FINISHES

Many of the projects are finished using clear, wood preserving solution which protects by soaking into the wood and forming a water-resistant barrier. The aviary is painted with creosote which has the advantage of being cheap. Do not, however, be tempted to use creosote on projects intended for wild birds and animals as the smell will deter them from using it. When creosote is applied, leave plenty of time before using the finished piece so that the smell can mellow.

BRUSHES

Most projects in this book can be painted or varnished using a range of four brushes: ½, 1, 1½, and 2in (12, 25, 38, 50mm). Brush quality will depend on price, but for applying the water sealing solution used for most of the projects, a 2in (50mm), low quality brush will suffice.

To get good results when applying varnish or paint, however, a good quality brush is required. Natural bristle brushes are excellent and, if from a quality manufacturer, the bristles will not break or fall out.

Always clean brushes thoroughly when the job is finished. Read the cleaning instructions on the tin of paint or varnish. Modern emulsion paints can be cleaned off using water, but many traditional oil-based paints require cleaning in a solution of white spirit, before washing with warm soapy water.

Roof Coverings

FELT

Roofing felt is a general purpose, low-cost roof covering that is sold in several different grades (thicknesses) and finishes. For substantial jobs, such as a flat roof for a house, several layers are used, stuck down with melted bitumen and finished with granite chips. For the small designs in this book, a single layer of felt secured with large-headed clout nails is sufficient.

PLASTIC FLASHING

Plastic flashing is a thick, flexible, plastic material with a self-adhesive back that is used for roof and guttering repairs. Where there is a requirement to waterproof small areas of roof this is ideal.

Wire Mesh

The wire mesh used for all of the projects is galvanized square mesh with welded corners. It comes in a range of sizes: I have used the variations with ½in (12mm) and ¼in (6mm) squares.

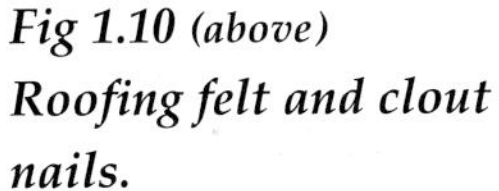

Fig 1.10** (above)* ***Roofing felt and clout nails.

Fig 1.11** (right)* ***Galvanized wire mesh and tin snips.

2

Tools and Techniques

Most of the projects described in this book require only simple techniques to make them. They provide an ideal way for a woodworking beginner to acquire new skills *and* end up with a useful project, or for a wildlife enthusiast without specific woodworking skills to obtain feeders and nesting boxes to enhance their pastime. Much of the work can be done using just the tools owned by most handymen, though the work is made easier if you have one or two power tools.

Tools

The list of tools that follows is not exhaustive, but with them most of the projects can be made. When a more specialized tool is required, it is mentioned in each particular project. A full complement of tools to mark out and measure the projects is mandatory. I used:

- pencils;
- a flexible rule;
- a long straightedge;
- a try square;
- a sliding bevel;
- and a marking gauge (for making some of the joints for the aviary).

I also used a tenon and a panel saw extensively and added to these a hand-held circular saw, which I used for converting large sheets of plywood and for forming angled edges, for example, on the top edge of the dovecote side, where it meets the roof. In a couple of the projects you will need to cut a square hole in the centre of a sheet of plywood: the easiest way to achieve this is to use a jigsaw.

A power drill is used for nearly all the projects, but if one is not available, a hand drill will do the job just as well. Nails, pins and screws are used to fasten parts, so a hammer and a screwdriver are essential. You will also need a centre punch to 'lose' the heads of the nails and pins by punching them below the surface of the wood. To fix wire mesh to a wooden frame, using a stapler is by far the quickest method and to cut the mesh, a pair of tin snips is required.

To get a straight edge on solid timber and plywood use a plane. Where this is not practical, for example on curved edges, use files and glasspaper.

Finally, for cutting some of the joints and for making the recesses to seat hinges, you will need a bevel-edged chisel.

Techniques

Fixing Nest Boxes to Trees

Which nails you use to fix nest boxes to trees depends on whether the trees will have any value as timber when they are eventually felled. Steel nails or screws, if left in place, will damage the machines that are used to convert the timber to planks. If the trees have no value as timber then these are fine because the tree will not be sawn up when it is felled. The alternatives for trees that will be sawn are copper or aluminium nails which will not damage a saw blade as much, and will not rust.

The environmentally friendly way of fixing them to the tree is to use hardwood pegs. These are shaped from a piece of oak or elm and inserted into a hole drilled into the tree.

Another good method, if the tree is not too thick, is to tie it on with a length of cord or a large plastic self-locking strap.

FIXING NEST BOXES TO MASONRY

Fixing a heavy object like the dovecote to a wall requires a strong fitting that can take a lot of weight. A masonry bolt is ideal for this and will make a secure fitting to brick, concrete, and insulation blocks. They consist of a threaded bolt that forces a plastic inset to expand when it is tightened.

First, bore a hole in the wall the same size as the plastic inset and push the inset into the hole. Next, put the bolt through the object to be hung up and screw it into the insert. Tighten the bolt so that the plastic sleeve expands in the hole.

For lighter objects, such as the wall-mounted seed tray, use a plastic wall plug. Drill a hole to take the plug, with a masonry bit. Put the screw through the object and into the plug before screwing it tight.

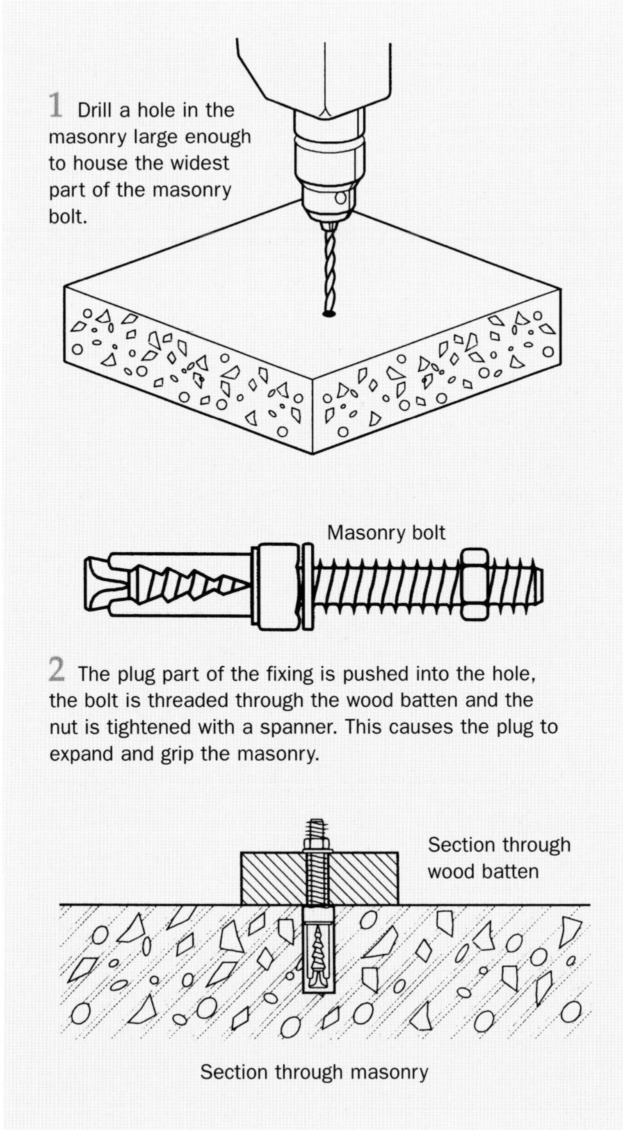

Fig 2.1
Heavy-duty masonry fitting.

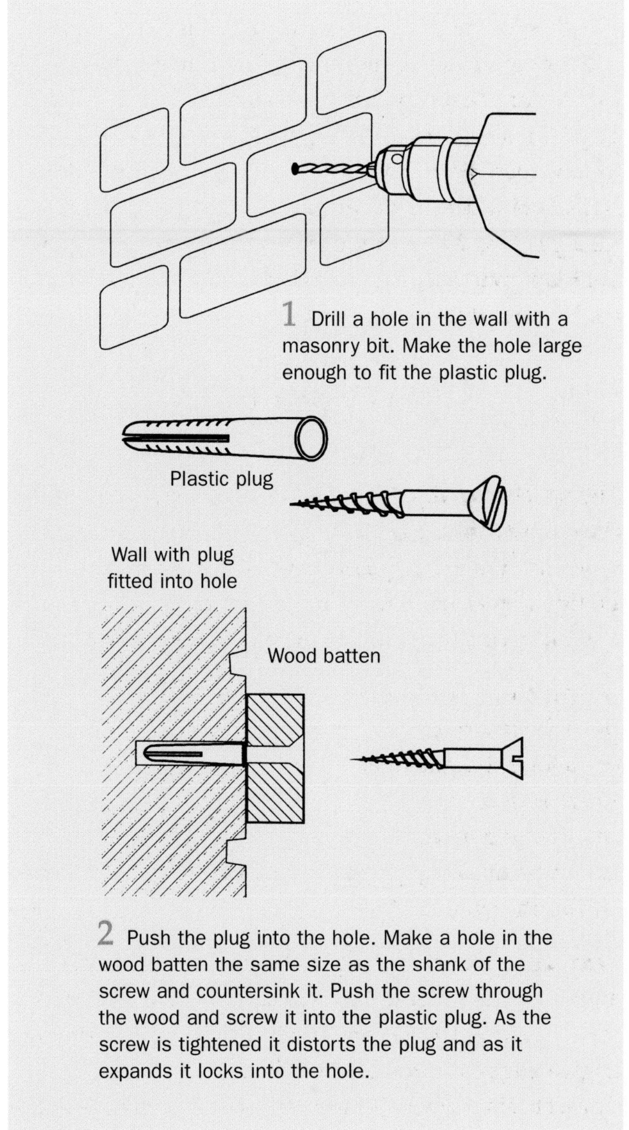

Fig 2.2
Light-duty wall fitting.

FITTING A HINGE

The only type of hinge used in these projects is a butt hinge. In most cases they are fitted in a shallow recess for added security, as the edges of the recess help to hold the hinge in place.

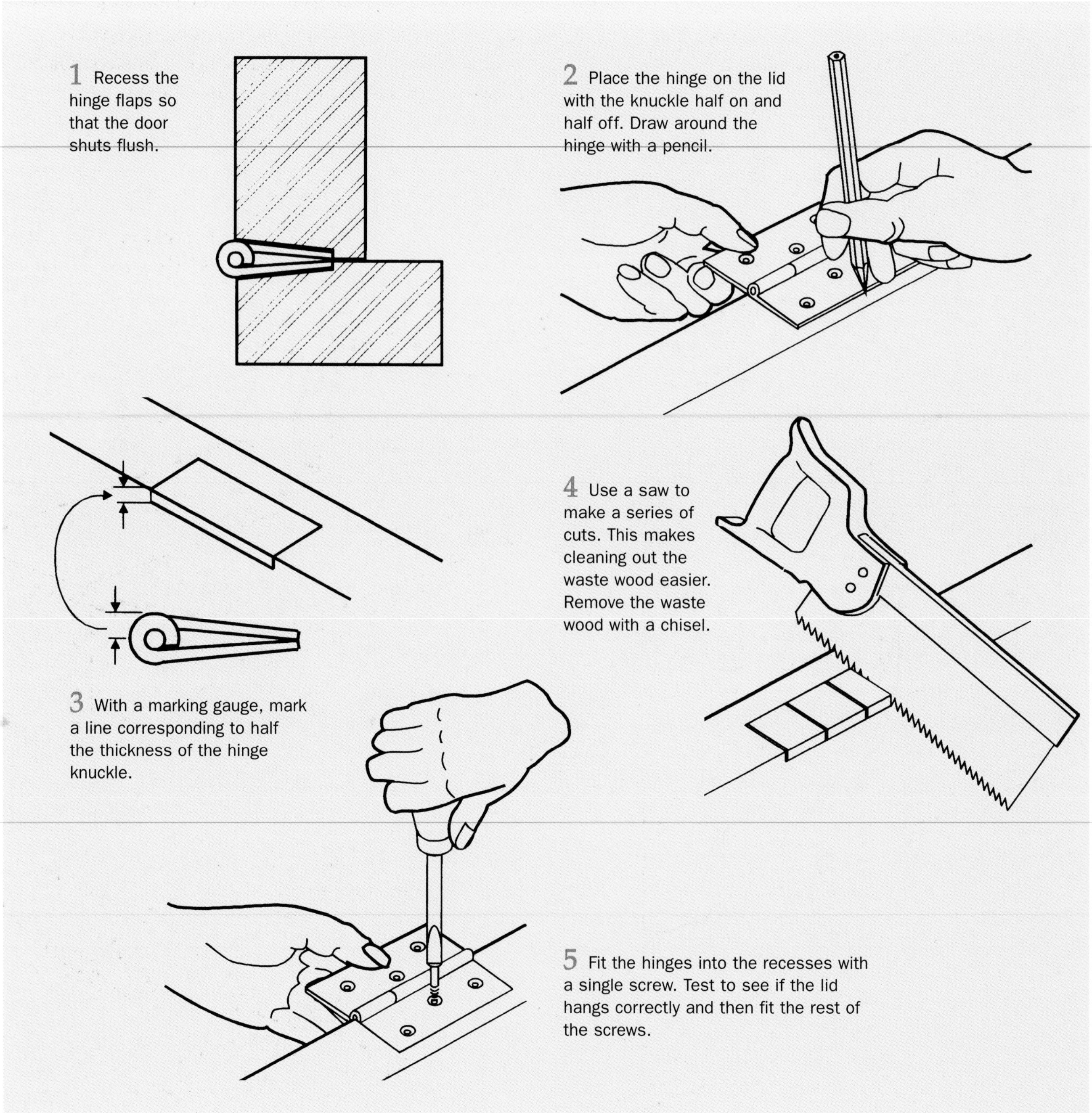

1 Recess the hinge flaps so that the door shuts flush.

2 Place the hinge on the lid with the knuckle half on and half off. Draw around the hinge with a pencil.

3 With a marking gauge, mark a line corresponding to half the thickness of the hinge knuckle.

4 Use a saw to make a series of cuts. This makes cleaning out the waste wood easier. Remove the waste wood with a chisel.

5 Fit the hinges into the recesses with a single screw. Test to see if the lid hangs correctly and then fit the rest of the screws.

Fig 2.3
Fitting a butt hinge.

USING NAILS

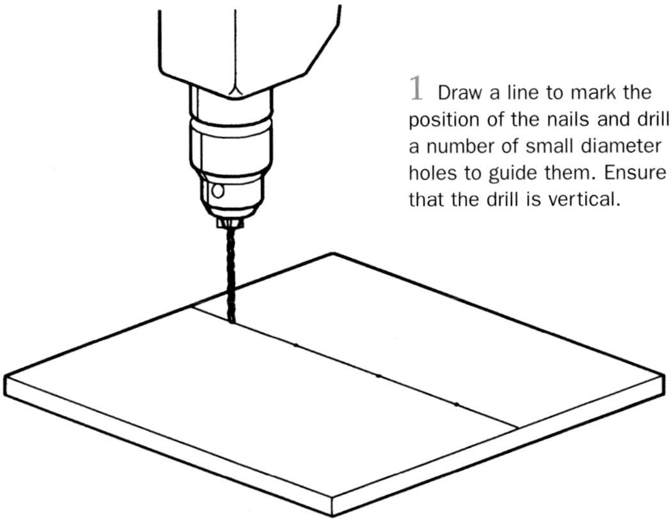

1 Draw a line to mark the position of the nails and drill a number of small diameter holes to guide them. Ensure that the drill is vertical.

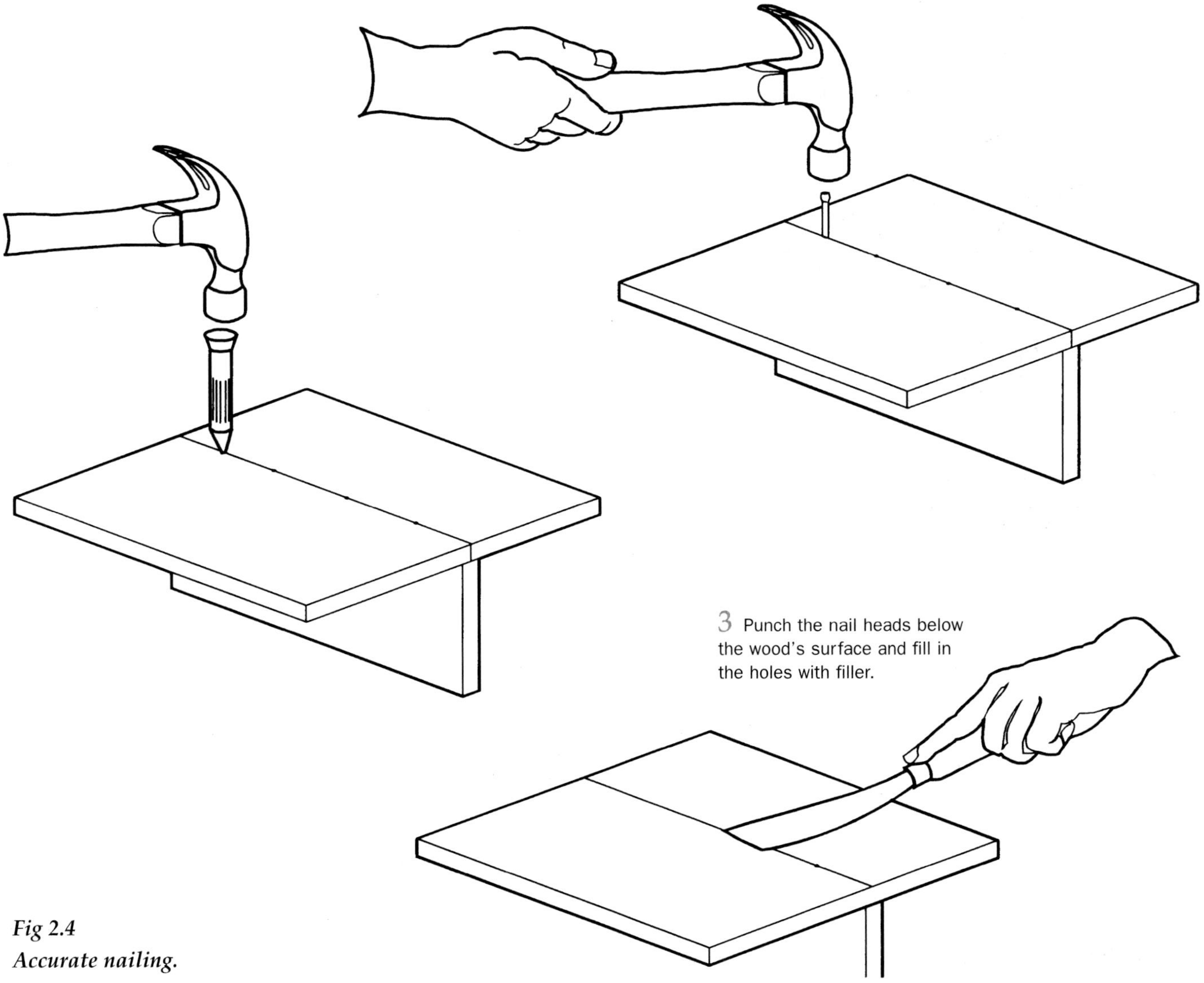

Use a nail that is two to three times longer than the thickness of the timber. If you are nailing one piece of plywood to another, it is important that the nails are upright and that they pierce the centre of the ply underneath. It helps if a line is marked, and a pilot hole slightly smaller in diameter than the nail is drilled in the top piece to locate the nail. When using oval nails, punch the heads below the surface of the wood with a centre punch, and fill the hole with filler.

2 Glue the edge and drive in the nails.

3 Punch the nail heads below the wood's surface and fill in the holes with filler.

Fig 2.4
Accurate nailing.

USING SCREWS

Screws provide a quick and effective way of making a joint in wood, and I use them extensively for construction work. Try to avoid screwing them into end grain as they are not very secure when used in this way. A screw needs to grip the grain of the wood to get a secure hold. All the strength of a piece of wood is along the grain, i.e. wood is difficult to break along the grain, but breaks easily with the grain (*see* Fig 2.6). When a

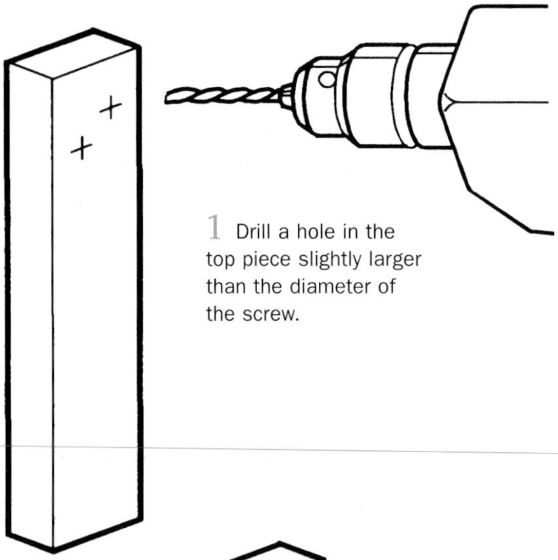

1 Drill a hole in the top piece slightly larger than the diameter of the screw.

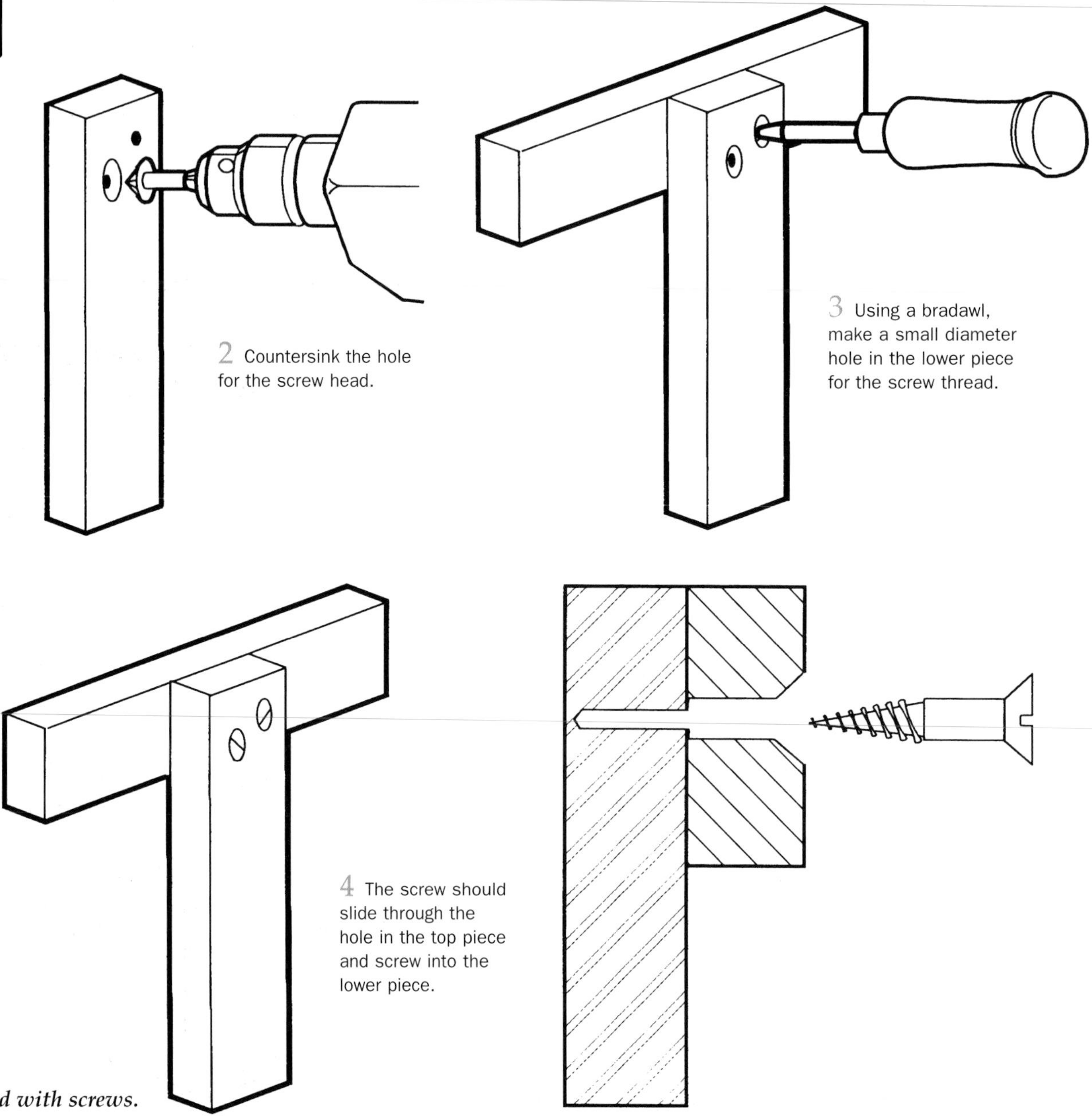

2 Countersink the hole for the screw head.

3 Using a bradawl, make a small diameter hole in the lower piece for the screw thread.

4 The screw should slide through the hole in the top piece and screw into the lower piece.

Fig 2.5
Joining wood with screws.

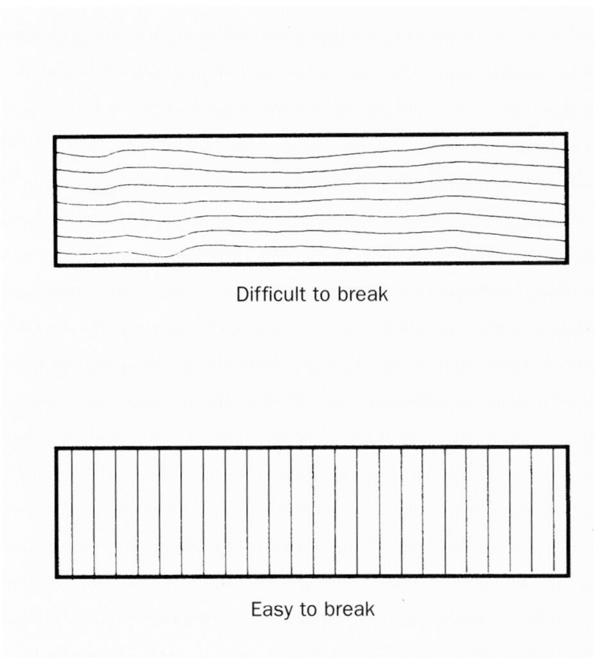

Fig 2.6
Grain direction and wood strength.

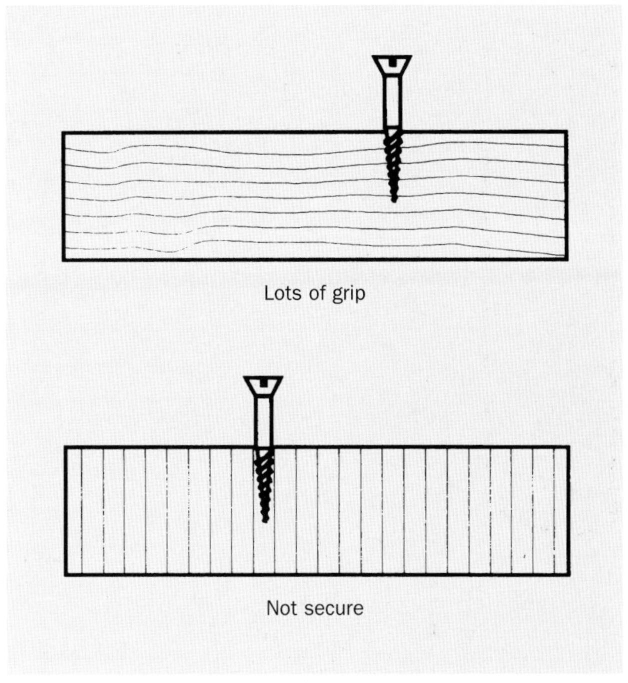

Fig 2.7
Grain direction and screw grip.

screw is inserted across the grain, it grips into the fibres (grain) and will not break out because the fibres are long and strong. When inserted into the end grain where the fibres are very short, the screw will tear out easily (*see* Fig 2.7).

If there are a number of large screws to be inserted in a project, it makes the job easier if they are lubricated with candle wax.

ENSURING STRUCTURES ARE SQUARE

When marking out rectangular shapes onto plywood prior to cutting them out, or when joining together wood battens to make a frame, it is important that the rectangles formed have 90° corners. To ensure that this is the case, make both of the diagonals the same length.

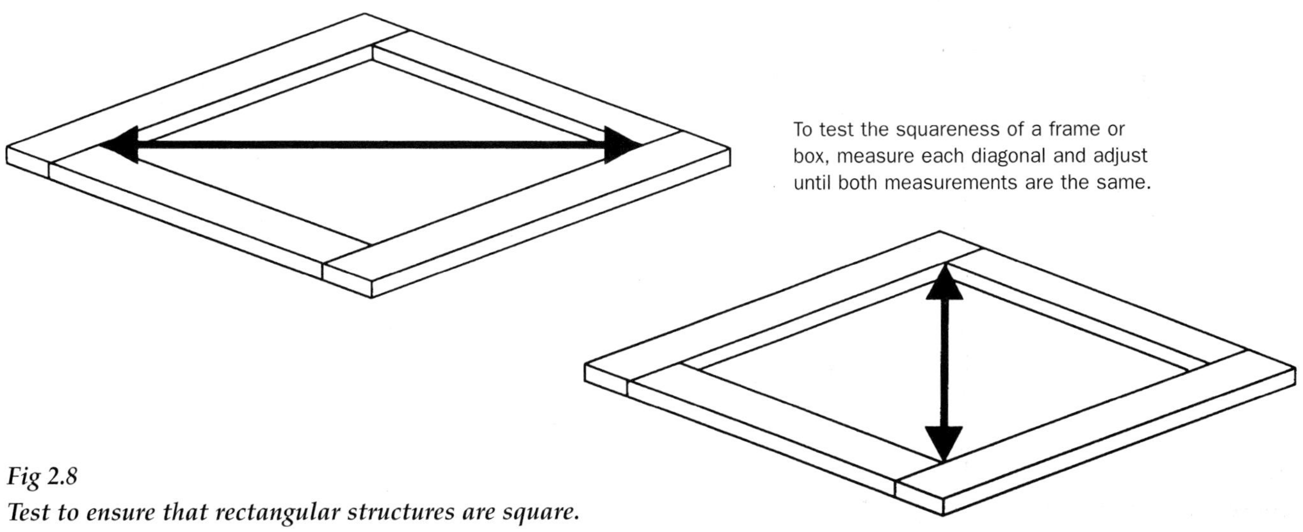

Fig 2.8
Test to ensure that rectangular structures are square.

MAKING A NAILED BUTT JOINT

A butt joint that is fixed together using glue only will vary in strength according to the size of the glued area: the bigger the area, the stronger the joint will be. One way to make the joint stronger when this area is not very extensive is to reinforce the joint with nails.

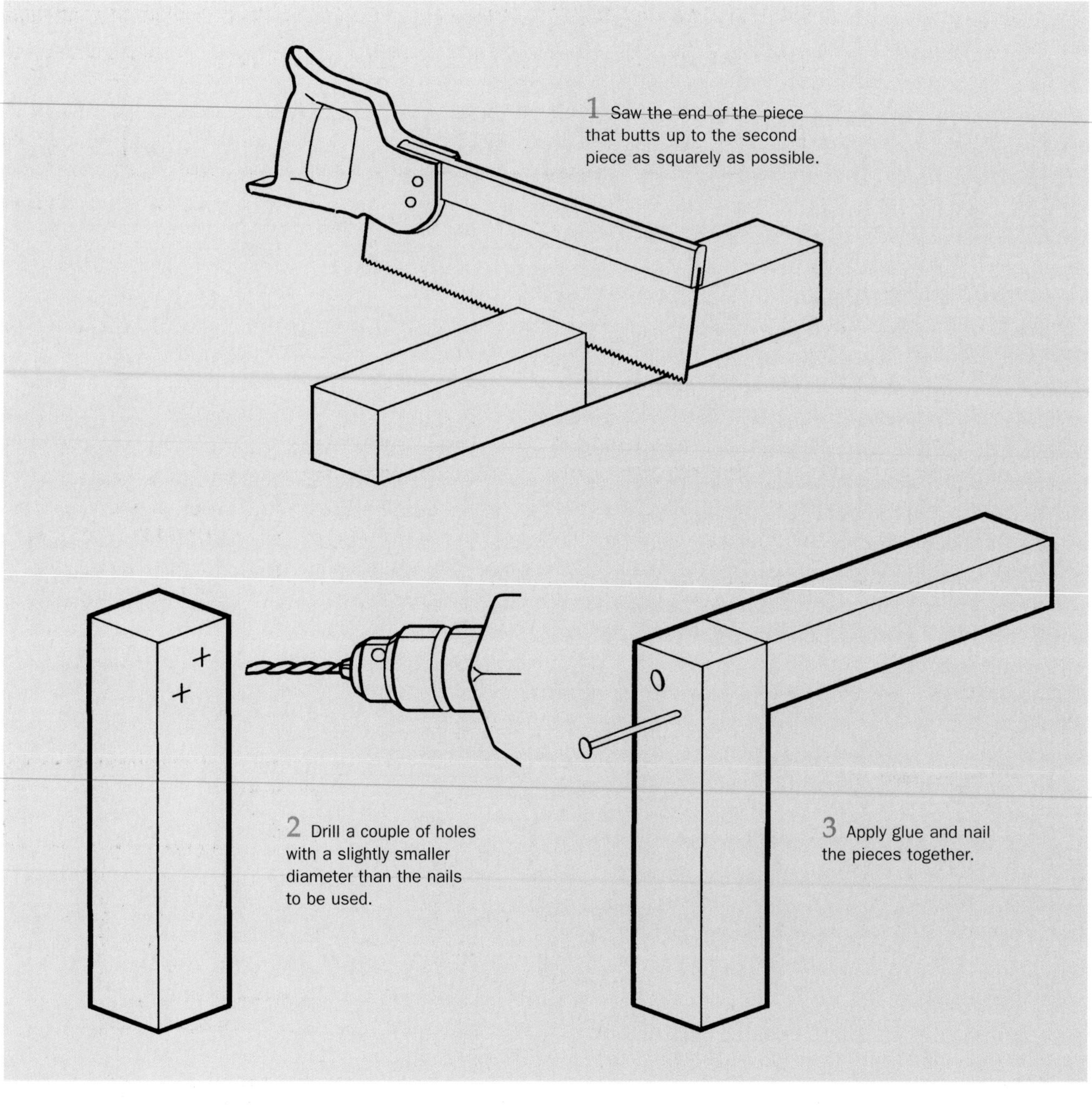

1 Saw the end of the piece that butts up to the second piece as squarely as possible.

2 Drill a couple of holes with a slightly smaller diameter than the nails to be used.

3 Apply glue and nail the pieces together.

Fig 2.9
A nailed butt joint.

SQUARING PIECES OF SOLID TIMBER

When joining together two pieces of wood, it is important that they have both been cut squarely so that the edges butt together and they have all of the available surface area in contact, as this facilitates a good glue joint. If they have not been sawn with square edges, use a plane and try square to make them square and flat.

Fig 2.10
Planing a piece of wood square and flat.

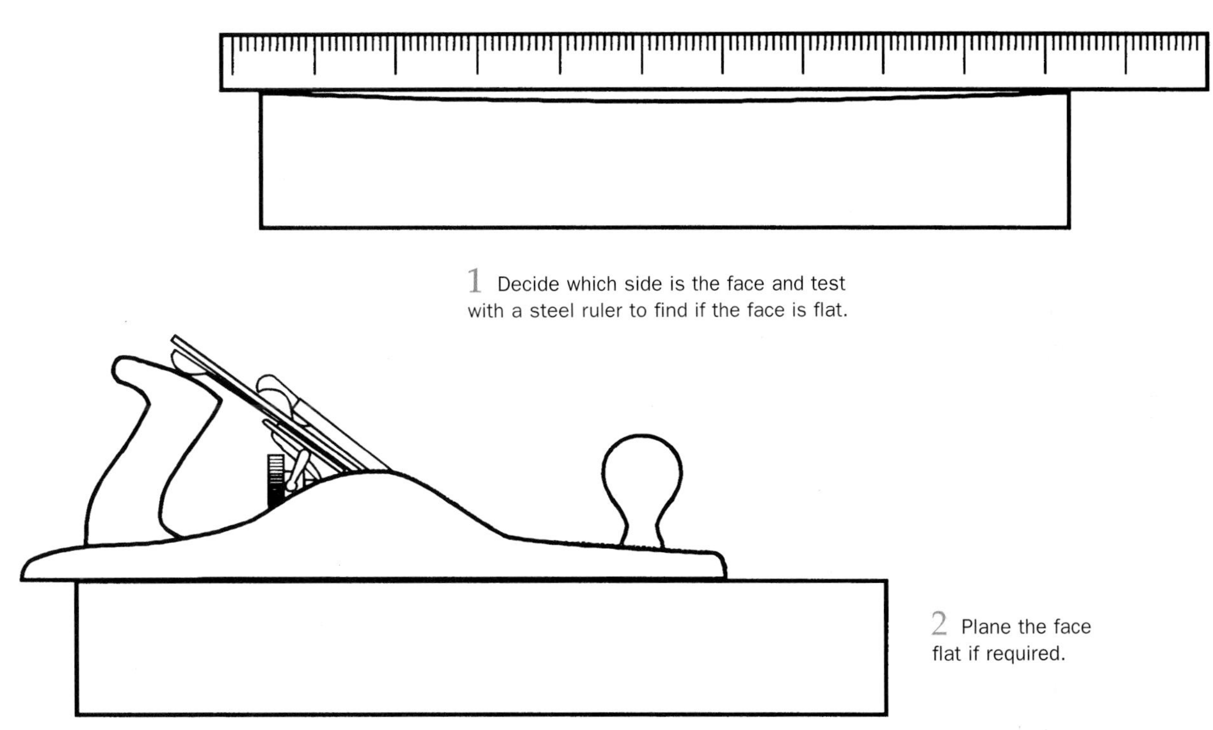

1 Decide which side is the face and test with a steel ruler to find if the face is flat.

2 Plane the face flat if required.

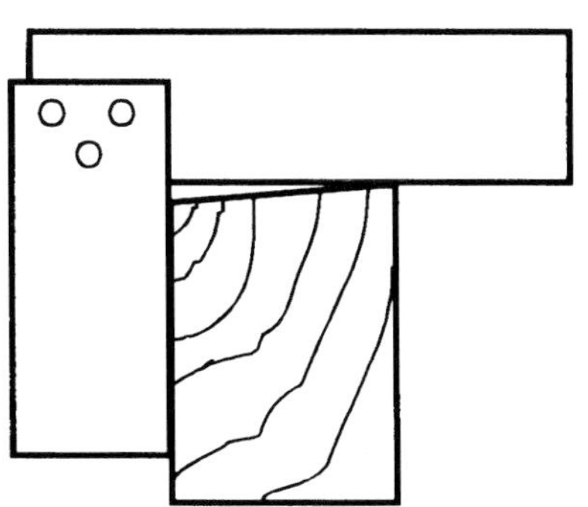

3 Test to see if the edge is square, placing the handle of the try square on the face.

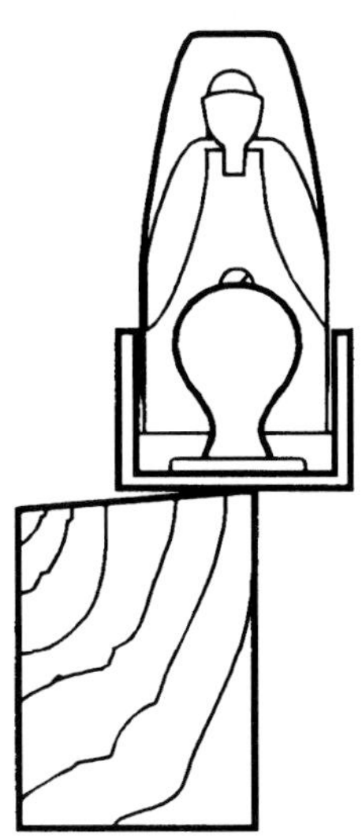

4 Plane the edge square by placing the plane off-centre.

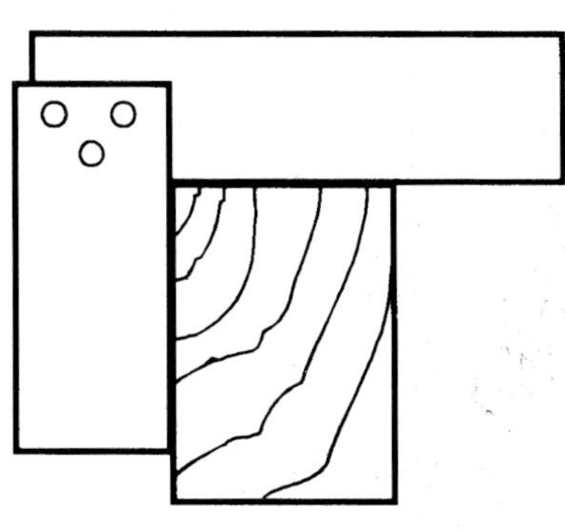

5 Retest and replane until it is square.

MAKING HALVING JOINTS

These are used in frame construction where simplicity is a prime consideration. Wherever an easy method of joining two rails or batons anywhere along their length is wanted, halving joints are appropriate.

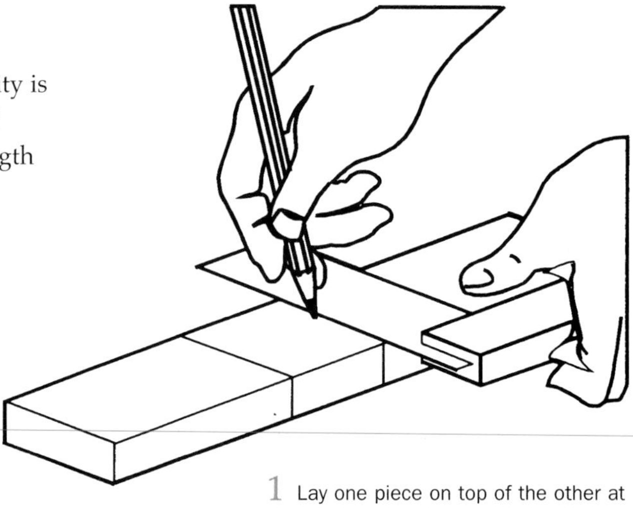

1 Lay one piece on top of the other at 90° and draw a mark on both sides of the top. Use a try square to ensure that these lines are square, and project them around all four sides. On the edge, use a marking gauge to find the centre, and scribe a line between the previously drawn lines.

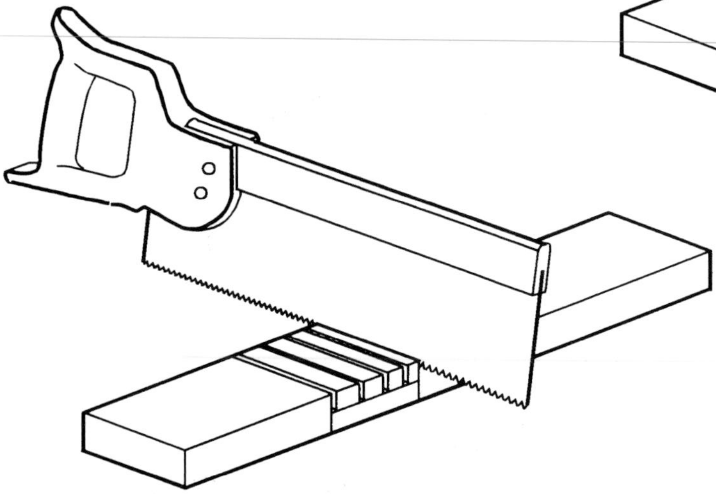

2 Cut down the vertical lines at the edges of the housing with a tenon saw, and make a number of cuts between these two to make it easier to remove the waste.

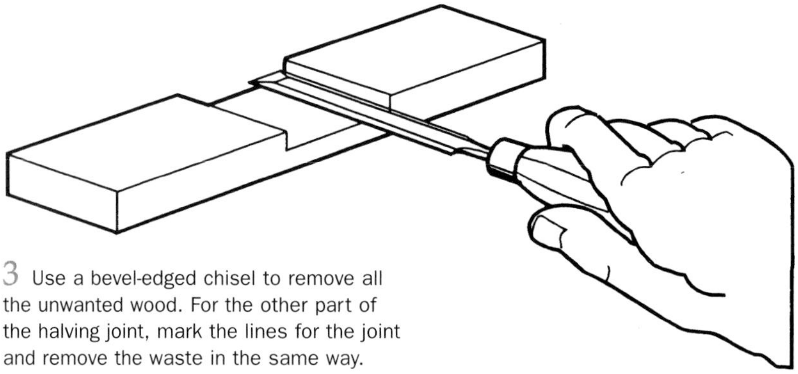

3 Use a bevel-edged chisel to remove all the unwanted wood. For the other part of the halving joint, mark the lines for the joint and remove the waste in the same way.

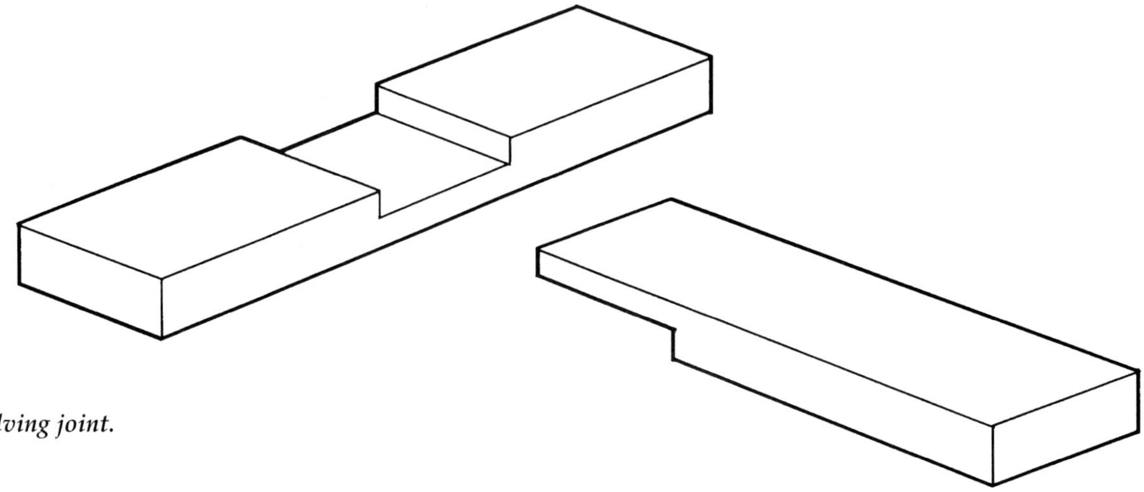

Fig 2.11
Making a halving joint.

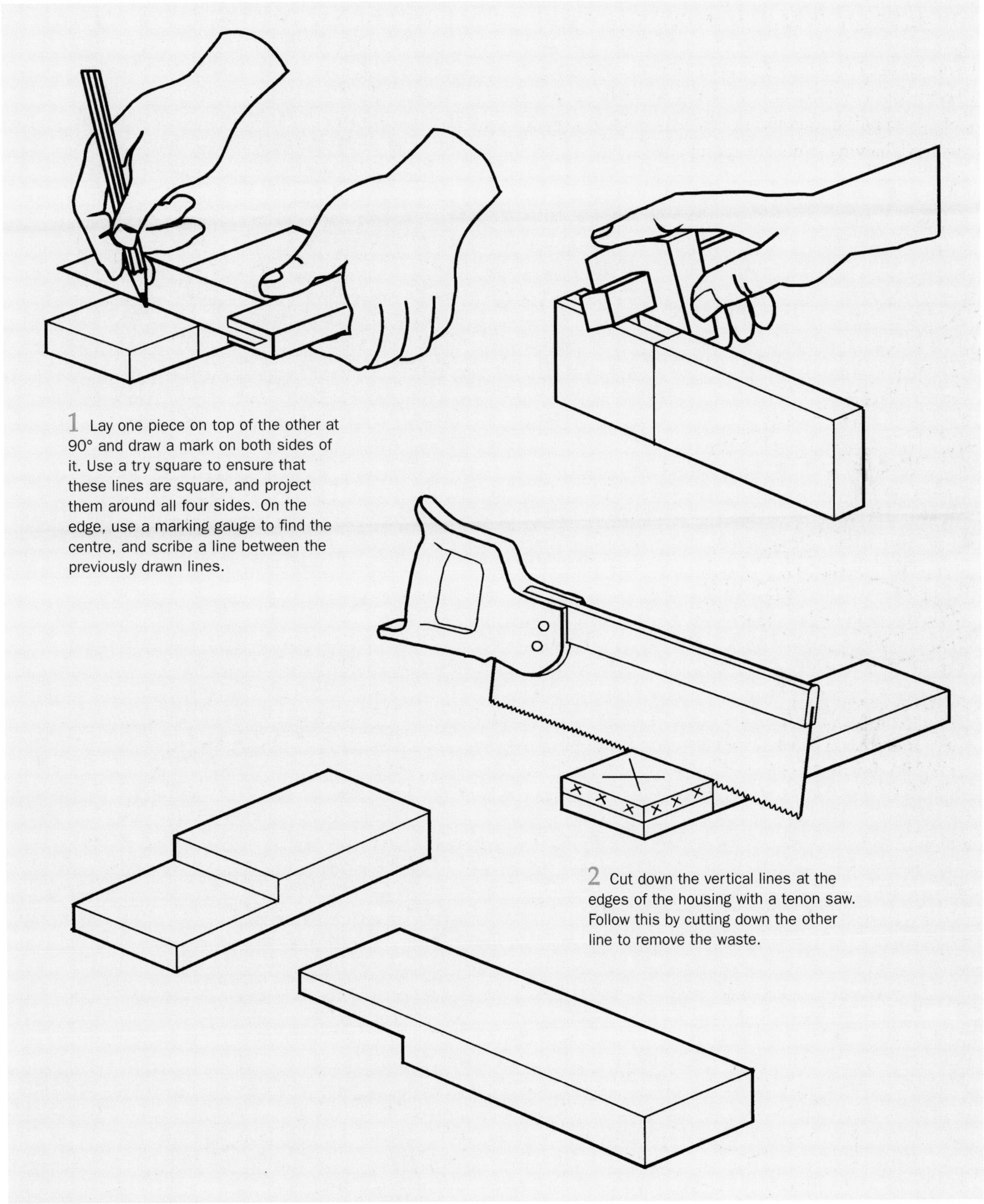

1 Lay one piece on top of the other at 90° and draw a mark on both sides of it. Use a try square to ensure that these lines are square, and project them around all four sides. On the edge, use a marking gauge to find the centre, and scribe a line between the previously drawn lines.

2 Cut down the vertical lines at the edges of the housing with a tenon saw. Follow this by cutting down the other line to remove the waste.

Fig 2.12
Making an end halving joint.

USING CLENCHED-OVER NAILS

When a joint has been made it is perfectly acceptable to rely on glue alone to secure it. However, this means that after gluing, the joint will require clamping until it dries. This is not always practical, so an alternative is to strengthen the joint with clenched-over nails. This makes a strong joint instantly, and becomes even stronger when the glue dries.

1 Drive a couple of long nails through the two parts of the joint.

2 Using a hammer, bend the nails over and hammer the points slightly below the surface of the wood.

Fig 2.13
Strengthening joints with clenched-over nails.

MAKING A HOUSING JOINT

Housing joints are mainly used for fixing one batten into another to form a 'T' shape. They require a housing, or recess, to be cut into one of the pieces, into which the other piece is fixed with glue.

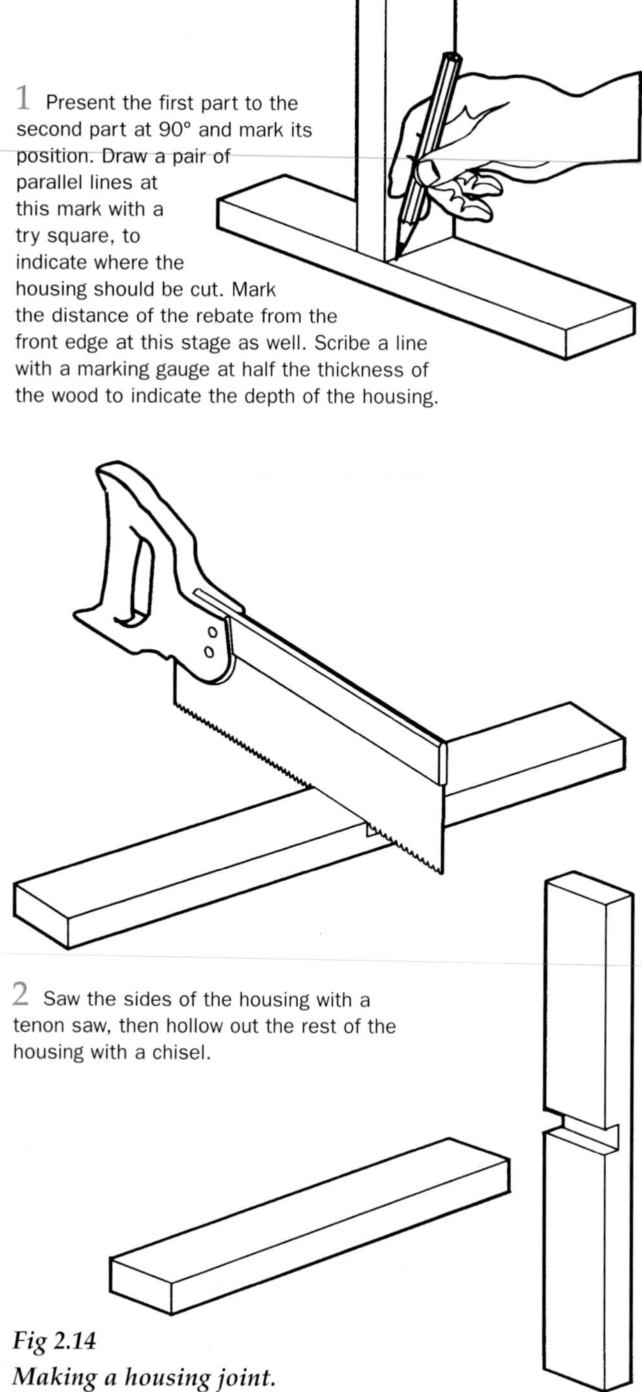

Fig 2.14
Making a housing joint.

FITTING PLASTIC FLASHING AND ROOFING FELT

PLASTIC FLASHING

Self-adhesive plastic flashing is a bitumen-based material used by builders for repairing leaky gutters and gullies. It comes in various widths, up to 12in (305mm). It is useful for placing on the roofs of bird boxes because it cuts easily with scissors and it does not have to be nailed down. In general, the way to fit it is as follows:

1 Cut a piece that is big enough to fit over the lid/roof and the edges.

2 Stick it in place on the top and cut out notches at the corners so that the edges of the flashing can be bent over the edges of the lid. Press it into place using a cork sanding block, particularly at the edges. Cut off any waste that overhangs the edges with a craft knife. (*See* Fig 2.15.)

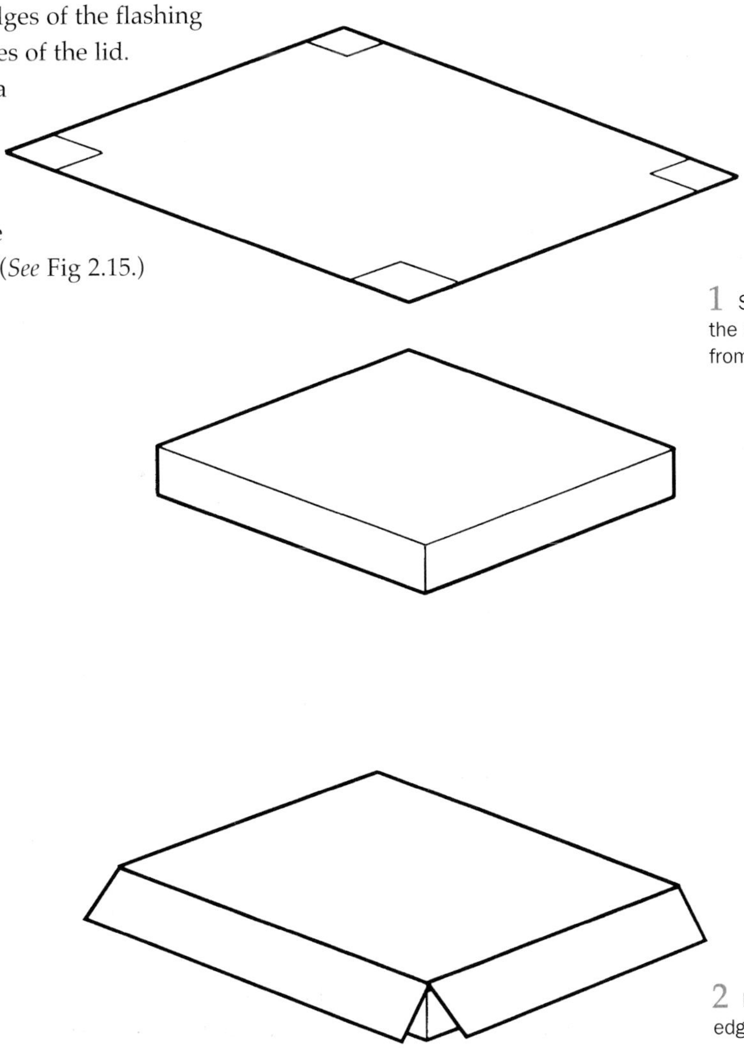

1 Stick the flashing on the wood and cut notches from the corners.

2 Bend flashing over the edges and trim.

Fig 2.15
Fitting plastic flashing.

ROOFING FELT

Felt is a fabric formed without weaving. It uses the natural tendency of fibres to interlace and cling together. Roofing felt is made from matted fibres impregnated with bitumen, and rolled flat. To fit roofing felt:

1 Cut a piece of felt large enough to cover the roof, allowing some to spare.

2 Choose one straight edge on the felt, and fix it to one edge of the roof with clout nails.

3 Pull the rest of the felt tightly over the roof and nail down the remaining edges.

4 To finish, trim the edges with a craft knife.

Painting

PREPARATION

Paint should be stirred before use, and if it is a tin that has been used before, it is a good idea to strain it through an old pair of tights or stockings first, particularly if you are going to apply a final coat of varnish or gloss paint.

For painting new wood, first fill any holes or flaws with a weatherproof cellulose filler, then rub down the surface with glasspaper and apply wood priming paint. When this is dry, rub it over with fine grade glasspaper, then apply the undercoat and finally, the top coat. Do not load up the brush with too much paint as this will cause runs. Apply the brush strokes from top to bottom and side to side. If the wood has knots and / or resinous patches, apply some 'knotting' paint before priming.

Knotting paint, as the name suggests, is designed specifically for painting over knots. In pine the knots sometimes contain a resinous substance that can leak out and spoil the paint. Knotting paint will prevent the resin seeping through and thus protect the final paint surface.

To varnish with a clear or coloured polyurethane varnish, rub down the wood with glasspaper before applying the first coat. When this is dry, rub over the surface with fine grade steel wool before applying a second coat.

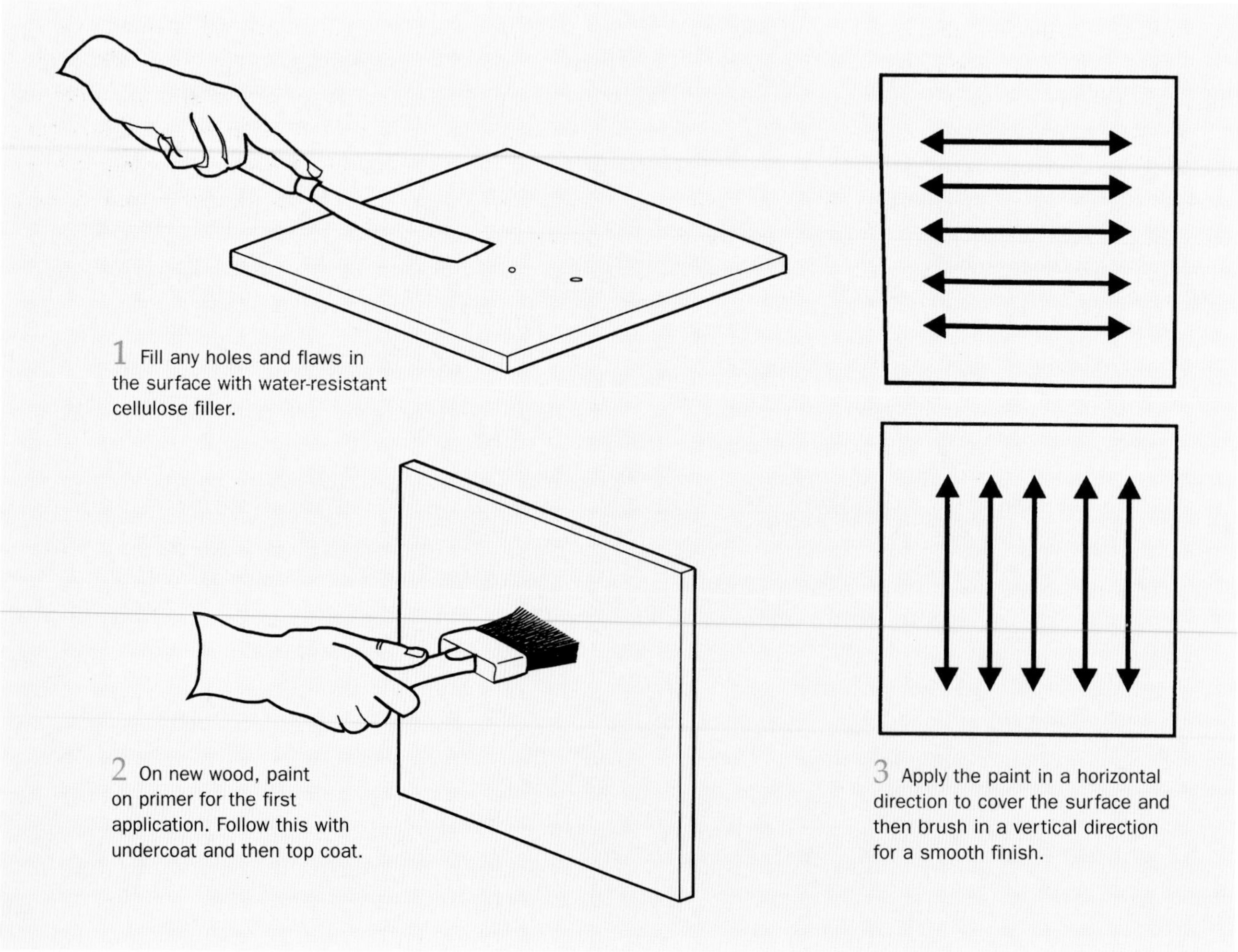

1 Fill any holes and flaws in the surface with water-resistant cellulose filler.

2 On new wood, paint on primer for the first application. Follow this with undercoat and then top coat.

3 Apply the paint in a horizontal direction to cover the surface and then brush in a vertical direction for a smooth finish.

Fig 2.16
Applying paint.

DECOYS

When painting birds, the best way to get the colour and form correct is to observe the live birds through binoculars. However, this is not always a practical proposition. The next best method is to obtain a good reference book from the library. One of the very best, in my opinion, is Tunnicliffe's book of measured drawings made from dead specimens, known as 'skins' in the trade (Tunnicliffe, C F, *A Sketchbook of Birds*, Victor Gollancz Ltd, London, UK, 1979). They are brilliant, and both a mallard and an oystercatcher appear. As well as being a good reference for colours, this book also shows the feather directions in great detail.

Use a palette knife when mixing the colours for a particular section, and mix enough of the constituent colours to cover the whole area. This is because, if a second batch is required halfway through the painting, it is difficult to obtain a good colour match. Apply the brush strokes in the direction that the feathers lie.

The alternative to mixing the paint with a knife is to use the brush you are painting with. This is fine for watercolours and oils thinned down with a lot of turps, but thick paint clogs the brush. The paint in the centre of the brush will stick there and not mix freely with the rest of the colour, resulting in an uneven mix. Using a palette knife avoids this problem.

In general, squeeze out a blob, about 1in (25mm), of the predominant colour, though this amount will vary according to the size of the area to be covered. Add small amounts of any colour other than black and white to this, to obtain the correct hue. Adjust the lightness/darkness by adding small amounts of white or black until it looks correct. White and black should always be added last, except when the colour required is grey. Grey colours are largely a mixture of white and black. For a light grey, start by squeezing out a blob of white, and adding black and for a dark grey, start by squeezing out black and adding small amounts of white.

When painting a bird, I generally work from dark to light colours. Most artists work this way when painting with oils and acrylics because the highlights and the brightest colours give the painting its impact. Starting with the dark tones enables you to judge the impact of the brightest colours in the finished work. To blend the edges of two colours, paint the second colour into the first whilst it is still wet. If a hard edge is required, wait for the first colour to dry.

3

ENVIRONMENT

One of the factors that influences the variety of birds and animals that appear in your garden is where it is situated. Whether you live in a town, the suburbs, open countryside or by the coast does make a difference. Naturally, a house deep in the countryside with a well-planted garden and some mature trees will attract a greater variety of birds than a small town garden, but the difference is not as large as you might think.

My house is situated in the suburbs of a medium-sized town and has a small garden, but I have recorded over 50 different bird species in or near it. Half a dozen different birds have nested here, including a mallard that reared 10 chicks near a pond measuring 6 x 4ft (1.8 x 1.2m). The other birds that have nested include sparrows, starlings, wrens, dunnocks, blackbirds, robins, thrushes and blue tits. We also get regular visits from squirrels, hedgehogs and, occasionally, a fox.

HABITAT

What can make a huge difference is the food and habitat provided: a garden that feeds the birds and provides other suitable facilities will be rewarded with far more visits than one that does not. However, it would be foolish of me to suggest that the rarer birds can be attracted to a small garden in the heart of a large industrial town, because the specialized habitat just does not exist there. However, some of the commoner birds are amongst the most entertaining, and they are all worth conserving.

The number and variety of trees and shrubs that grow in a garden affects the variety of the wildlife that will want to live there. Native trees, such as oak, beech

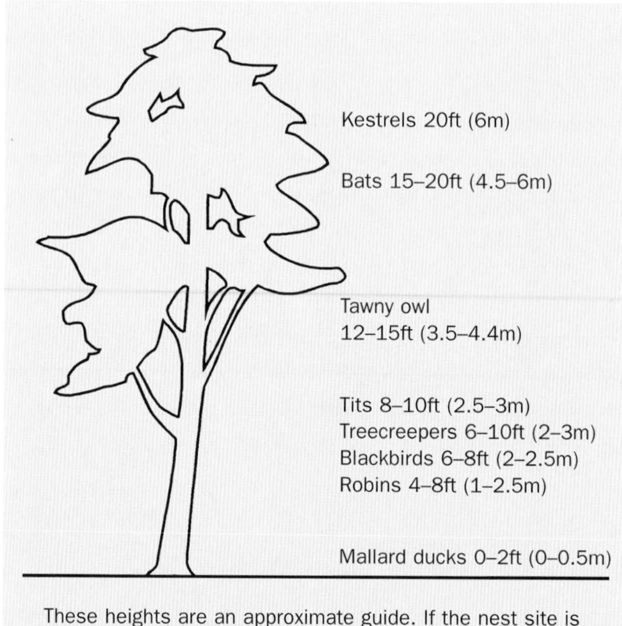

Fig 3.1
Height for nest boxes.

and birch, will attract more insects than trees that are not indigenous. This, in turn, encourages more birds because they feed on the insects. Any shrub that has berries in the winter or autumn will encourage birds, such as blackbirds and thrushes, looking for a free meal. Good examples of these plants are pyracantha, viburnum, holly, and rowan. Dense foliage plants like ivy, and closely-planted evergreen hedges are also good because they provide shelter.

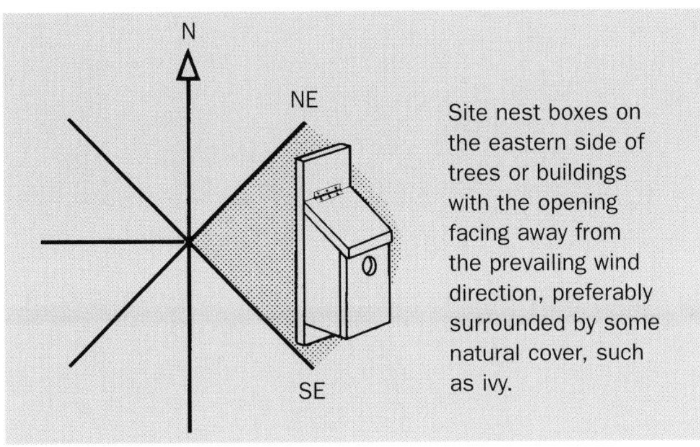

Fig 3.2
Direction to face nest boxes.

Do not keep your garden too tidy. If there is enough room, leave a neglected corner with clumps of brambles and nettles and some long grass and weeds. A pile of dead leaves and twigs will do very nicely for hedgehogs.

A water feature such as a pond not only makes the garden more interesting for the owner, but also makes it more helpful for birds and animals, who use it for drinking and bathing. It is important that one of the sides slopes gently to give easy access: one or two strategically placed large stones near the water's edge have the same effect. If there is not enough room for a pond then a bird bath is an acceptable alternative.

BENEFITS

There are many benefits to be gained from turning your garden into a miniature wildlife sanctuary, but the principal one for many people is entertainment. Watching the birds feeding and bathing or seeing frogs hop around the lawn after it has rained is amusing, and also satisfying, knowing that you are aiding wildlife conservation.

In addition, more birds and animals means less insects to eat your flowers and vegetables. Blue tits are voracious consumers of aphids and caterpillars and a pipistrelle bat will eat up to 3,000 insects in a single night.

Nest Boxes and Feeders

By providing nest boxes and a well-stocked feeder we draw many birds to the garden, but in doing so we must not make their lives more hazardous. Site the boxes and feeders in appropriate positions that are safe from predators (*see* Figs 3.1, 3.2 and 3.3).

Feeders should be kept clean so that the birds do not catch any diseases from stale or mouldy food. Scrape off any old food that is left uneaten and scrub the table with a 5% bleach solution. Nest boxes should be cleaned out after the young have fledged. If there are insects in the box, a dusting with pyrethrum powder will kill the insects without harming the birds.

In the spring, to encourage the birds to nest, leave some scraps of nest building material in the garden. A friend who likes walking in the countryside collects scraps of sheep's wool from fences and hedges. At the right time of year she leaves them in her garden and they are snapped up by eager nest builders within a few hours.

Use of Chemicals

Controlling weeds with herbicides does harm to the environment. It's more beneficial, but slightly harder work, to hoe the weeds. The work involved when hoeing also gives a good excuse for leaving a small area of the garden in a wild state. Encouraging birds will help to minimize the insect population. Gardeners who use insecticides will also control the numbers of bugs, but in doing so will deprive the birds of a valuable food source. Both ways control the insects, but the natural way means that there will be more birds, hedgehogs and frogs for us to enjoy in the future.

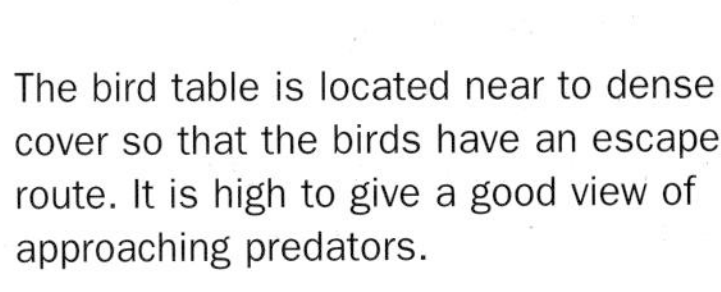

Fig 3.3
Location of bird table.

4

Food

In the summer most birds prefer food that is available naturally. This consists of insects, caterpillars, worms, bugs and seeds. It is during the winter, when natural food is hard to get, that they require 'artificial' food to supplement their diet. This is not to say that it is wrong to feed birds through the summer, but it is not necessary. The only caveat is that in the spring it is best not to put out whole peanuts in a way that allows birds to carry them to their chicks in one piece. Of course, if they are put out in a ¼in (6mm) mesh feeder, the birds have to break them up to get them out.

There is a wide range of nuts and seeds available from specialist dealers for both birds and mammals (*see* Figs 4.1–4.9), but if you don't want to go to this expense, most kitchen scraps will be suitable, with the exception of very salty or spicy food. Thrushes and blackbirds like slices of apple or windfalls and birds of the tit family like fatty food. To give them a treat in the winter try making a birdcake using the following recipe.

> Melt a small quantity of suet in a saucepan and add approximately three times the weight of this in mixed seeds. Stir it together and pour it into a mould such as a plastic vending cup. Put it in the fridge to set, then hang it in a tree or place it on a bird table. If you need to, you can add peanut flour to thicken the mixture.

It is important that a supply of clean water is readily available as well as food.

FOODS SUITABLE FOR BIRDS

Cheese	Peanuts (NOT WHOLE IN SPRING)	Fruit
Cooked rice		Moist bread
Seeds and nuts	Mealworms	Cooked potatoes
Fat and suet	Uncooked pastry	Tinned cat food
Porridge	Raisins	Tinned dog food

Fig 4.1
Mixed corn.

Fig 4.2
Niger (thistle seed).

Fig 4.4
Whole peanuts.

Fig 4.3
Flaked maze.

Fig 4.5
Birdcake mix (peanut flour and seeds).

Fig 4.6
Black sunflower seeds.

Fig 4.8
Feeder seed (sunflower seeds, peanut granules, canary seed and pinhead oatmeal).

Fig 4.7
Table seed (a mixture of various seeds).

Fig 4.9
Peanut granules.

PRESENTING THE FOOD

Food should be presented to birds and animals in the most attractive way. There is no best way as many of them are specialist feeders, so what is good for one species is not so good for another. For example, some birds, such as dunnocks, like to pick their food off the ground, but others, including long-tailed tits, prefer a feeder. I have never seen goldfinches use a peanut feeder, but they are drawn to thistle seeds in a seed dispenser.

Blue tits, great tits, siskins, greenfinches, nuthatches and even treecreepers will all take

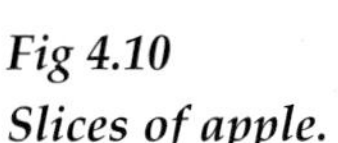

Fig 4.10
Slices of apple.

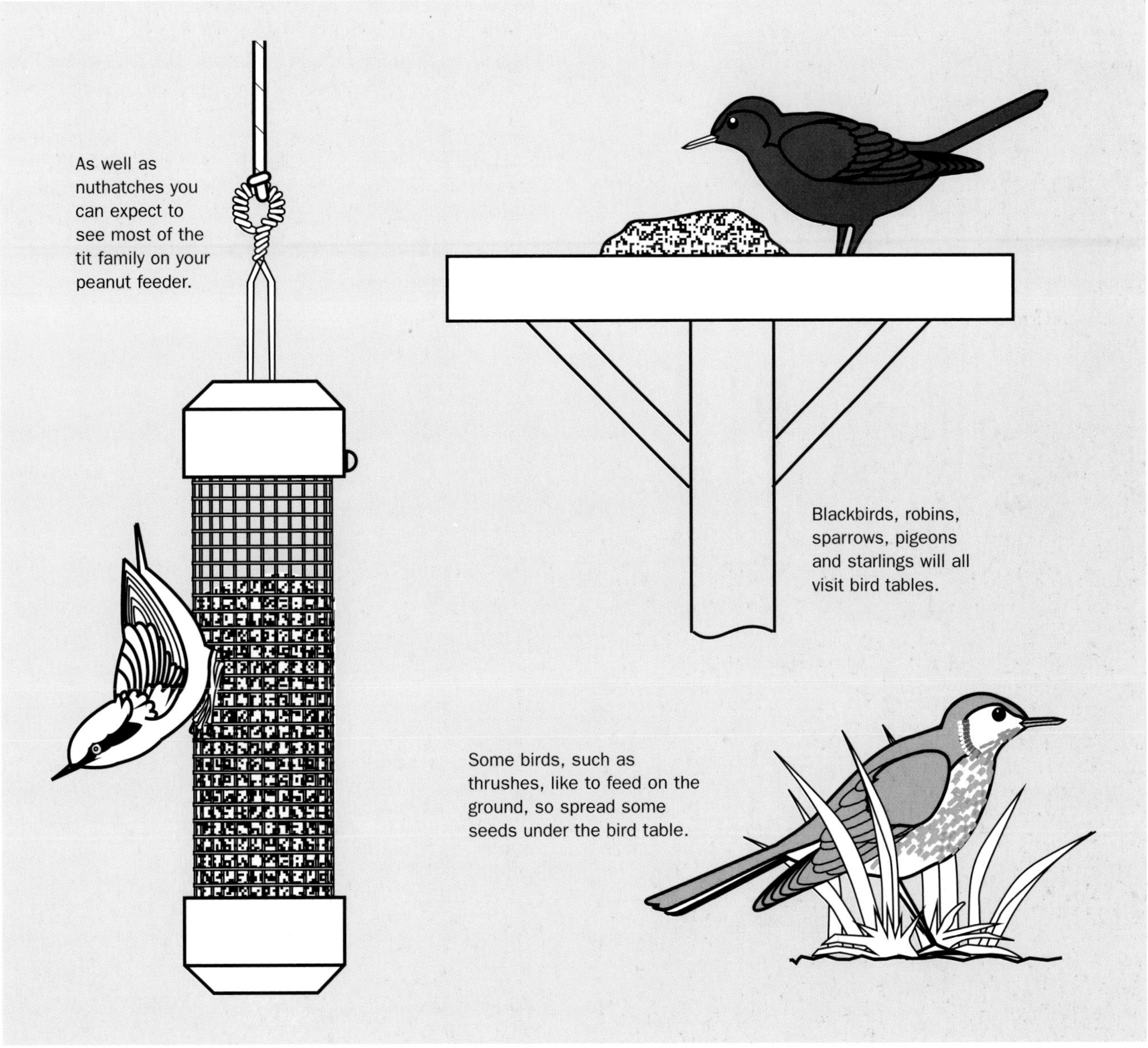

Fig 4.11
Presenting food to birds.

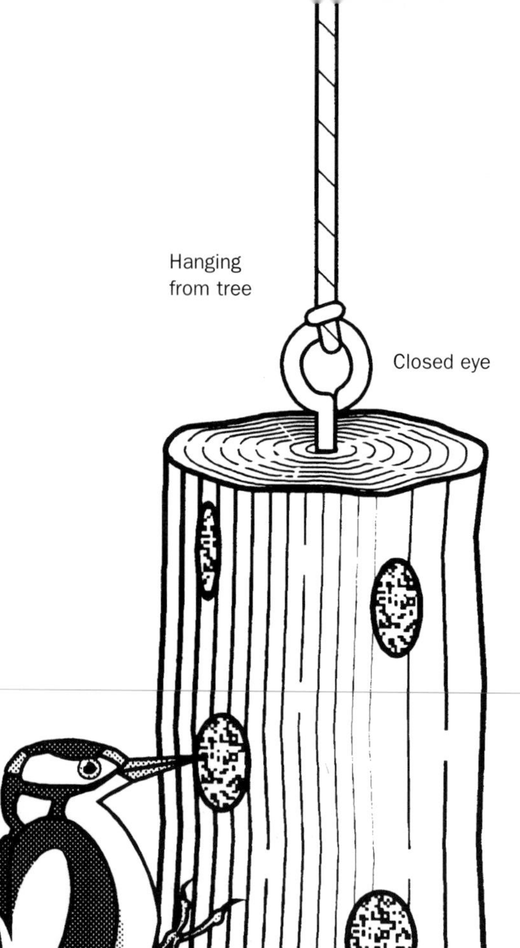

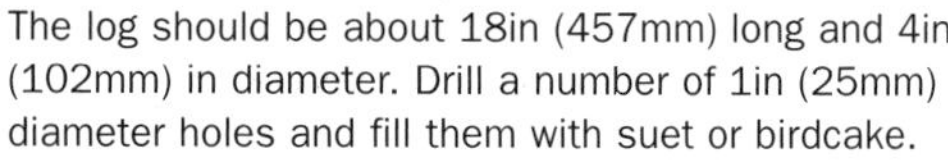

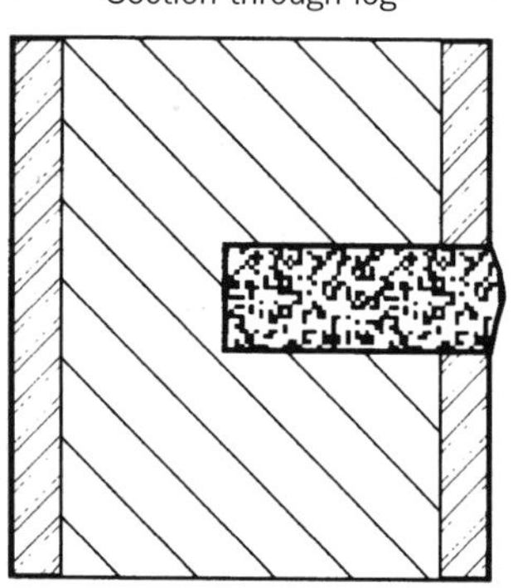

Fig 4.12
Woodpecker log.

peanuts from a hanging feeder. Great spotted woodpeckers will visit a peanut feeder, but to really excite their interest, it's hard to do better than a suet mixture served in holes in a log (*see* Fig 4.12).

Birdcake can also be put into a tit bell (*see* Fig 4.13). The advantage of this is that the larger, less acrobatic birds, such as starlings, find it difficult to get into the birdcake.

To make a tit bell, find an old ceramic flower pot (the plastic ones are too slippery), and attach a length of cord to a small piece of plywood that will fit into the base of the pot. Thread the cord through the drainage hole in the pot, and place the plywood piece neatly in the base to block the hole. Pour in the birdcake mixture and leave to set. When it is ready, hang the pot from a tree.

To feed your local badgers and hedgehogs, put out tinned cat and dog food, or buy food for them from a specialist dealer. For hedgehogs, place the food out in the open, but near some dense ground covering plants so they can approach it without being seen, as they can be a little shy at first.

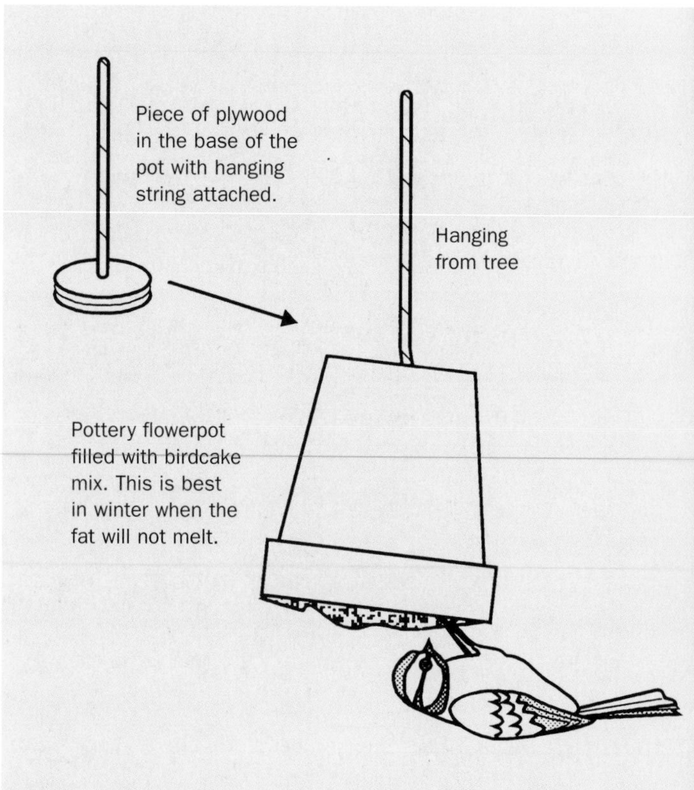

Fig 4.13
Bell feeder for tits.

Town Gardens

It is often thought that living in a large town means the only birds that are likely to be seen are sparrows, starlings and pigeons, but this is far from the truth, particularly if there are shrubs or small trees in the garden or the house is situated near a park or an open space. For example, in Greater London, more than 50 different breeding birds have been recorded.

A garden is not a prerequisite to success: if a bird table is fixed to the windowsill of a flat, it will still attract most of the birds that are common to the area.

The simple projects in this chapter are designed to attract any birds that are in the vicinity. They will provide lots of enjoyment for the observer, and for the birds. Remember that although the birds will not worry about the quality of the woodwork, if it is made well, it will be durable and look attractive. Gaps left between the components of the nest box will result in draughts, which will lower the temperature inside the box and lessen the chances of the birds breeding successfully. They will also let in rain – and a bird box should be waterproof.

WOODPIGEON

SCRAPS BOX

5

Nesting Box for Tits

This box is made entirely from ½in (12mm) interior grade plywood, so it requires painting with several applications of clear wood preserver – the type that soaks into the wood. It has a lid so that it can be cleaned out easily after the nesting season. If possible, you should resist the temptation to peek inside too often when the birds are nesting, as too much attention will inhibit breeding success.

The size of the hole in the front of the box affects which birds breed in it. A hole that is between 1in (25mm) and 1⅛in (28mm) allows both blue tits and great tits to use it. If the hole is much larger then sparrows will take up occupation, which might not be what you want to happen. A small hole also inhibits the access of cats and squirrels, which kill chicks if they get the chance.

When completed, the nesting box should be sited 8–10ft (2.5–3m) from the ground, in a sheltered position on a tree or building.

CUTTING LIST

Back (1)	Plywood	18 x 6 x ½in (457 x 152 x 12mm)
Lid (1)	Plywood	6¼ x 6 x ½in (158 x 152 x 12mm)
Front (1)	Plywood	9¼ x 6 x ½in (235 x 152 x 12mm)
Base (1)	Plywood	5 x 4½ x ½in (127 x 114 x 12mm)
Sides (2)	Plywood	12 x 4½ x ½in (305 x 114 x 12mm)
ALSO REQUIRED:		
Brass hinge (1)		2in (50mm)
Roofing material		9½ x 7in (241 x 178mm)
Gate latch (1)		2in (50mm)

CONSTRUCTION

1 On a sheet of plywood, mark out all the rectangular shapes required with a pencil, ruler and try square, ensuring that the square for the lid is big enough to accommodate the bevel on the front and back edges. Cut them out with a panel saw and smooth the edges with a jack plane. To mark the slope at the top of the sides, use a sliding bevel set to an angle of 25°. When one side is made, use it as a template to mark out the second side. The same angle is used for the top edge of the front, and the front and back edges of the lid. I used a power saw set at the required angle to form the edges, but it can be done, with a little more effort, using a plane.

Fig 5.1
Plan with dimensions.

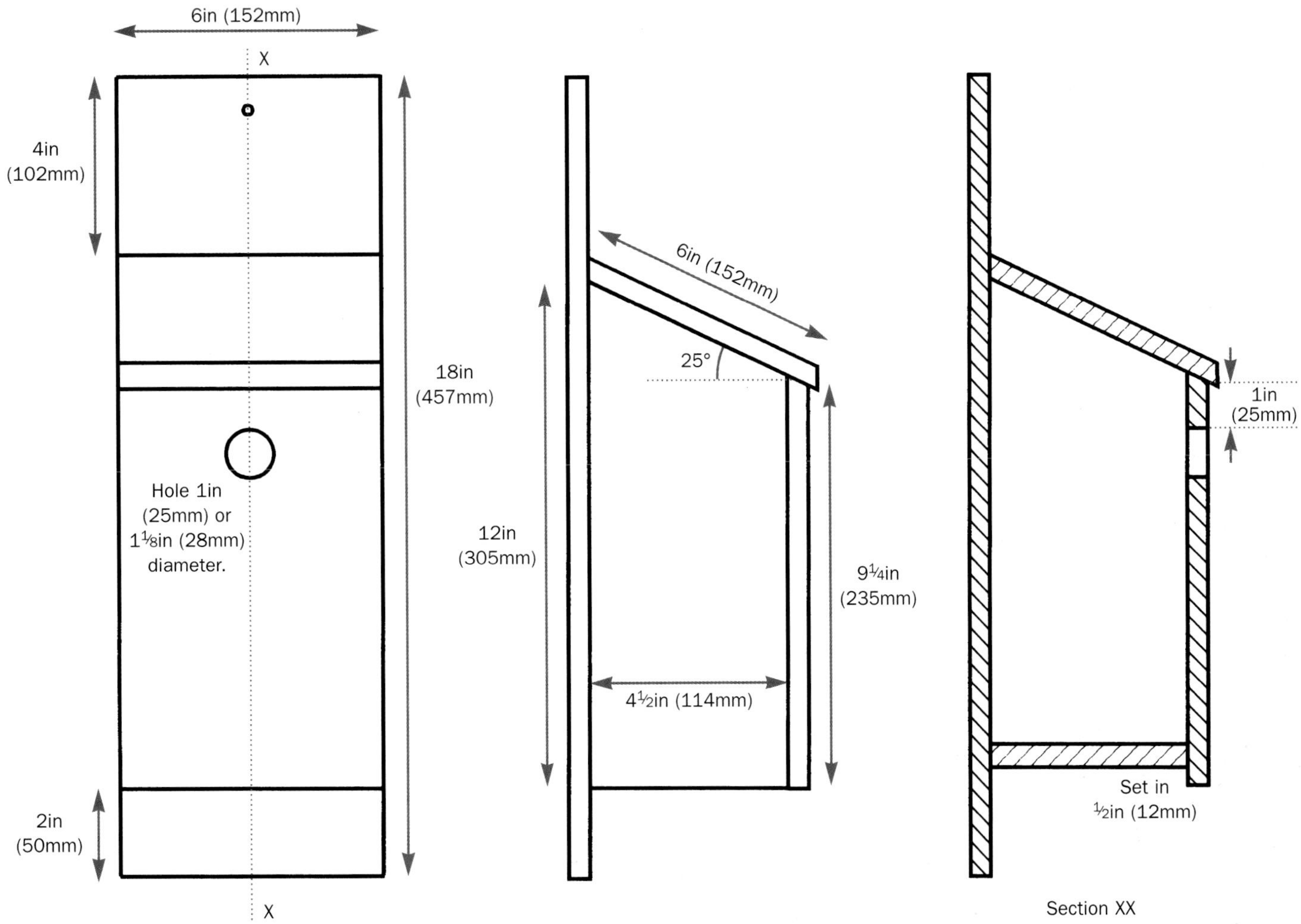

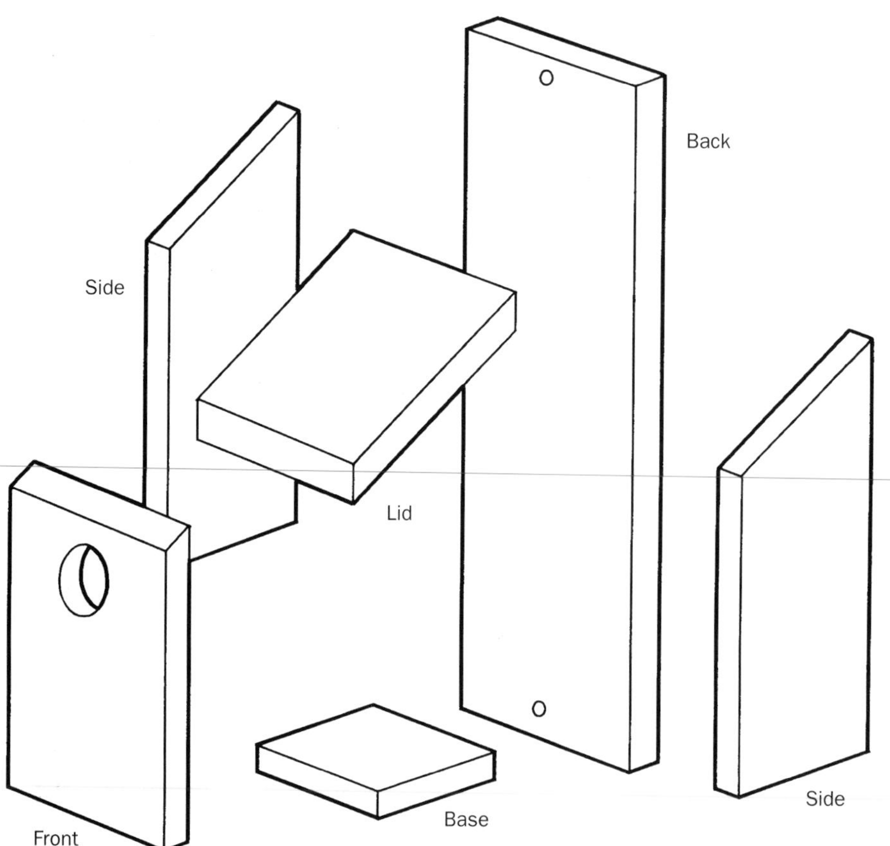

Fig 5.2 (left)
All the wooden parts of the nest box.

Fig 5.3 (below)
The plan of the roofing scheme, plus folding method.

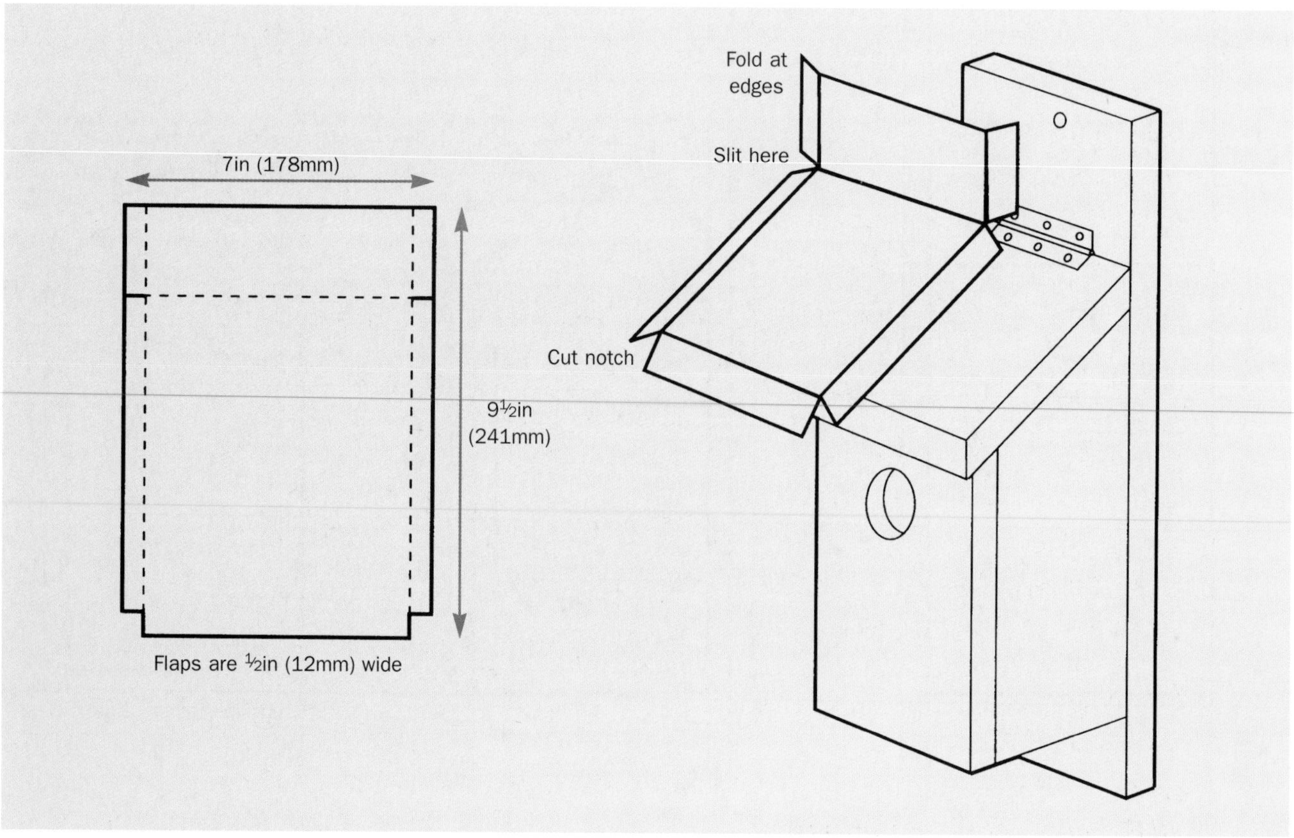

7in (178mm)
9½in (241mm)
Flaps are ½in (12mm) wide
Fold at edges
Slit here
Cut notch

Fig 5.4
The angle at the top of the sides is found with a sliding bevel.

Use a hole saw in a power drill to make the access hole in the front panel. The technique is to drill a small diameter pilot hole and then cut part of the way through from both sides with the hole saw. This will stop the wood on the back from tearing when the blade emerges. At the same time, drill two holes in the back so that the nest box can be fixed to a tree or wall when it is finished.

Fig 5.5
The entrance hole is cut using a hole saw.

Fig 5.6
All the parts, ready to be assembled.

2 To join the panels together, use waterproof glue and 1¼in (32mm) galvanized nails. Fix the front to the two sides first, then put in the base and follow this by nailing and gluing the back into place.

I used a 2in (50mm) brass hinge to fix the lid to the box. To locate the hinge, hold the lid and hinge in position and mark where the screws will go with a gimlet. Because the hinge is held with brass screws, which are easily damaged, pre-drill the holes with a fine drill and lubricate the screws with candle wax – this will ensure they are easily screwed in.

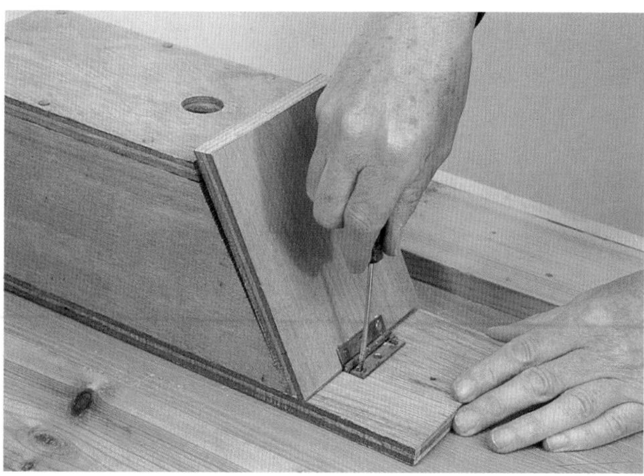

Fig 5.7
A brass hinge is used for the lid so that it will not rust.

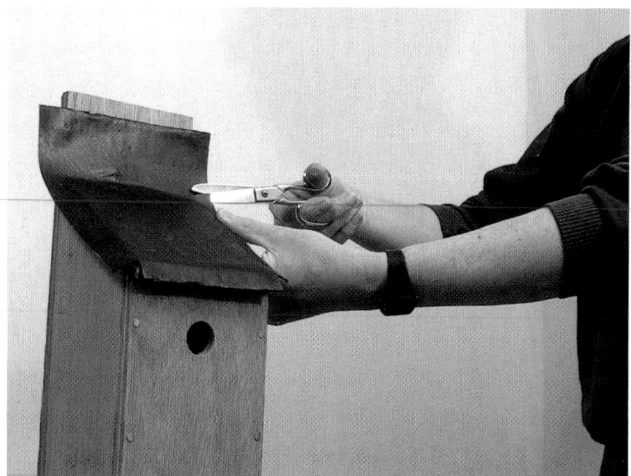

Fig 5.8
The lid-covering materials are trimmed using scissors.

FINISHING

1 With the lid in place, apply two coats of clear wood preserver.

2 Fit some self-adhesive flashing on the top of the lid (*see* Chapter 2, page 19). Cut slits in the edges so that it bends where the lid hinges.

3 Fix a galvanized gate latch to the lid to hold it down and prevent predators getting into the box. If you refer to the drawing of the gate latch in Fig 1.4 (*see* page 3), you will notice that there are two screw eyes. One is the catch and one the latch. To fix the gate latch in place, drill two small holes, one in the lid and one in the body of the box and simply screw in the screw eyes.

Fig 5.9
The completed nesting box.

6

Scraps Box

Some leftovers, such as baked potatoes or the fat from a Sunday joint, are ideal for feeding tits and robins, and can be placed out on the bird table, or in a scrap feeder. The advantage of the feeder is that large birds such as crows, magpies and black-headed gulls, can't carry off big pieces, giving the smaller birds a better chance to feed before it all disappears.

Stale cake, uncooked pastry and soft biscuits can all be put into the feeder, but don't put in too much bread without wetting it, as some birds have difficulty digesting dry bread. Others, such as crows and magpies, if given dry bread, will dunk it in the bird bath before eating it.

What you put into the feeder will determine the mesh size you need. For chopped bacon rind, a ¼in (6mm) mesh is best, but for general use the ½in (12mm) mesh I used for my scraps box is satisfactory. Mesh is used not only on the front of the box, but also underneath so that birds will be able to get at the last crumbs. This also allows bits and pieces to fall onto the ground where birds that have difficulty using the feeder, such as thrushes, will get their share.

When completed, the feeder should be installed at least 5ft (1.52m) from the ground.

CUTTING LIST

Back (1)	Pine	10 x 8 x ¾in (254 x 203 x 18mm)
Lid (1)	Pine	8⅜ x 4³⁄₁₆ x ¾in (212 x 106 x 18mm)
Sides (2)	Pine	6 x 4 x ¾in (152 x 102 x 18mm)
Cross rail (1)	Pine	8 x ¾ x ¾in (203 x 18 x 18mm)

ALSO REQUIRED:

Brass hinge (1)	2in (50mm)
Roofing material	10 x 7in (254 x 178mm)
Gate latch (1)	2in (50mm)
Wire mesh, ½in (12mm) square	8 x 10½in (203 x 266mm)

CONSTRUCTION

THE MESH

1 Cut out a piece of mesh measuring 8 x 10½in (203 x 266mm). You need to bend this mesh to form the shape shown in Fig 6.1. First, make the bend to form the front and the underside of the box.

To do this, measure the position of the bend and mark it with a felt-tip pen, then bend it around a straight-edged piece of wood held in a vice. With the mesh thus formed into an 'L' shape, mark the ¾in (19mm) flaps at the top and bottom edges and bend them inwards by 90°, using a pair of pliers. Cut out the notches in the four corners with tin snips and cut the mesh at the ends of the original bend as well. Next, form the flaps at the sides, using pliers. Put the mesh to one side whilst the wooden parts are made.

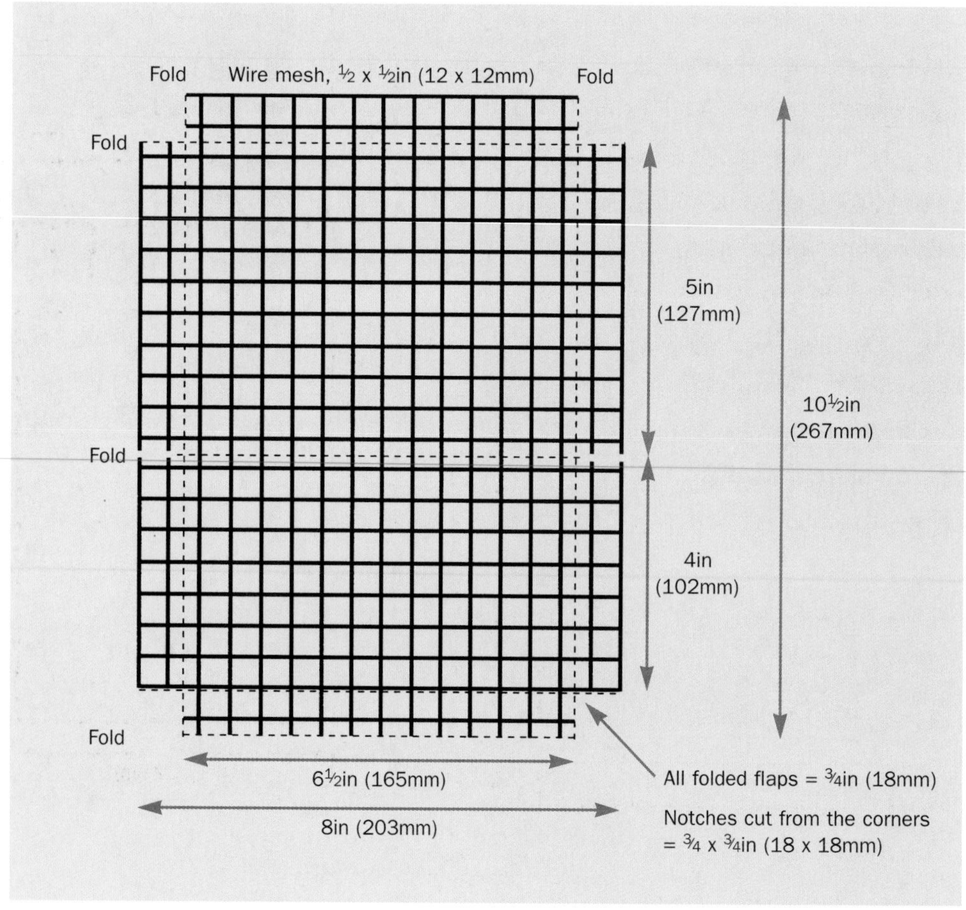

Fig 6.1 Cutting information for the wire mesh.

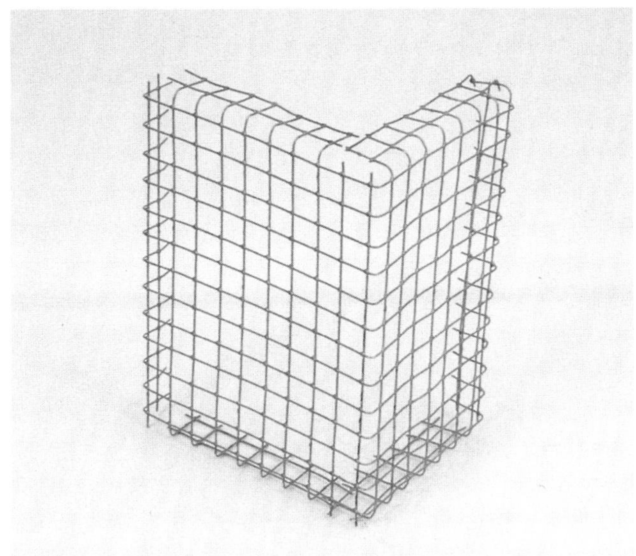

THE BOX

1 Cut the two sides and the front rail that joins them together to the required size. Form halving joints at the ends of the cross rail with a tenon saw, and cut the recesses to house them in the sides, using a tenon and a coping saw.

Check the fit of the joints and fix them with waterproof glue (*see* Fig 6.5).

Fig 6.2
The mesh cage before being fitted into the sides.

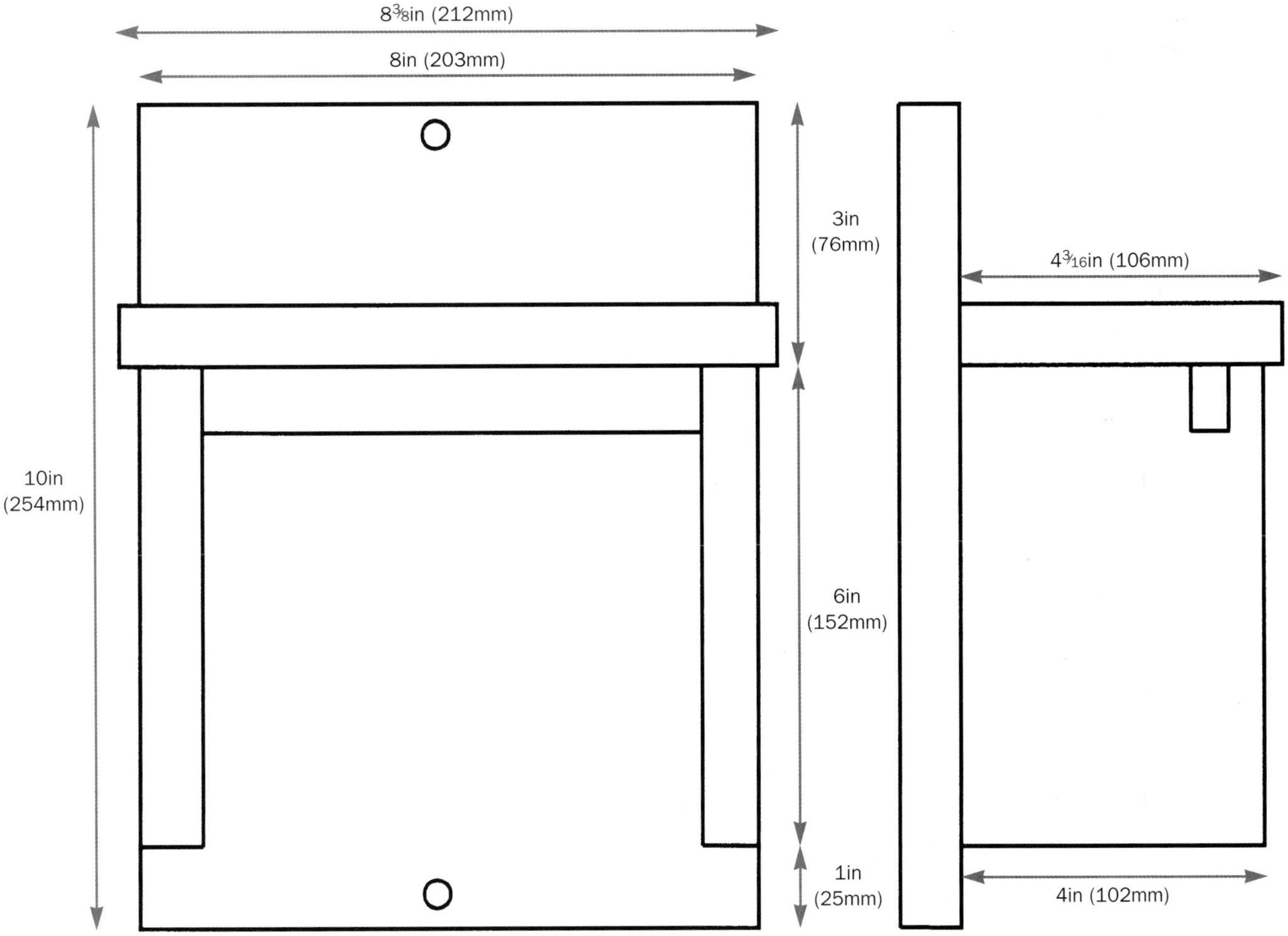

8$\frac{3}{8}$in (212mm)

8in (203mm)

3in (76mm)

4$\frac{3}{16}$in (106mm)

10in (254mm)

6in (152mm)

1in (25mm)

4in (102mm)

Fig 6.3
Plan with dimensions.

Fig 6.4
All the wooden parts for the scrap feeder.

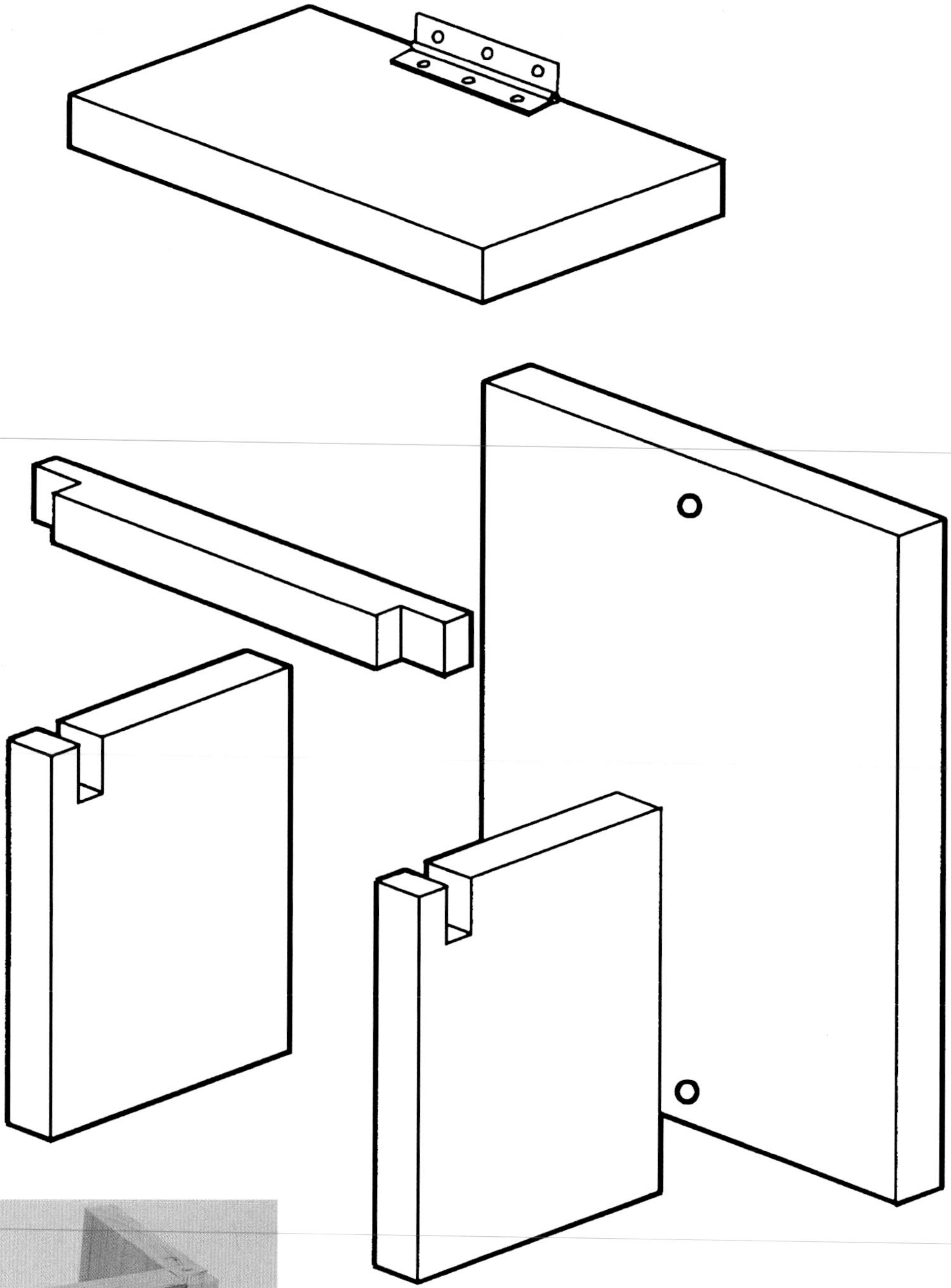

Fig 6.5
The two sides are assembled with the front rail before being fitted to the back.

2 To get a piece of board wide enough for the back, glue a couple of lengths of ¾in (18mm) thick tongue-and-groove floorboards together (*see* Fig 6.6), and drill two holes in the back, so that the feeder can be hung up with nails or screws. To make it easier to nail the back to the sides, drill small pilot holes in the back for the nails. (The actual joining of back to sides will be done later.)

3 The next step is to fix the mesh cage to the underside of the front rail and the base of the back, using a stapler. If this is left until after the back and sides have been joined, the limited remaining space makes it difficult to use the stapler.

4 With the mesh partially attached, the sides can be fixed to the back with glue and galvanized nails, and the mesh fixed at the sides, again using the stapler. It is possible to leave the sides until this stage, because there is more clearance for the stapler (*see* Fig 6.7). Cut a lid from a suitable piece of pine and fit it with a brass hinge.

FINISHING

1 Give the box two applications of clear wood preserver. Cut a piece of self-adhesive flashing, and fit it to the top of the lid. (*See* Chapter 2, page 19.) Fix a galvanized gate latch to the lid to hold it down and prevent squirrels getting into the box. (*See* Chapter 5, page 34.)

***Fig 6.6** (above)*
To make up the wide backboard, two pieces of tongue-and-groove boarding are joined together.

***Fig 6.7** (right)*
Fixing the mesh to the sides with a stapler.

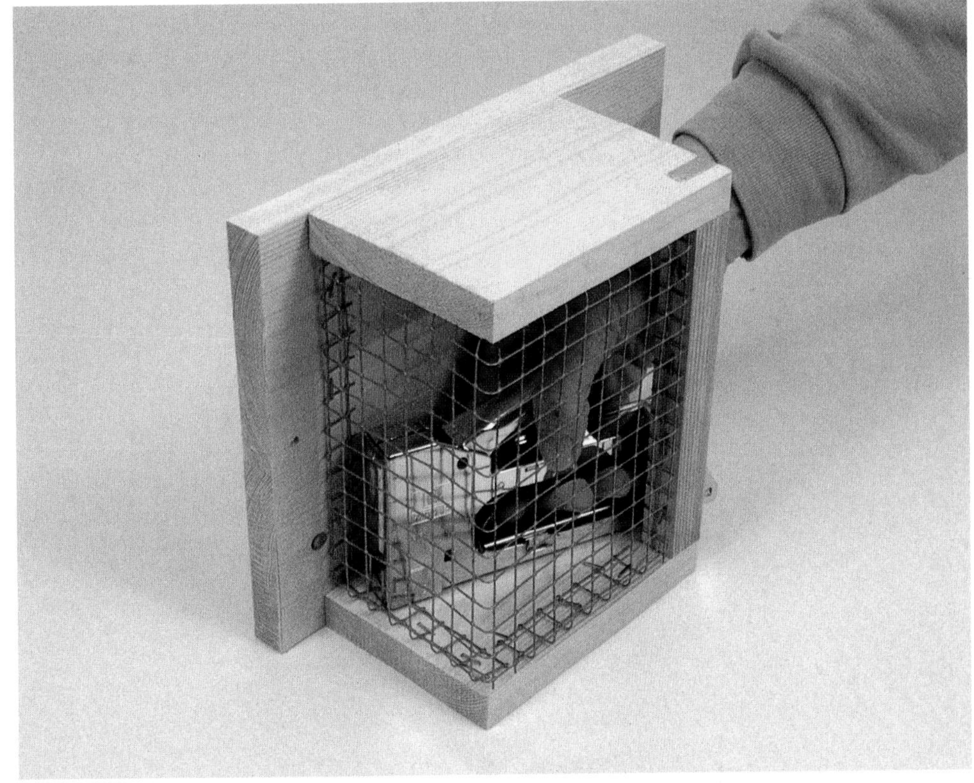

Fig 6.8
Plan with dimensions and method of folding the roof covering.

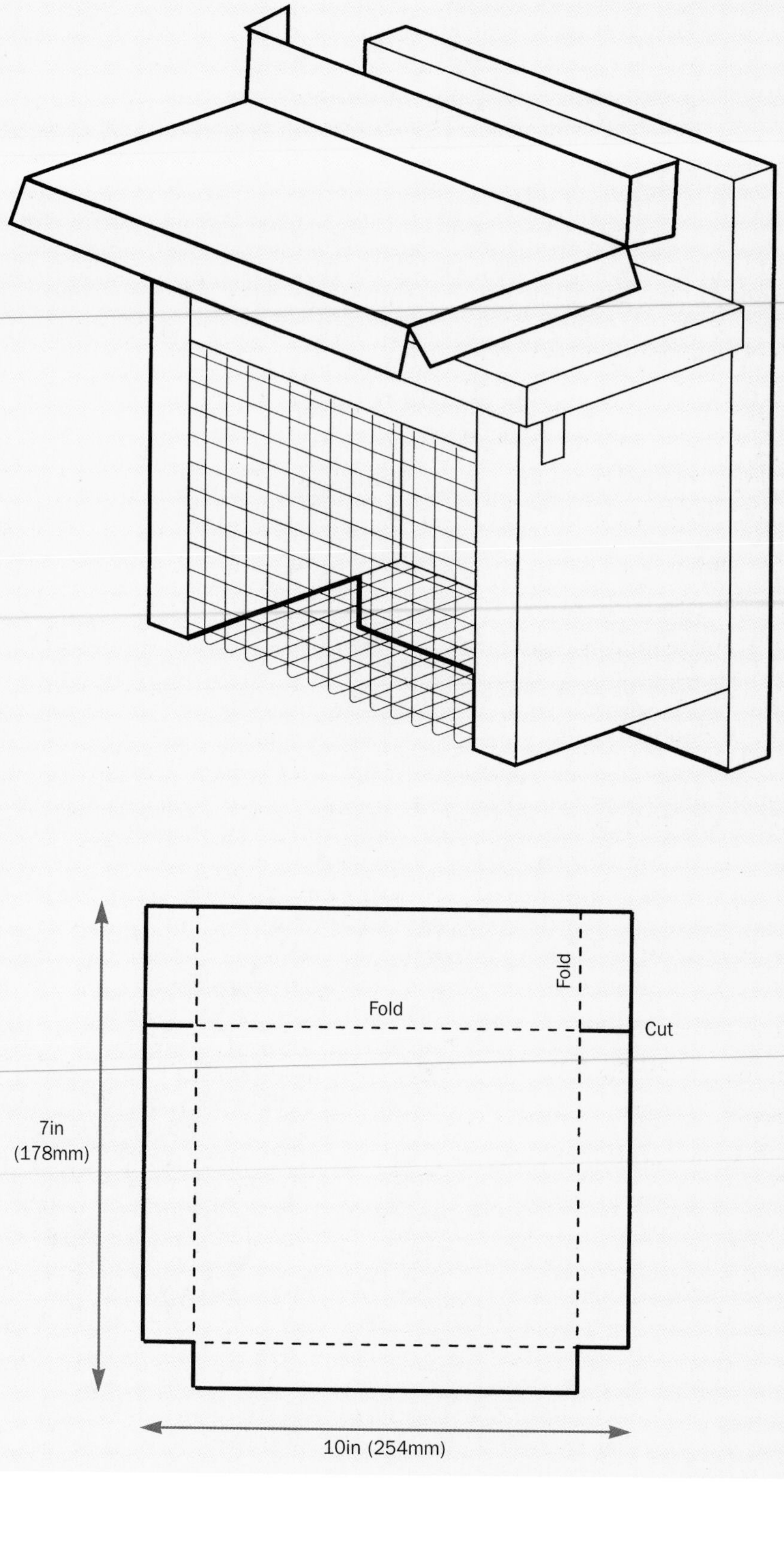

Fold

Fold

Cut

7in
(178mm)

10in (254mm)

7

Bird Table on a Stand

A table is one of the best ways of attracting birds to your garden: the type of bird will depend on the food offered and the area in which you live. Finches and tits like nuts and seeds, whereas blackbirds favour pieces of apple. Most birds like fatty foods and starlings are very fond of most scraps, even fish and chips. The table must be kept clean as any rotting food left on it will spread disease. To this end, I have left a gap in the small fence around the table top so that leftover food can be easily brushed off, but the fence will still prevent seeds from blowing away in the wind.

The plans given are for a bird table on a stand that can be moved around the garden, but if mobility is not important then the job can be simplified by dispensing with the stand and putting the post into a metal fence post holder – these can be obtained from garden centres (*see* Fig 7.3).

The table should be about 4½ft (1.42m) above the ground to make it difficult for cats to sneak up on the birds as they eat.

GREENFINCH

CUTTING LIST

Base of table top (1)	Plywood	14 x 14 x ½in (356 x 356 x 12mm)
Front of table top (1)	Pine	14 x 1½ x ¾in (356 x 38 x 18mm)
Back of table top (1)	Pine	15½ x 1½ x ¾in (394 x 38 x 18mm)
Sides of table top (2)	Pine	14 x 1½ x ¾in (356 x 38 x 18mm)
Post (1)	Pine	52½ x 2 x 2in (1,334 x 51 x 51mm)
Table top supports (2)	Pine	7 x 2 x 1in (179 x 51 x 25mm)
Base supports (4)	Pine	12 x 2 x 1in (305 x 51 x 25mm)
Base (2)	Pine	24 x 2 x 2in (610 x 51 x 51mm)

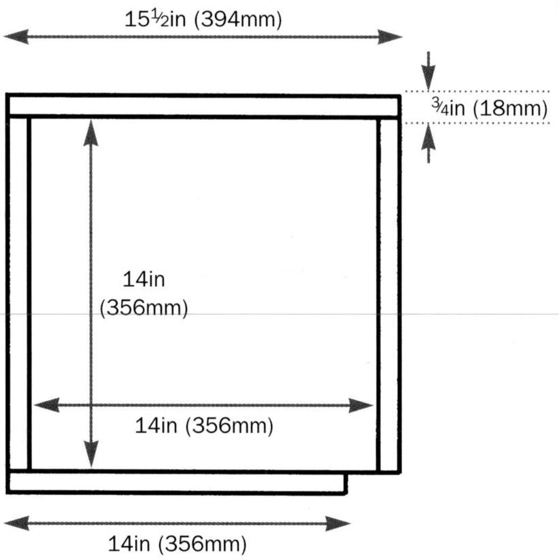

15½in (394mm)
¾in (18mm)
14in (356mm)
14in (356mm)
14in (356mm)

Plan view of top

15½in (394mm)
1½in (38mm)
7in (179mm)
56in (1,422mm)
52½in (1,334mm)
2in (51mm)
12in (305mm)
1in (25mm)
2in (51mm)
24in (610mm)

Side view of table

Fig 7.1
Sizes for the table on a stand.

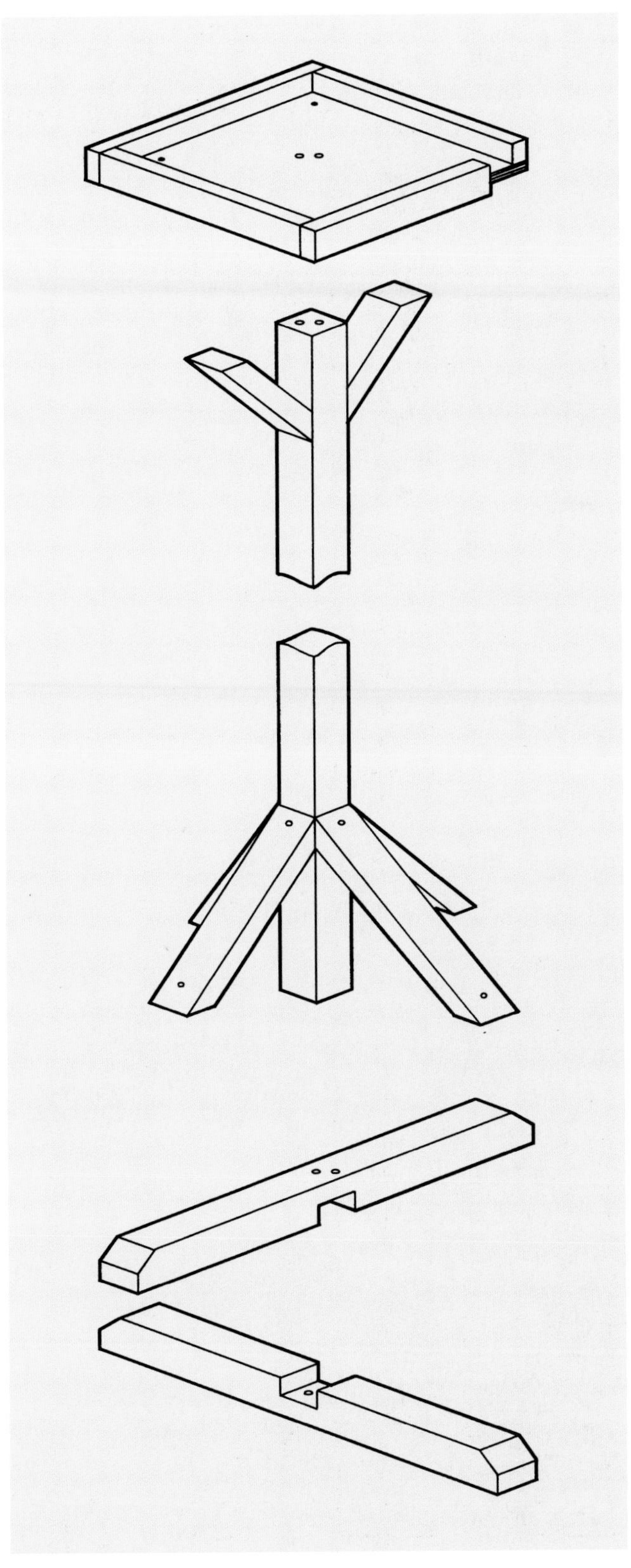

Fig 7.2
Construction details for the table and stand.

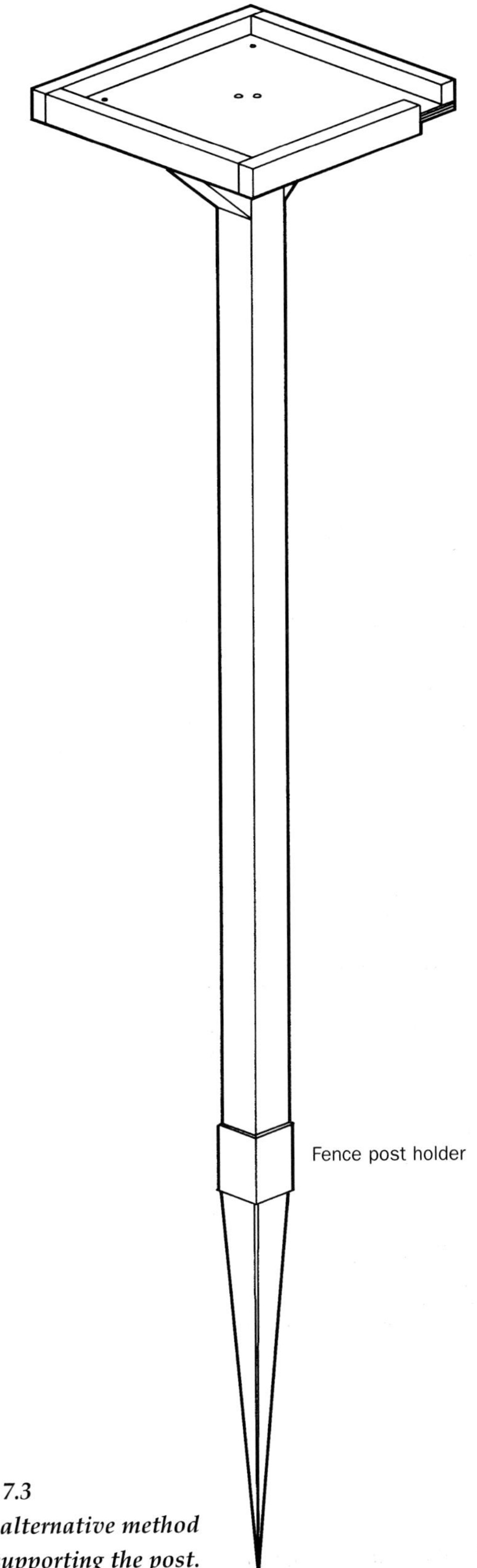

Fig 7.3
An alternative method of supporting the post.

Construction

THE BASE

1 Cut a piece of 2 x 2in (51 x 51mm) pine to length for the post. Use a try square to ensure that the ends are square – this will help to make the stand upright when joined to the base.

Cut the pieces of wood that will form the cross for the base to size and mark the position of the halving joints in the centres (*see* Fig 7.4). Use a tenon saw to cut the cheeks of the recess before removing the waste with a bevel-edged chisel. Mark the chamfers on the ends of the pieces with a 45° square before sawing them off. Clean up any rough edges with a plane and test the joint for fit. If the fit is accurate, glue the joint together with waterproof glue and clamp until dry.

2 To fit the base to the post, use two 4in (100mm) nails. Drill two, small-diameter holes through the centre of the cross pieces of the base, with the drill held upright. These holes are to guide the nails and prevent the wood from splitting. Put the post in a vice to hold it upright and nail through the base into the end grain of the post.

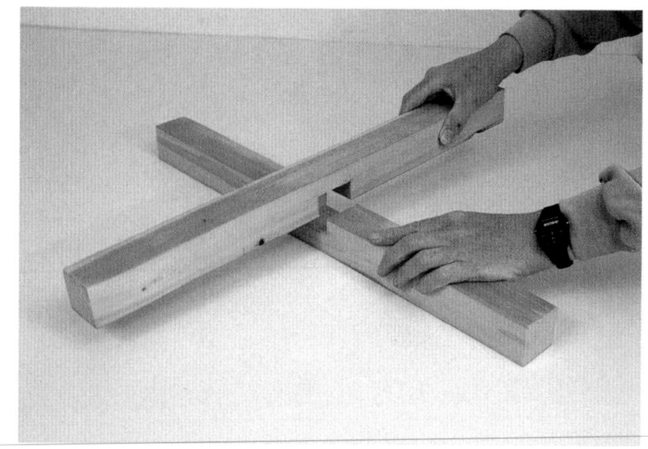

Fig 7.5
Testing the halving joints for accuracy.

3 The base supports are the next parts to be made and attached. These are the same width as the post and have 45° bevels on each end so that they fit flush with the post at one and the base at the other. Cut the pieces to the length shown in Fig 7.1 and make the mitres on the ends using a power or panel saw in a mitre box. Drill holes in the ends to guide the nails (*see* Fig 7.6), then fix the supports permanently in place using galvanized nails and glue (*see* Fig 7.7).

STARLING

Fig 7.4
Marking the halving joints on the base.

Fig 7.6
Drilling pilot holes in the base supports to guide the nails.

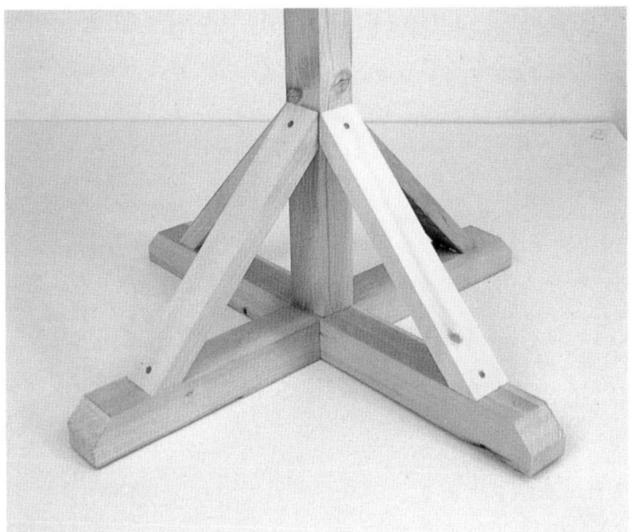

Fig 7.7
The finished base.

THE TOP

1 Cut the baseboard for the top from ½in (12mm) plywood and drill a hole in each corner so that any surplus water will drain off when it rains. The edge strips are made from ¾in (18mm) thick pine. After cutting these to size, fix them with glue and small copper-plated nails, punched below the surface. Fill the punch holes with neutral-coloured filler to hide them.

2 Use two 2in (50mm) nails to fix the top to the post in a way similar to how the base was fixed. To find the centre of the table, so that the nails are in the correct place, trace lines along a ruler placed across the diagonals. The top is secured by two supports only, and they are cut and fixed in the same way as the base supports. However, take care not to use nails that are too long, because the base of the top is not very thick.

FINISHING

1 Pine is not very rot-resistant and if exposed to the weather without any protection it will deteriorate fairly rapidly. To prevent this, give the table a couple of coats of weatherproofing solution. I used a variety that was also a wood dye to brighten up the appearance of the stand.

Fig 7.8
The assembled table and stand.

8

Suspended Bird Table

Another effective way of presenting food to birds is on a suspended bird table. If squirrels are not a problem in your garden, a good reason to make it is simply that it looks decorative.

For hanging the table in a tree, a long length of thin garden wire is best, as this is difficult for squirrels to climb down, although if the table is close to the trunk they will be able to jump onto it. As an optional extra, there is a bracket for hanging the table from a wall.

The surface of the table is partitioned so that different types of foods, like nuts, seeds and fruit, are kept separate. Observing which food disappears the quickest will indicate the best and most popular things to offer, in order to attract more birds. The partition will also prevent the food, especially light seeds, from blowing away and being deposited on the floor.

CUTTING LIST

TABLE

Base (1)	Plywood	15 x 11 x ½in (381 x 279 x 12mm)
Curved sides (2)	Plywood	14 x 11 x ½in (356 x 279 x 12mm)
Front and back (2)	Plywood	16 x 2 x ½in (406 x 51 x 12mm)
Wide roof panel (1)	Plywood	17 x 8 x ½in (432 x 203 x 12mm)
Narrow roof panel (1)	Plywood	17 x 7½ x ½in (432 x 191 x 12mm)
Long partition (1)	Plywood	15 x 1 x ½in (381 x 25 x 12mm)
Short partitions (2)	Plywood	11 x 1 x ½in (279 x 25 x 12mm)

ALSO REQUIRED:

Self-adhesive flashing pieces (3)	18 x 9in (457 x 229mm)

SUPPORT

Horizontal arm (1)	Pine	15 x 2 x 1in (381 x 51 x 25mm)
Diagonal support (1)	Pine	12¾ x 2 x 1in (324 x 51 x 25mm)
Vertical wall plate (1)	Pine	25½ x 2 x 1in (648 x 51 x 25mm)

ALSO REQUIRED:

Brass or galvanized chain (1)	3ft (1m)
Brass cup hook (1)	1in (25mm)
Brass eyes (2)	1in (25mm)

CONSTRUCTION

BASE AND SIDES

1 Make a start by cutting the base from some ½in (12mm) interior plywood and planing the edges smooth. Mark and cut out two rectangles from the same material, big enough to form the two side panels that support the roof. At one end, cut the slopes that conform to the pitch of the roof. Use the base of any convenient plate or container with a diameter of approximately 7½in (190mm) as a template to mark the semicircular cut-outs on the edges of the sides (*see* Fig 8.3). Once the curves have been drawn, cut them out with a coping saw. Clean up the straight edges with a plane and smooth the semicircular cut-outs with a drum sander (*see* Fig 8.4).

2 Cut the two narrow table sides and the three partitions to size, and form small halving joints where the partitions cross, using a tenon saw for the sides of the joint and a coping saw to remove the waste. Round the top edges of the partitions slightly, using a plane followed by glasspaper, before testing the accuracy of the joint.

BLACKBIRD

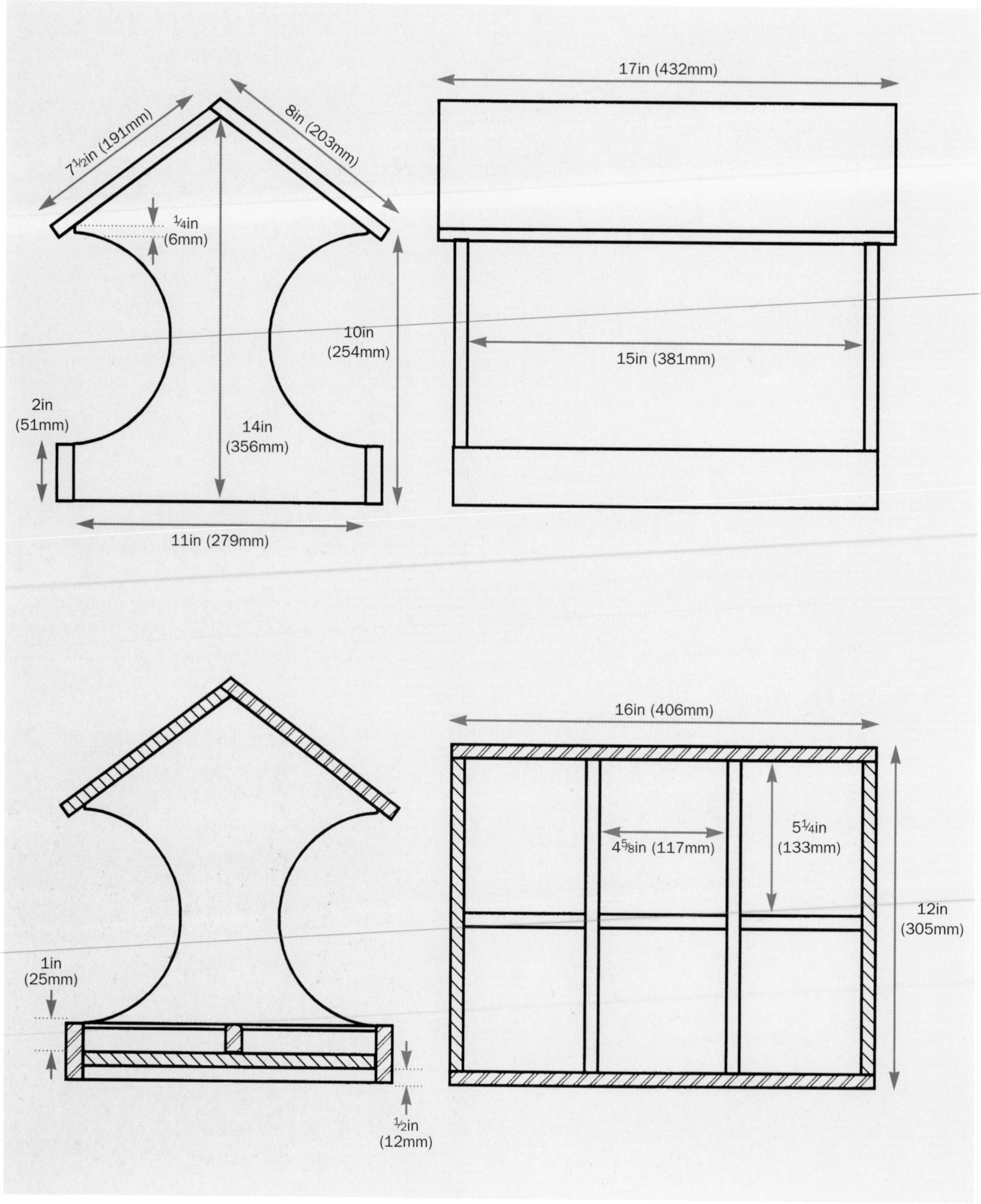

7½in (191mm)
8in (203mm)
¼in (6mm)
10in (254mm)
2in (51mm)
14in (356mm)
11in (279mm)
17in (432mm)
15in (381mm)
16in (406mm)
4⅝in (117mm)
5¼in (133mm)
12in (305mm)
1in (25mm)
½in (12mm)

Fig 8.1
Dimensioned plan.

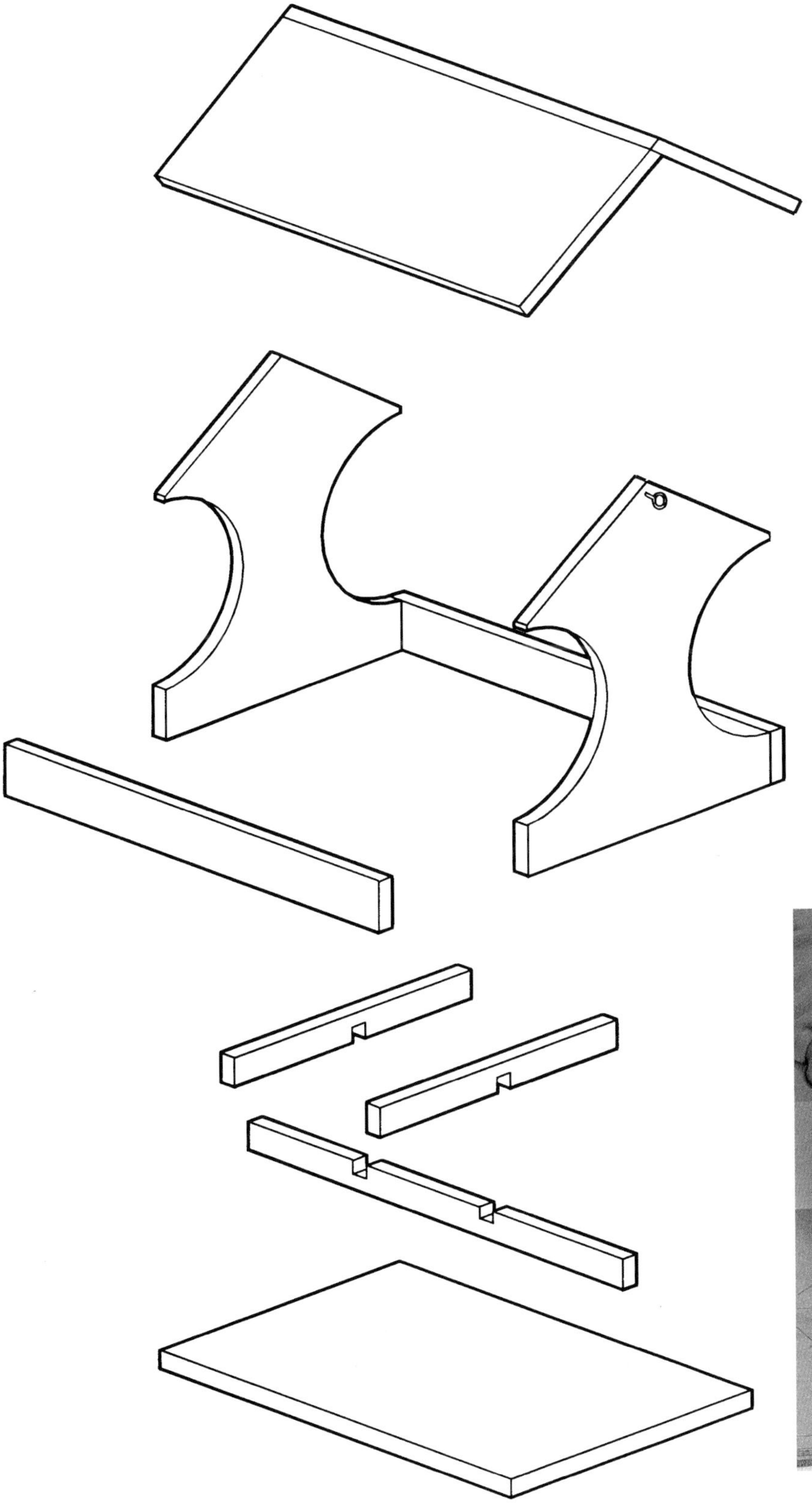

Fig 8.2
Construction details.

Fig 8.3
Using a circular container as a template to mark the curved shapes on the sides.

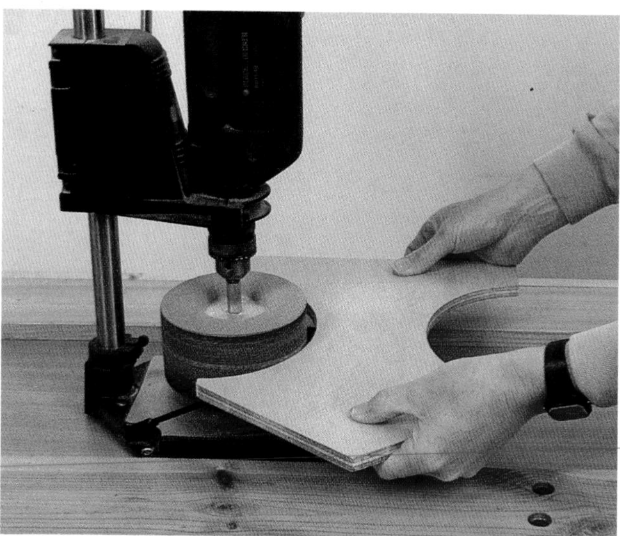

Fig 8.4
A drum sander is used for smoothing the curved shapes.

Fig 8.5
The table before the roof covering is fitted.

3 Fix the base to the sides, ½in (12mm) from the bottom edge of the sides. To locate the correct position, draw a line around the inside edge of the four sides as a guide. When this is marked, fix the base to the two sides that support the roof with waterproof glue and 1in (25mm) oval brads. To help prevent them rusting, punch them below the surface and fill the resulting holes with an appropriately coloured wood filler.

ROOF

1 Saw two rectangular panels from ½in (12mm) interior plywood for the roof, and bevel their edges where they meet at the top, using a plane. The angle of the bevel corresponds to the pitch of the roof.

The two roof panels are fixed in the same way as the base and sides, although it is not necessary to cover the nail heads with filler as the entire roof is protected with a waterproof covering.

2 Next, glue and nail the two narrow sides into place. Unlike the bird table on a stand (*see* page 41), there is not a gap in the sides for cleaning purposes. This is because scrap food can be emptied out by turning the table upside down. Fix the partitions in place with glue, and drill drain holes into the base, one in each compartment (*see* Fig 8.5).

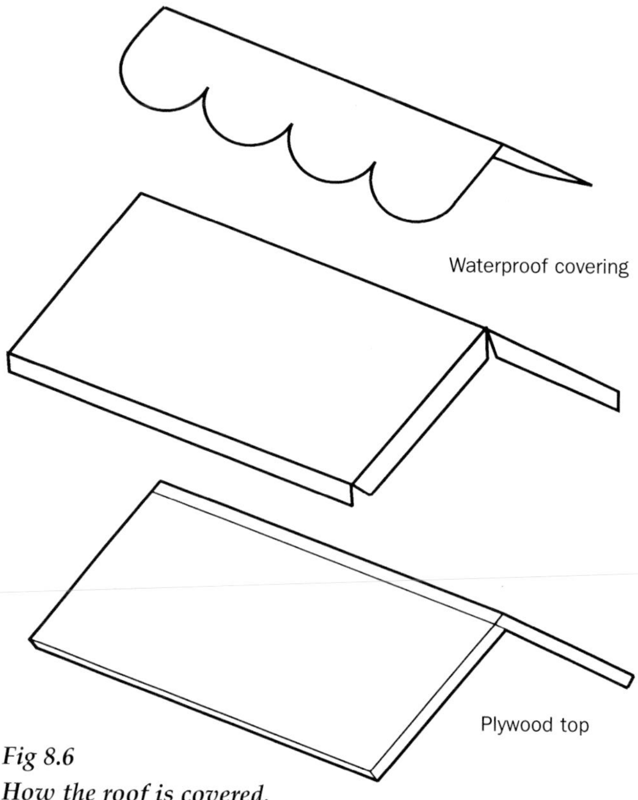

Fig 8.6
How the roof is covered.

WALL BRACKET

1 Using pieces of planed timber with a section of 2 x 1in (51 x 25mm), cut the three pieces that make up the bracket to length. Drill holes in the ends of the

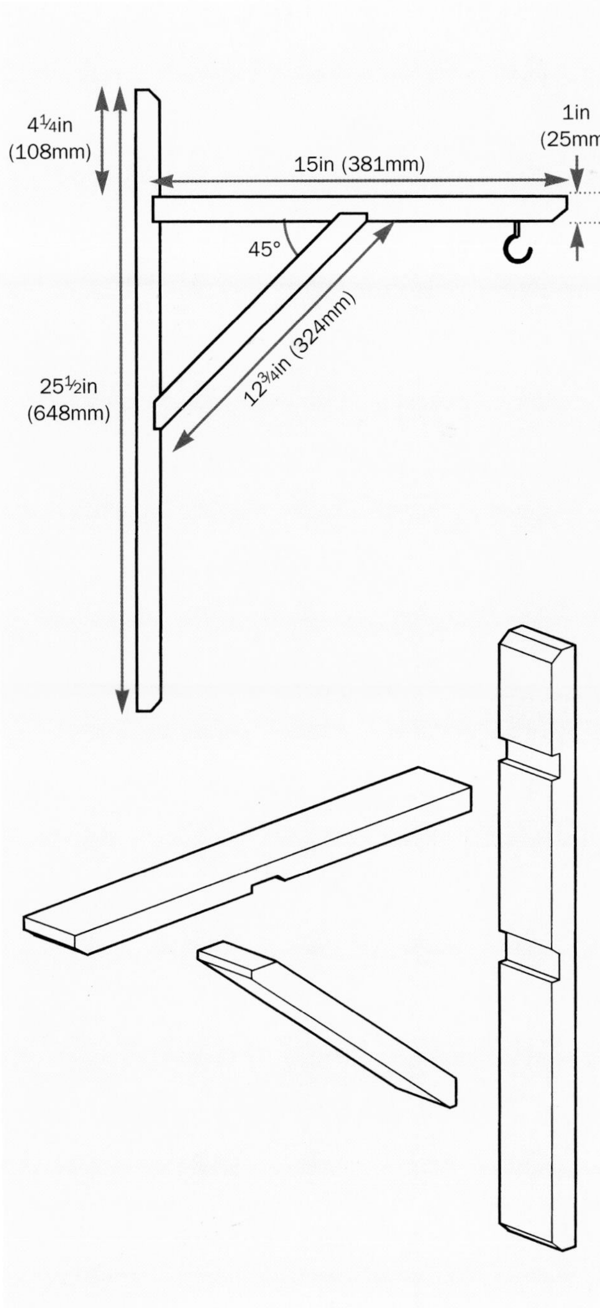

Fig 8.7
Plan, with sizes and construction details, for the wall bracket.

vertical wall plate so that it can be fixed to the wall, and chamfer the ends with a plane. Fix the horizontal support to the wall plate with a housing joint. Make this joint by sawing the sides with a tenon saw before cleaning out the waste with a bevel-edged chisel.

2 On the diagonal support, cut a double chamfer on the ends with a tenon saw, after marking them with a 45° set square. Fit the horizontal support into the wall plate and, after ensuring that they are at exactly 90°, lay the diagonal support in the correct position and draw around the ends onto the vertical and horizontal pieces to indicate where the housing joints are to be made. Cut the housings using the same method as before. Fix all the parts together with glue and a brass screw through the back of the joint.

FINISHING

BIRD TABLE

1 Paint the entire structure with two coats of cedar-coloured wood preserver, except the roof which should be left untouched so that the roofing material will stick to it.

Three pieces of self-adhesive flashing are used to cover the roof. To begin, stick two rectangular pieces to the roof panels, wrap them around the edges, and then trim them to size with scissors. On the third piece, make scallop shapes. Draw them on the backing paper first, using a paint tin as a template, and then cut them out with scissors.

Screw two zinc-plated eyes into the top of the sides that support the roof so that the table can be connected to a chain and hung up.

WALL BRACKET

1 Finish the bracket with wood preserver so that it matches the table, and fix a brass cup hook into the end of the horizontal arm so that the table can be suspended. Do not use a long length of chain as this will allow the table to swing against the wall and cause damage: 3ft (1m) is about right.

Wall-Mounted Feeding Tray

This bird table, designed to fit onto a wall, is simple to make and ideal for flat dwellers without access to a garden. It can be fixed beside a window and has 'keyhole' slots for the fixing screws so that it can be easily detached for cleaning. For houses with wooden window frames, fixing it to the frame so that it rests on the sill is an alternative to wall fixing.

CUTTING LIST

Base (1)	Plywood	13 x 10 x ½in (330 x 254 x 12mm)
Sides (2)	Pine	11 x 2 x ⅜in (279 x 51 x 9mm)
Back (1)	Pine	13 x 3¾ x ¾in (330 x 95 x 18mm)
Front (1)	Pine	13 x 2 x ⅜in (330 x 51 x 9mm)

CONSTRUCTION

1 From ½in (12mm) plywood, cut the base to size and clean up the edges with a plane. Follow this by cutting the two short sides and the front from ⅜in (9mm) pine – wall cladding is ideal for this. The back is made from ¾in (18mm) thick pine. It needs to be more substantial, as it is the part that is fixed to the wall. Drill

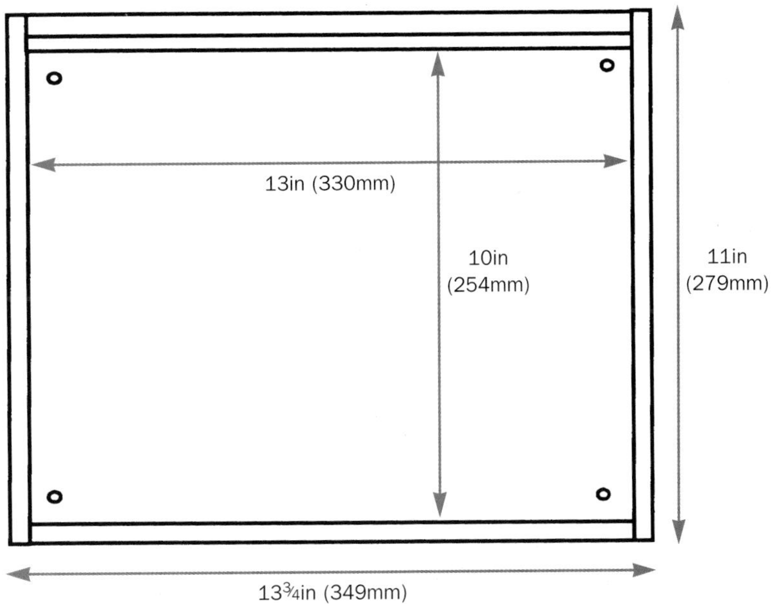

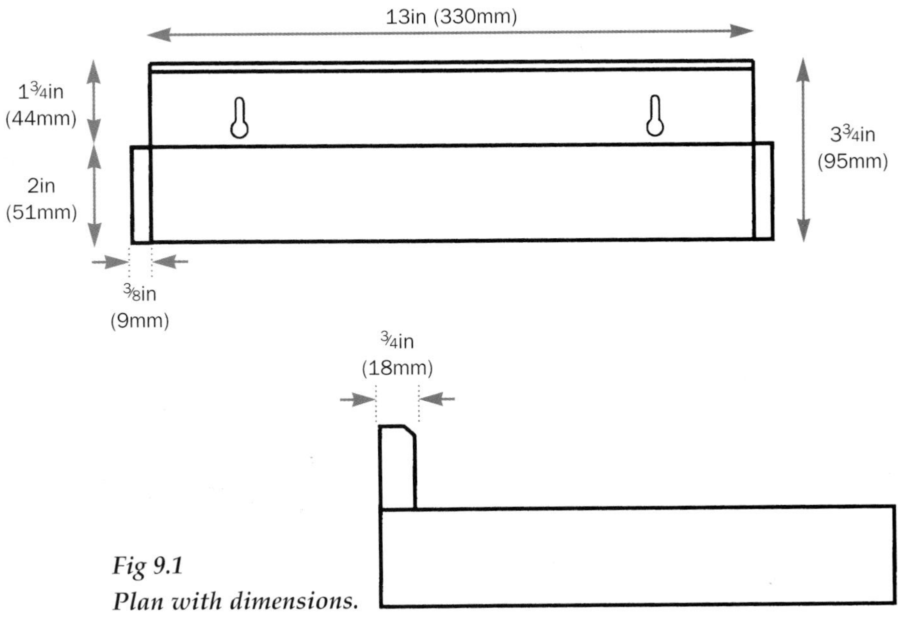

Fig 9.1
Plan with dimensions.

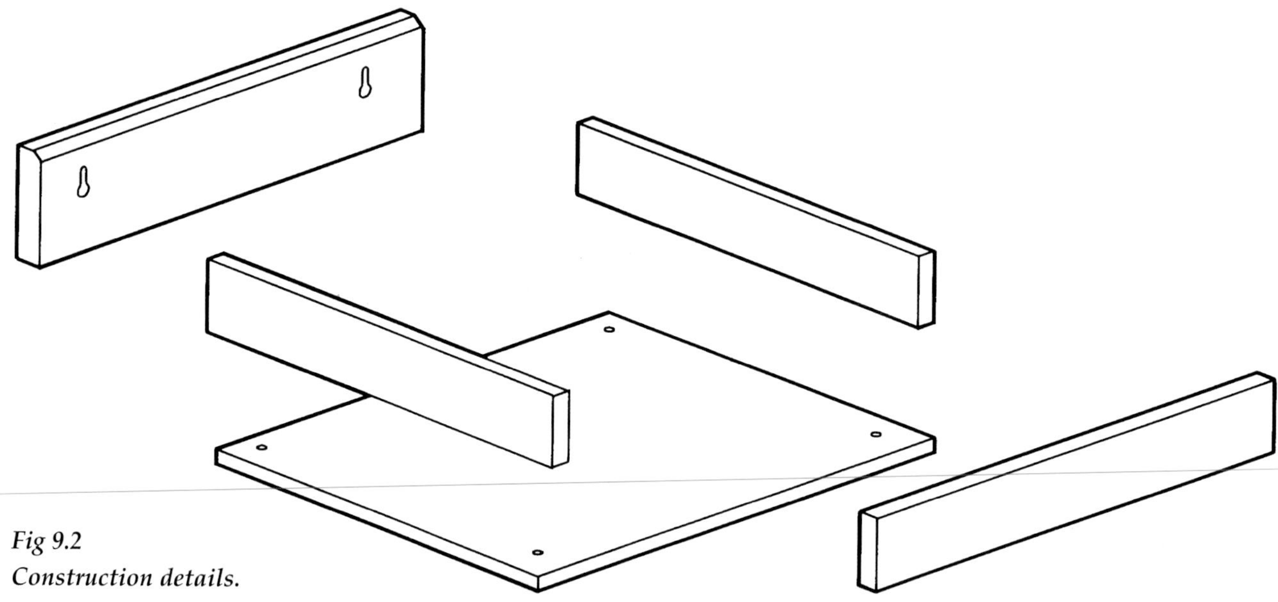

Fig 9.2
Construction details.

Fig 9.3
Cleaning up the 'keyhole' slot with a file.

two keyhole slots in the back to accommodate the screws that will fix the tray to the wall. The idea is that the largest part of the slot will pass over the screw head and the tray can then be pushed down, so that the head is in the narrow part of the slot and holds the tray onto the wall.

To make these slots, drill a ½in (12mm) hole at the lower end of where the slot will be, and a couple of 3⁄16in (4mm) holes for the narrow part of the slot. Remove the waste wood between these holes with a chisel, and clean it up with a file (*see* Fig 9.3).

2 Nail and glue the sides to the base and to each other, using 1in (25mm) oval brads, except at the corners where the sides and front meet – use 1in (25mm) panel pins here instead. Punch the heads of all the nails below the surface of the wood, and fill the holes with a neutral-coloured filler.

Finishing

1 When this is dry, clean it up with glasspaper and smooth the end grain of the sides with a plane.

2 On the top front edge of the back, cut a decorative chamfer with a plane and drill drainage holes in the base with a ¼in (6mm) bit.

3 Finish the tray with two coats of clear, water-repellent wood preserver.

Fig 9.4
The tray is easily fixed to a wall.

Suburban Gardens

The dividing line between a town and the suburbs is indistinct in wildlife terms, but there are differences. The gardens in suburbs are usually bigger, there are generally more trees in the streets and possibly overgrown railway embankments and roadside verges. There is also a higher percentage of space given to public parks, playing fields and open areas, all of which add to the diversity of wildlife that can be attracted to a suburban garden.

In an urban environment it should be possible to attract up to 50 different species of bird, depending on what part of the country the garden is situated, although not all of them will nest. The more variation there is in the habitat, the greater the variety of birds that will be encouraged to visit. If there are plants that attract insects, the insects will attract the birds, and dense foliage plants, such as ivy, will encourage them to nest once they have visited.

PEANUT FEEDER

GREAT TIT

SLOTTED NEST BOX

10

Slotted Nest Box

Robins and spotted flycatchers will take readily to this form of nest box, particularly if it is fixed to a wall or tree that is covered in ivy or a dense shrub of some kind. Because it has an open front, it is essential that it be situated so that the prevailing direction of the wind and rain does not drive into the opening.

The box is made from ½in (12mm) plywood that is not very weather-resistant, so when finished it must be given a couple of coats of clear wood preserver. The alternative is to make it from weather-resistant ply or one of the more durable timbers, such as oak, elm, or cedar.

CUTTING LIST

Back (1)	Plywood	18 x 6 x ½in (457 x 152 x 12mm)
Sides (2)	Plywood	11 x 6 x ½in (279 x 152 x 12mm)
Base (1)	Plywood	6 x 5 x ½in (152 x 127 x 12mm)
Roof (1)	Plywood	7½ x 7 x ½in (190 x 178 x 12mm)
Front (1)	Plywood	6 x 4 x ½in (152 x 102 x 12mm)
ALSO REQUIRED:		
Plastic flashing		8 x 8½in (203 x 216mm)

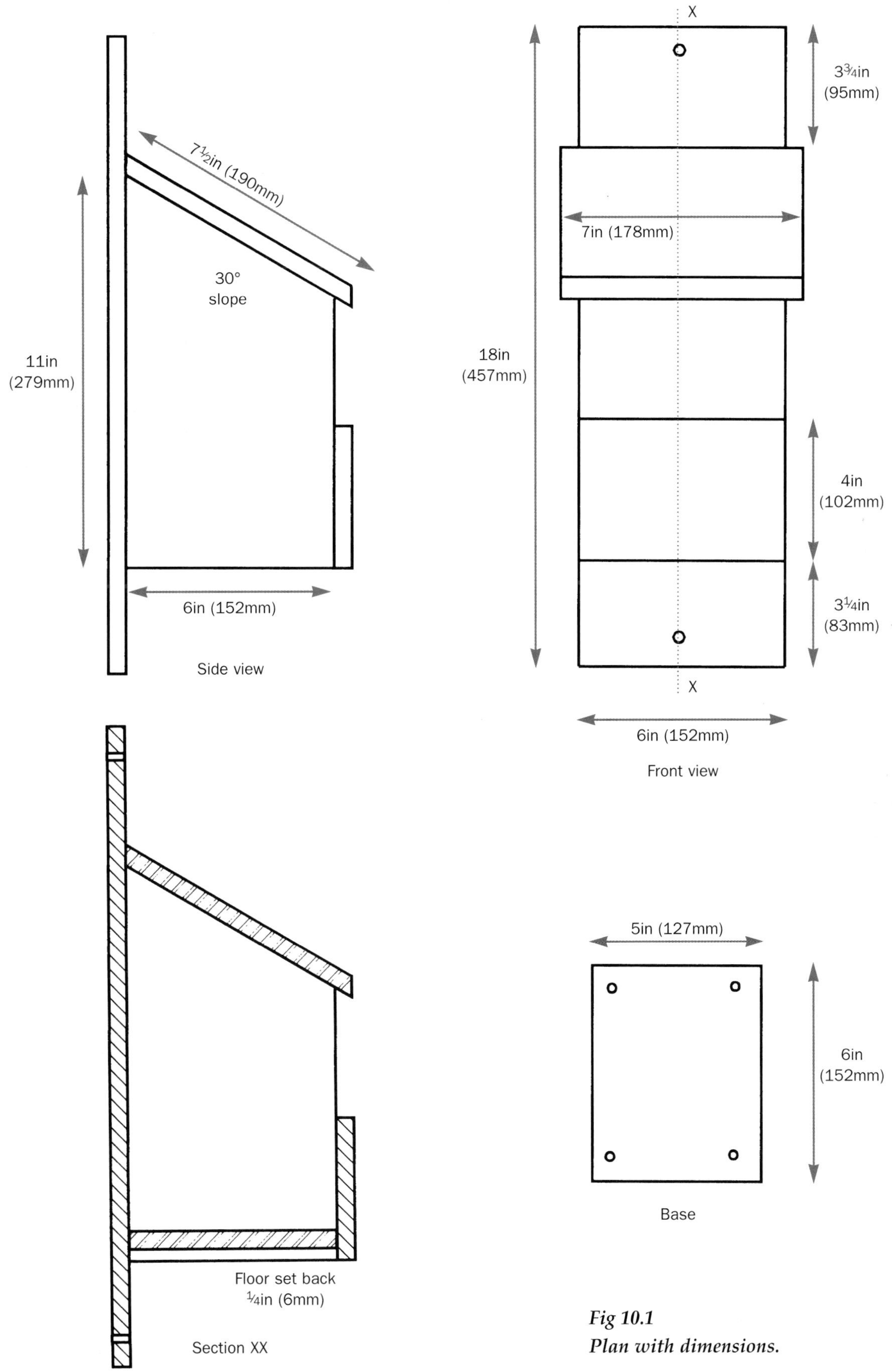

X

7½in (190mm)

30° slope

11in (279mm)

6in (152mm)

Side view

18in (457mm)

3¾in (95mm)

7in (178mm)

4in (102mm)

3¼in (83mm)

X

6in (152mm)

Front view

Floor set back ¼in (6mm)

Section XX

5in (127mm)

6in (152mm)

Base

Fig 10.1
Plan with dimensions.

Construction

1 On a sheet of plywood, mark all of the shapes, using a long rule and a try square for accuracy. Mark the 30° slope on the top of the sides using a sliding bevel, and do the same with the chamfers on the front and back edges of the roof. Use a panel saw to cut out the shapes and a plane to smooth the edges.

Drill holes in the back of the box at the top and bottom so that it can be fixed to a tree or the wall of a house.

2 Mark the positions where the sides will join the back and drill small pilot holes in the back to guide the nails (*see* Chapter 2, page 11). Use glue and 1in (25mm) oval brads to fix the sides to the back and when this is done, fit the base of the box in the same way. As you work, keep a damp rag handy to wipe away any surplus glue. Where the nails pierce the front and sides, punch the heads about ⅛in (3mm) below the surface of the ply and fill the resulting holes with a neutral-coloured plastic filler. This will prevent the nails from rusting and improve the appearance of the finished piece.

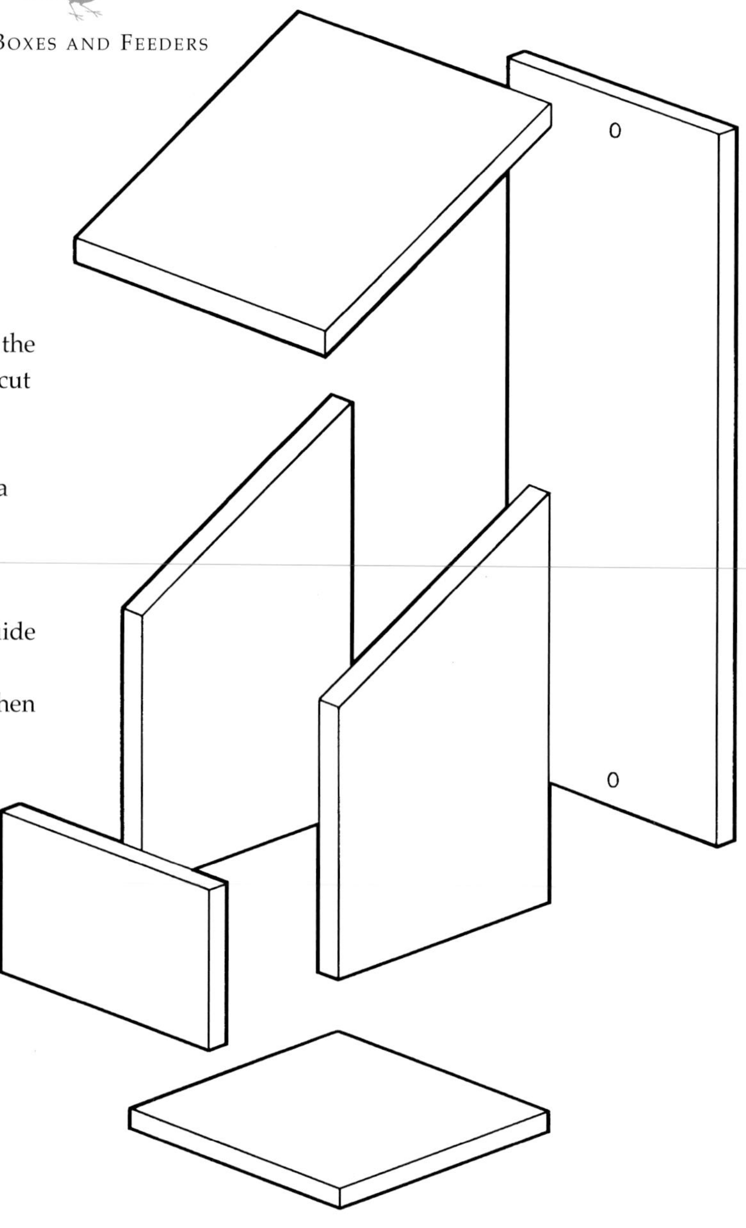

Fig 10.2 (above) Construction details.

Fig 10.3 (left) The completed plywood parts.

Fig 10.4
The back, sides and base ready to be assembled.

Fig 10.5 (below)
Roof-covering details.

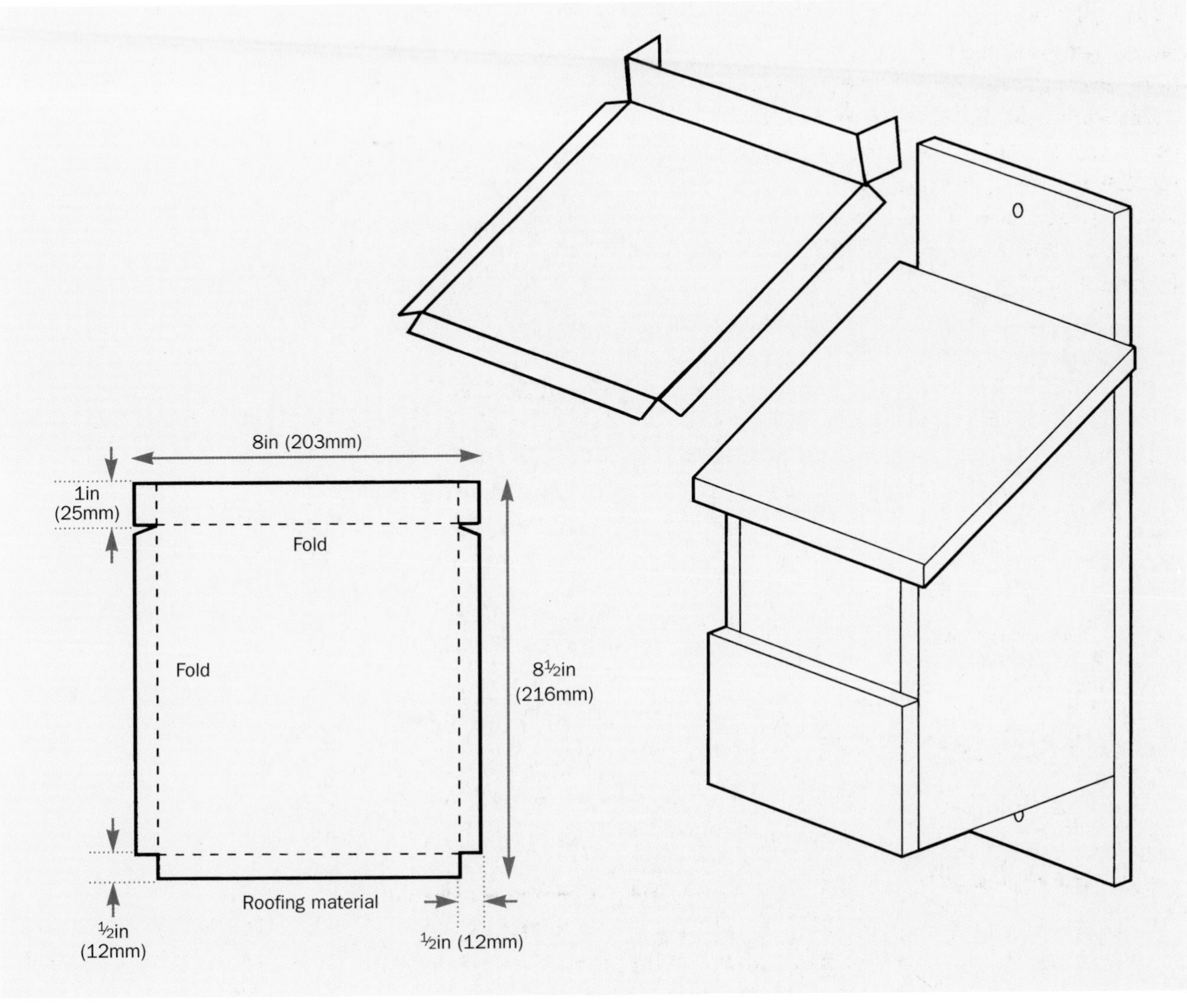

Fig 10.6
Fitting the plastic flashing to the roof.

3 Fix the roof in place by nailing and gluing: this time it is not necessary to punch the nails below the surface, as they will be covered by the roofing material. Follow this by drilling some drainage holes in the base, so that any rain that gets in through the front slot will not form a puddle in the bottom.

Finishing

1 Waterproof the entire box before the roofing material is applied, by applying two coats of clear wood preserver. (*See* Chapter 2, page 20.) At the fold between the roof and the back, cut small slots in the edges, so that the flashing bends easily into position. Press firmly all over to ensure that it stays in place.

Fig 10.7
The completed nest box.

11

Peanut Feeder

Dispensing shelled peanuts in a feeder is one of the best ways of persuading many small birds to enter your garden. Blue tits, great tits, coal tits, greenfinches, and siskins are all attracted to this type of food. In a suburban garden, with some large, mature trees in the immediate area, it is also possible that nuthatches and great spotted woodpeckers will be enticed.

I used oak for the two turned ends, not only because it is ideal for this application, but also because I had some logs available from a friend who was clearing an oak stump from his garden. If you use this type of material it is not important if the log is still green, as long as there are no large cracks in it and you have a microwave oven: I have given a quick-drying method. Of course, if you have some seasoned pieces of oak or other hard wood, ignore the drying instructions.

TO MAKE THIS PROJECT A LATHE IS REQUIRED.

CUTTING LIST

Base (1)	Oak	4 x 4 x 3½in (102 x 102 x 89mm)
Top (1)	Oak	4 x 4 x 3½in (102 x 102 x 89mm)

ALSO REQUIRED:

Wire mesh, ¼in (6mm) square	8 x 8½in (203 x 215mm)
Wire, approx. 1/16in (2mm) thick	36in (914mm) long
Fuse wire, 15amp	

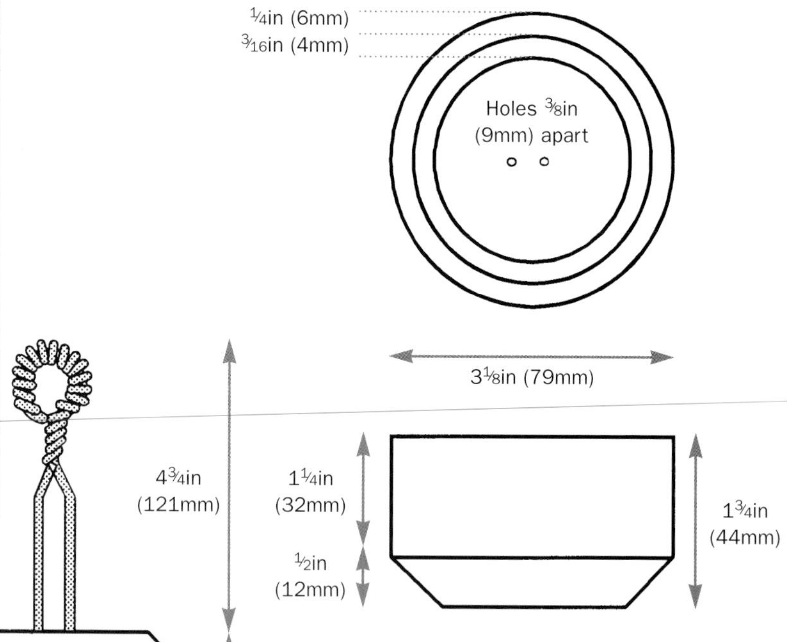

¼in (6mm)
3/16in (4mm)
Holes ⅜in (9mm) apart
3⅛in (79mm)
4¾in (121mm)
1¼in (32mm)
½in (12mm)
1¾in (44mm)
2½in (64mm) diameter 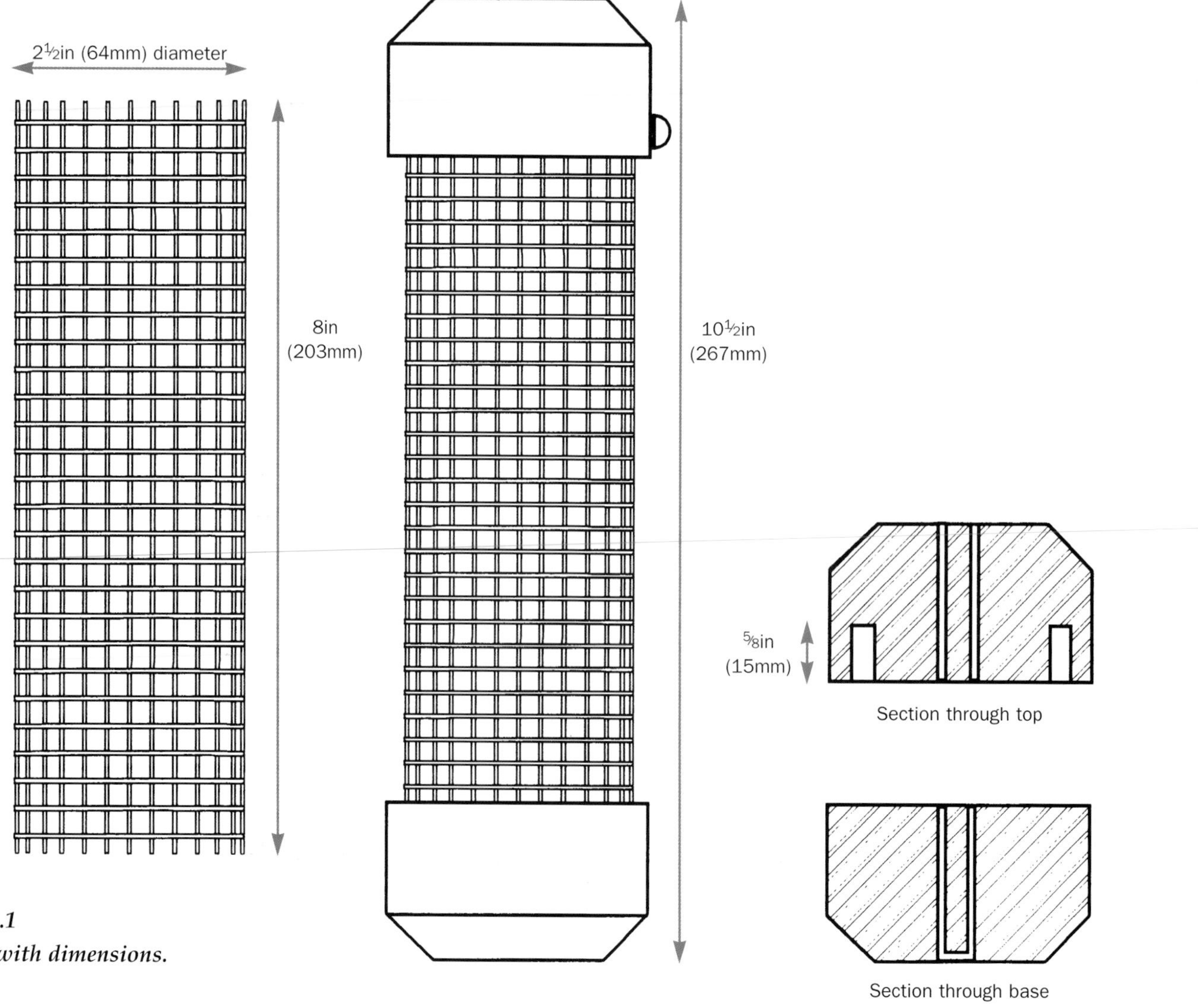
8in (203mm)
10½in (267mm)
⅝in (15mm)
Section through top
Section through base

Fig 11.1
Plan with dimensions.

Construction

Mesh Body

1 From a sheet of galvanized wire mesh with a ¼in (6mm) mesh size, cut a piece measuring 8 x 8½in (203 x 215mm) using a pair of tin snips. This will make a cylinder that is 8in (203mm) long and approximately 2½in (64mm) in diameter.

Bend the wire into a cylinder, using a plastic bottle of appropriate dimensions as a former, so that the ends overlap by two squares. If they are not overlapped by two squares then the final diameter of the cylinder will not be 2½in (64mm). Hold the wire in this shape temporarily by wrapping a couple of pieces of tape around it. To fix the wire permanently in the cylindrical shape, 'sew' the edges together with thin wire (*see* Fig 11.2 and 11.3). I found that 15amp fuse wire is about the correct gauge for this. Do not be tempted to solder or braze the edges together as the galvanized zinc coating will give off toxic fumes if heated to a high temperature.

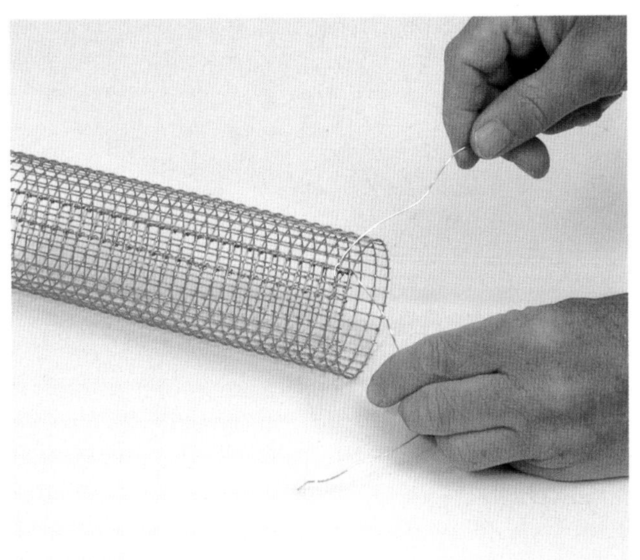

***Fig 11.2** (above)*
Binding the cylinder with thin wire.

***Fig 11.3** (below)*
Binding the wire mesh.

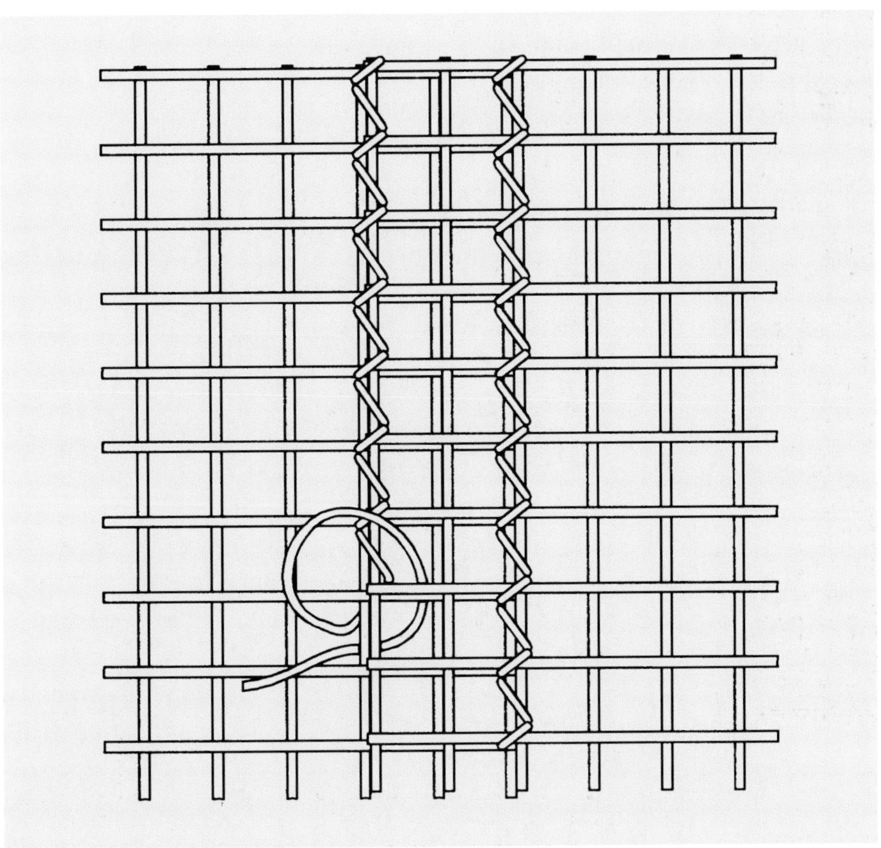

TOP AND BASE

1 To make the top, cut a square of oak measuring approximately 4 x 4 x 3½in (102 x 102 x 89mm), with the grain running in the direction of the 3½in (89mm) dimension, and mark the centre of the block. To speed up the turning process, cut off the corners using a panel saw, pierce a hole at either end and mount the piece between centres on the lathe. Turn to a smooth cylinder, with a diameter approximately ¼in (6mm) larger than required for the final size.

2 Take the cylinder from the lathe and put it into the microwave for one minute on a medium setting. The reason drying is done after some waste wood has been cut away is that there is a limit to the penetration of the microwaves. If the wood is too thick, the centre will not dry. However, the piece is not completely finished before it is dried because the drying process will distort the shape. Enough wood is left so that the shape can be turned once again, into a true cylinder.

After the first minute in the microwave, take the block out and allow it to cool for half an hour. Do this approximately 10 times and the wood will be dry and ready for remounting on the lathe. Do not be tempted to leave it in any longer than one minute or reduce the cooling period as this may cause the wood to burn.

Pieces that have a lower moisture content may not need so many sessions in the oven. The guesswork can be eliminated by weighing the wood before you start, taking a note of the weight and reweighing it every time it comes out of the oven. When it ceases to lose weight, the wood is dry enough to use and will not crack.

3 Remount the cylinder and turn it to the correct diameter of 3⅛in (79mm), using a ½in (12mm) gauge. Mark the required length of 1¾in (44mm) in pencil, then reduce the area outside these marks to approximately 1in (25mm) in diameter. Using a scraper, cut the faces square, then form a decorative 45° chamfer. Set the diameter of the wire cylinder accurately on a pair of dividers and use these to mark the position of the recess for the wire cylinder on the inside face of the top. Hollow out this slot to a depth of ⅝in (15mm), with a ⅛in (3mm) parting tool (*see* Fig 11.4). Clean up the outside with glasspaper and, while it is still mounted on the lathe, saw off the two ends. Flatten and smooth the sawn ends with glasspaper.

Produce the base in exactly the same way, and test the top and base to ensure that the wire cylinder fits in the recesses.

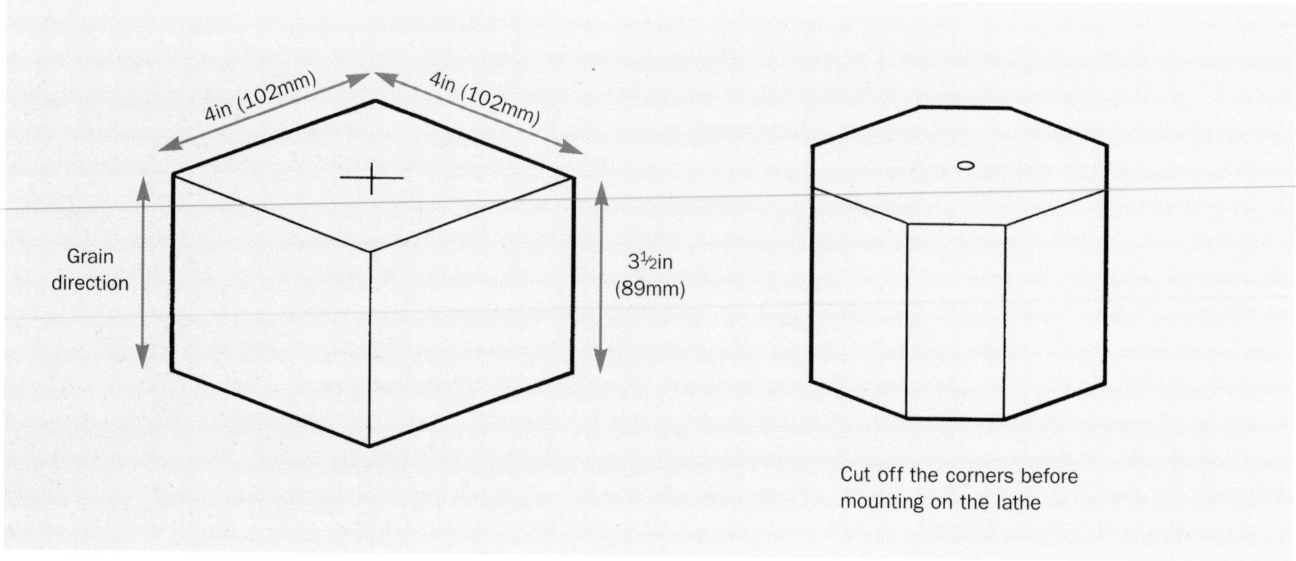

Fig 11.4
Preparing the block for turning.

4 Drill two ⅛in (3mm) diameter holes in the top and the base to house the wire used to hang the feeder. On the bottom of the base, use a chisel to cut a small recess between the two holes so that the wire will be hidden from sight when it is threaded.

Fig 11.5 (above) Measuring the turned cylinder.

SISKIN

HANGING WIRE

1 Obtain a length of stiff wire with a diameter of approximately 1/16in (2mm): I used a straightened wire coathanger. Bend this into an elongated 'U' shape with the base of the 'U' the same length as the distance between the two drilled holes.

The method of filling the holder with peanuts is to slide the top up the hanging wire. It is possible that a squirrel might learn how to slide up the top and so plunder the contents. To stop this, fit a 1in (25mm) dome-headed brass screw to lock it into place. It should pass through the side of the top and through the wire mesh.

Fig 11.6 (right) Excavating the recess that houses the wire cylinder.

Assembly and Finishing

1 Before assembling the feeder, paint the two oak ends with clear, water-repellent finish.

2 Thread the hanging wire through the base and ensure that the bottom of the 'U' shape fits into the recess. Fit the wire cylinder into the slot in the base. This is not glued in any way as the fit should be quite snug. However, if it is not a snug fit, fix it in place with a filling paste such as 'plastic padding'. Thread the top onto the hanging wire and twist the wires together using pliers (*see* Fig 11.7). Ensure that enough wire is left untwisted to allow the top to slide up so you can fill the feeder. Finally, bend the twisted end into a hook shape for hanging the feeder up.

To help protect the peanuts from marauding squirrels, I use a length of fairly stiff garden wire, about 6ft (1.8m), to hang the feeder in a tree. Because the wire is stiff the squirrels cannot pull it up from above (as they can if it is too flexible), and because it is thin, they can't get a grip on it to climb down. In my garden they attempt to slide down the wire, but because of the length they gather so much speed that by the time they get to the feeder, they inevitably drop off the end. This also makes their paws hot and you can see them blowing on them to cool them off after attempting this. The only other way they can get at the nuts is by jumping from a nearby tree, so ensure the feeder is at least 6ft (1.8m) from the nearest branch or trunk.

Fig 11.7
Assembly and hanging wire scheme.

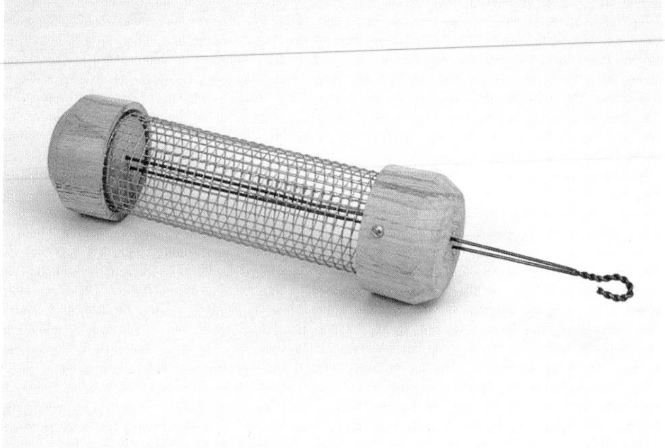

Fig 11.8
The assembled peanut feeder.

12

Seed Hopper

A seed hopper is used to dispense any available varieties of bird seed, such as sunflower seed, millet or mixed bird seeds. This design has a glass front so that it is obvious when the hopper needs refilling. It is also fitted with a squirrel screen, made from ½in (12mm) square wire mesh. The squirrel guard works by having holes cut into the mesh, large enough to let birds through, but not big enough for squirrels. The hole size can also be chosen in order to exclude some birds, such as starlings and sparrows. If the access holds are 1in (25mm) square, it will let blue tits and coal tits through, but exclude sparrows. With a 1½in (38mm) hole, sparrows, greenfinches and great tits will have access, but not starlings, wood pigeons or squirrels. Site the seed hopper on a tree or fence, 4–5ft (1–1.8m) from the ground.

A number of different materials would be suitable for this hopper, but for the example shown I used pine floorboards, ⅝in (15mm) thick. Pine is not very durable when left out in the elements, so it needs a couple of coats of wood preserver to finish.

I made the hopper quite large so that it doesn't require filling up very often. It takes approximately 3lb (1.4kg) of mixed seed, which will last several days. The hopper is wedge-shaped so that seeds are not trapped in any corners: if any seed is trapped, it can cause problems if it rots.

CUTTING LIST

Back (1)	Pine	15 x 5¾ x ⅝in (381 x 146 x 15mm)
Sides (2)	Pine	10¾ x 5¾ x ⅝in (273 x 146 x 15mm)
Floor (1)	Pine	4½ x 4½ x ⅝in (114 x 114 x 15mm)
Floor front (1)	Pine	4½ x 1½ x ⅝in (114 x 38 x 15mm)
Brace (1)	Pine	4½ x ⅝ x ⅝in (114 x 15 x 15mm)
Lid top (1)	Pine	5¾ x 5$\frac{13}{16}$ x ⅝in (146 x 148 x 15mm)
Lid sides (2)	Plywood	5$\frac{13}{16}$ x 1½ x ¼in (148 x 38 x 6mm)
Lid front (1)	Plywood	6¼ x 1½ x ¼in (159 x 38 x 6mm)
Seed holder front (1)	Glass	10⅛ x 4⅞ x ⅛in (257 x 124 x 3mm)

ALSO REQUIRED:

Roofing material	8 x 8¾in (203 x 222mm)
Gate latch (1)	1½in (38mm)
Butt hinge (1)	1in (25mm)
Wire mesh, ½in (12mm) square	17½ x 10½in (445 x 266mm)

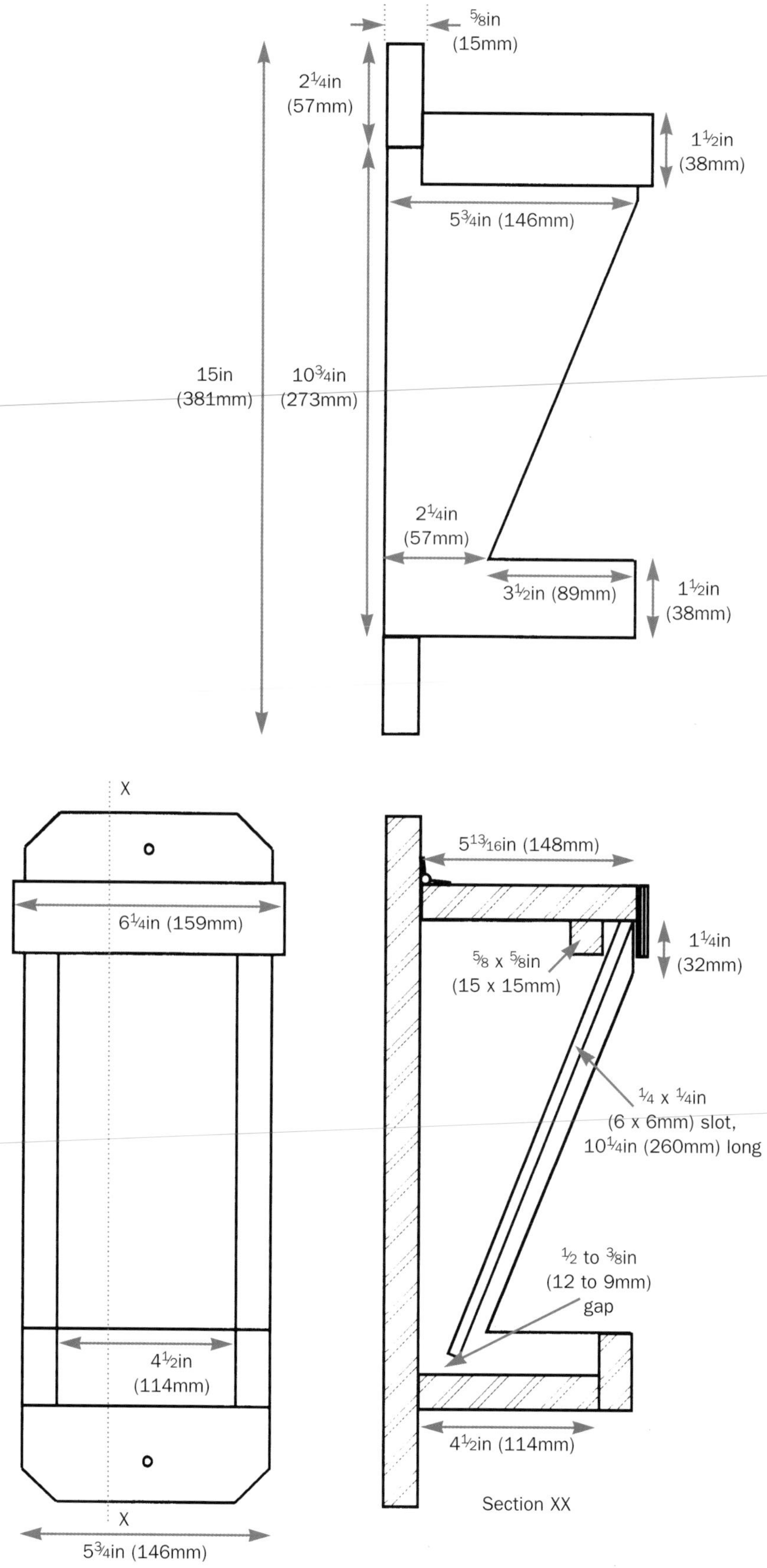

Fig 12.1
Plan with dimensions.

Fig 12.2
Construction details.

Construction

Back and Sides

1 Cut the back to size with a panel saw, plane the edges and cut the recess that houses the sides with a tenon saw and a coping saw. Chamfer the corners before glasspapering the end grain and drilling holes in the ends for the nails that will eventually be used to hang the hopper up.

2 Shape the sides with a panel saw and, using a router with a ¼in (6mm) straight cutter, form the groove for the glass front (*see* Fig 12.3). If you do not have a router, lengths of ¼in (6mm) plastic channel stuck to the surface of the sides will be equally effective.

Cut the groove so that it ends about ½in (12mm) from the floor of the hopper. This gap is to allow the seeds to flow out of the storage compartment onto the floor of the feeder, but not so large that it empties out completely. For large seeds this gap size is about right, but if smaller foods such as chopped peanuts and thistle seeds are used, then the gap should be slightly smaller.

Drill pilot holes along the back edge of the sides to accommodate the galvanized nails that are used, together with waterproof glue, to fix the sides to the back. (*See* Chapter 2, page 11.)

3 Cut and plane the floor and front ledge, and fix them in place with nails and glue as for the back and sides. Because I used budget-priced wood, I had a problem with it being slightly warped which caused the two sides to lean towards the centre. To hold the two sides the required distance apart, in order to avoid problems when I put the glass in the slot, I cut a small part to brace the sides, and glued it at the top front of the seed compartment.

4 Before fitting the wire mesh, paint the hopper with clear, water-repellent solution.

Glass and Mesh

1 Cut a piece of glass for the front of the seed compartment. If you can't cut the glass, get a shop to do it for you. Once it has been cut, smooth the edges by rubbing them with a piece of sharpening stone to make them safe, but do not fit the glass until the job is complete.

2 From a piece of ½in (12mm) mesh, cut a panel to fit around the front and sides of the hopper for the squirrel guard. Carefully mark the corners and bend them to form right angles (*see* Fig 12.4). To do this, fold the mesh around a piece of wood held in a vice.

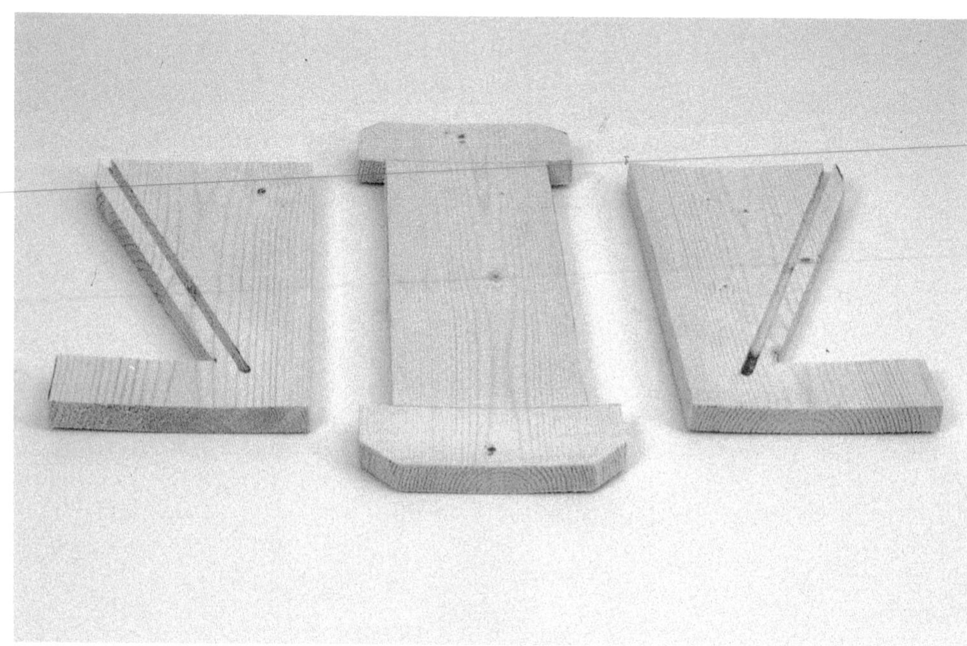

Fig 12.3
The softwood parts before starting assembly.

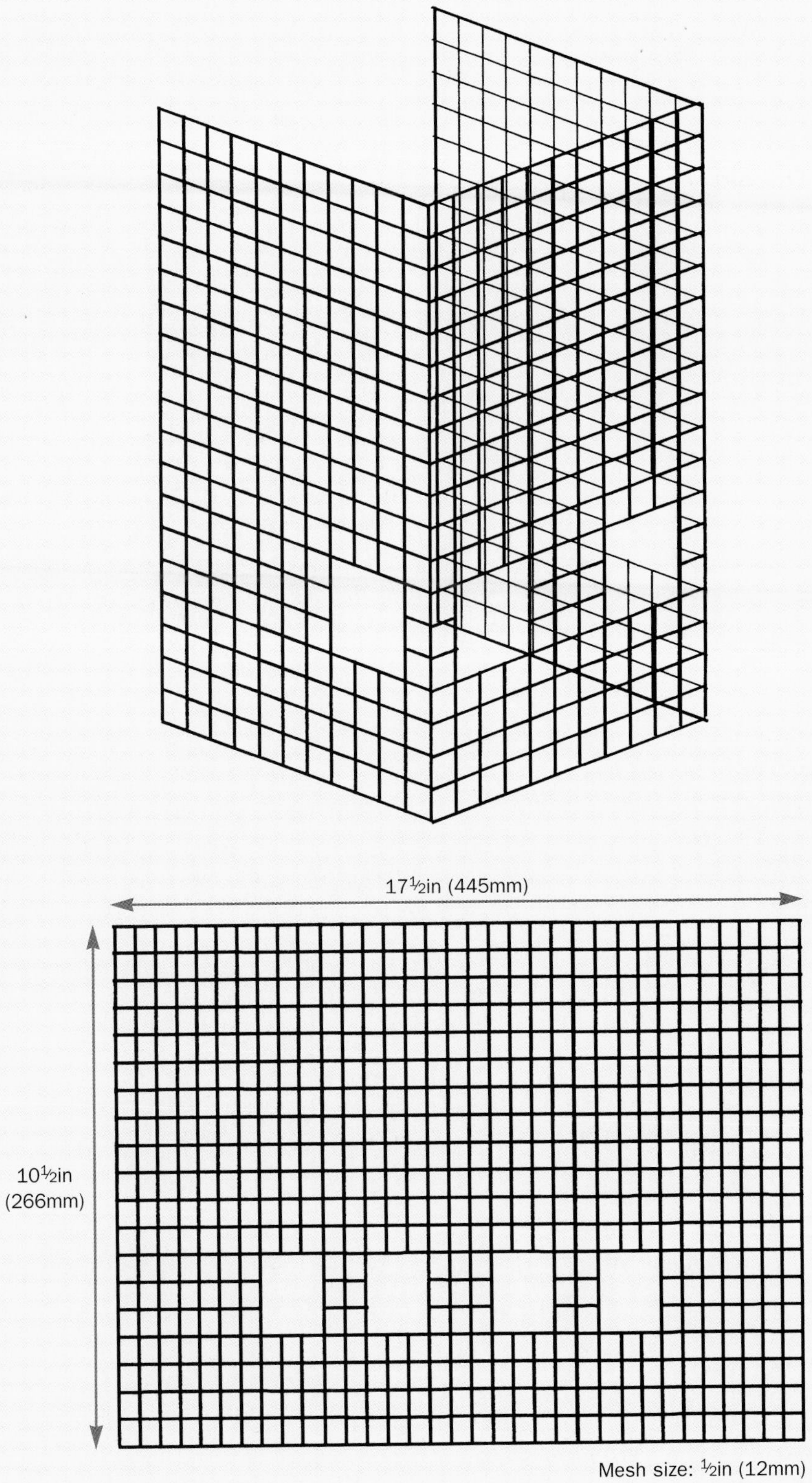

Fig 12.4
Wire squirrel guard.

17½in (445mm)

10½in (266mm)

Mesh size: ½in (12mm)

Fix the mesh to the outsides of the hopper with staples. Cut the access holes for the birds with wire cutters and file off any small spikes of wire that are left sticking into the holes after the unwanted mesh is removed. The idea of this is to stop the birds harming themselves on the spikes, but as they hop around on thorn bushes without any ill effects it is probably not a problem.

LID

1 The top of the lid is made from a piece of ⅝in (15mm) pine, and the sides from ¼in (6mm) plywood. Cut the parts to size and join them together with glue and panel pins.

FINISHING

1 Paint the wood with a clear, water-repellent finish before fitting the lid to the hopper with a 1in (25mm) butt hinge, fixed onto the surface and not recessed (*see* Fig 12.5).

2 From a piece of self-adhesive plastic flashing, cut the roof covering and fit it into place (*see* Chapter 2, page 19). Slide the glass into the slot and fit a 1½in (38mm) gate latch to secure the lid and prevent squirrels prising it open to get at the seeds. Fit the glass and the job is complete.

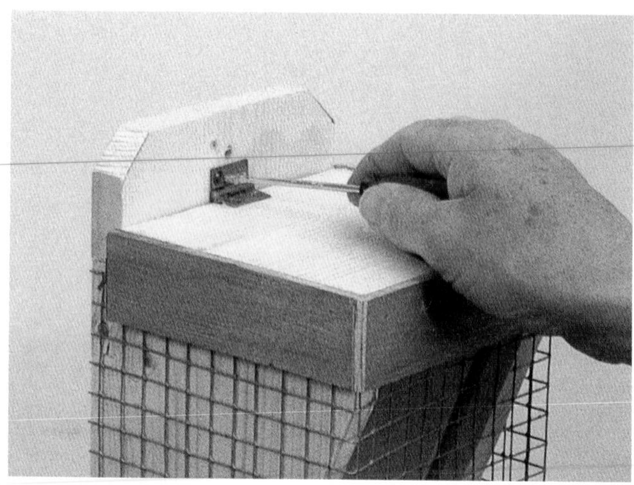

Fig 12.5
Fitting the butt hinges on the surface.

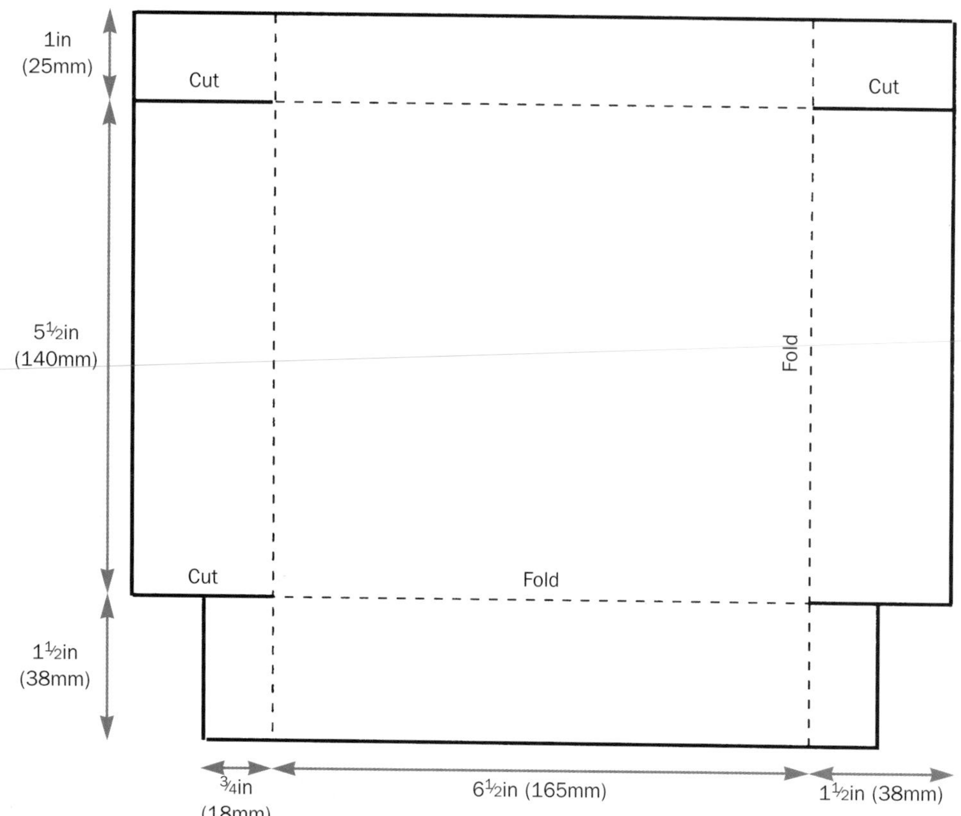

Fig 12.6
Roof-covering plan with dimensions.

13

Bird Bath

Providing birds with water is as important as providing them with food. They need it to drink and also to bathe in. A bird bath does not have to be very large, but it must have gently sloping sides so that small birds will not get into difficulties when using it.

My bird bath is made from wood, which might seem a strange choice at first. However, it is not necessary for the bath to hold water for weeks at a time as it should be replenished every day with fresh water. This is not only for the health of the birds, but also because when birds bathe, it is so vigorous that most of the water gets sprayed over the surroundings and the bath quickly empties.

This bath has been designed to sit on the ground to encourage birds that feed on the ground, such as dunnocks, to use it. It should be placed on a level surface such as a patio or terrace.

I chose European redwood for my bird bath. Although it is not as weatherproof as Western redwood, which comes from the USA, when treated properly, it will last for many years. Other suitable woods that stand up to the weather are oak, elm, or larch.

CUTTING LIST

Sections (3)	Pine	13½ x 4½ x 2¾in (343 x 114 x 70mm)

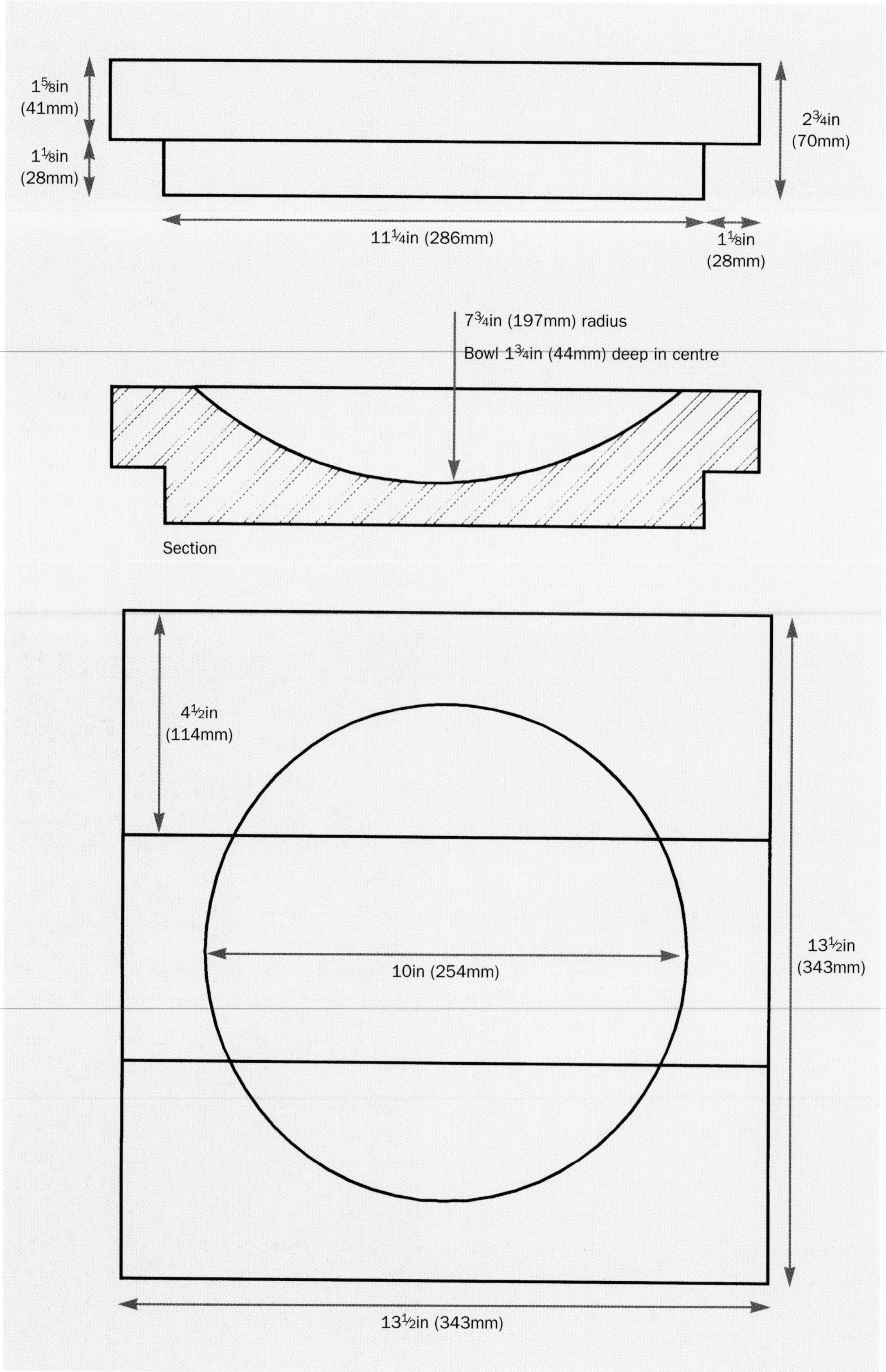

1⅝in (41mm)
1⅛in (28mm)
2¾in (70mm)
11¼in (286mm)
1⅛in (28mm)
7¾in (197mm) radius
Bowl 1¾in (44mm) deep in centre
Section
4½in (114mm)
10in (254mm)
13½in (343mm)
13½in (343mm)

Fig 13.1 Plan with dimensions and section.

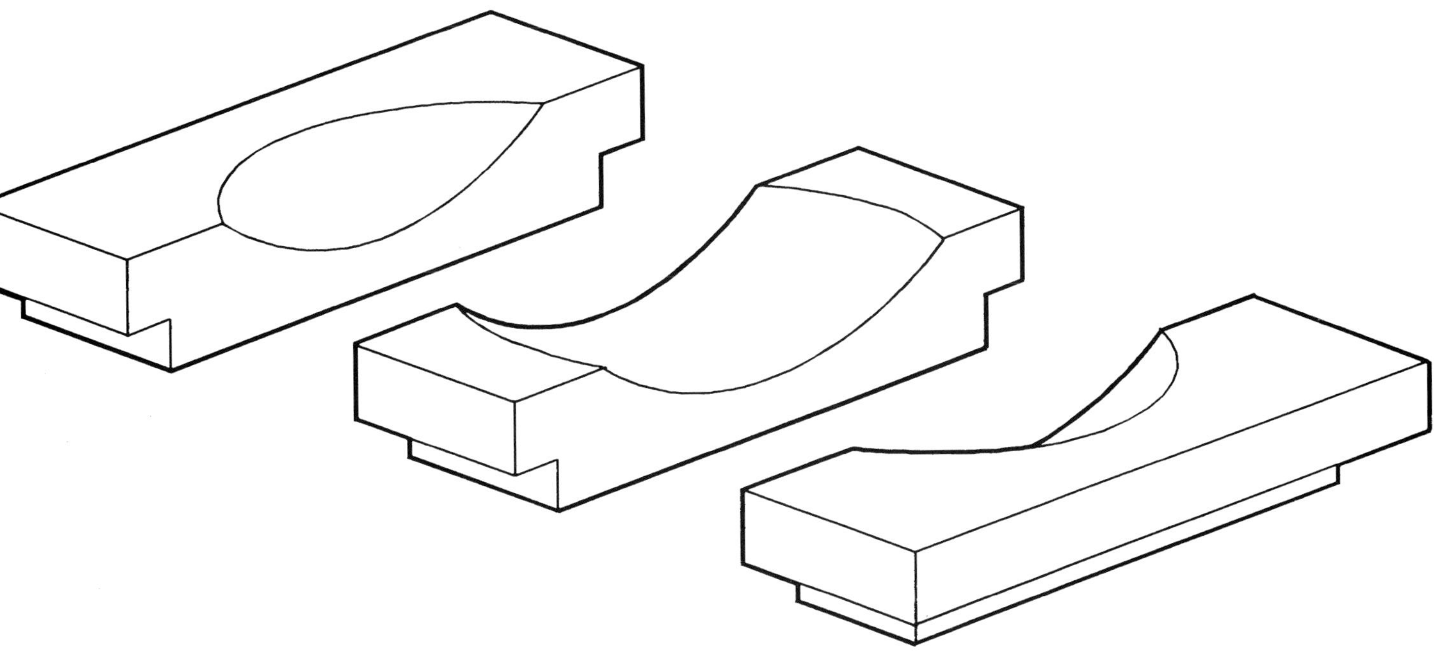

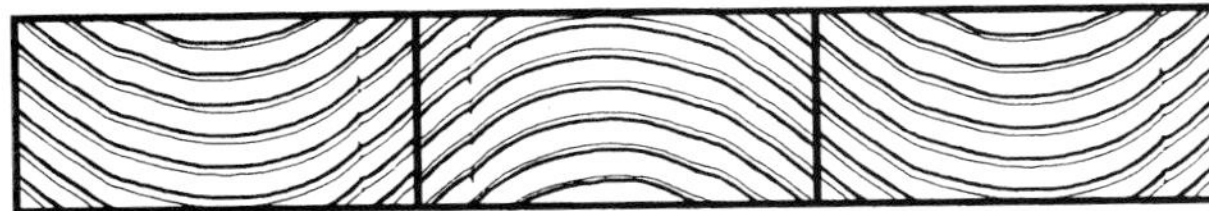

Fig 13.2
Construction details.

Fig 13.3
The clamps are placed in an alternating position to avoid distorting the assembly.

Construction

1 Cut three pieces of wood about 14in (356mm) long and plane the edges square. To do this, plane the face on each piece so that they are flat and mark them with a pencil so that you will not use the backs by mistake, when planing the edges. With a try square laid on the flat side, test each edge to see if it is at 90° to the face. If the edges are not square, plane them until they are. To remove wood from one side of the edge, position the centre of the plane over that edge (*see* Chapter 2, page 15).

2 Lay the three pieces together, alternating the grain direction, and draw the outline of the bath in the centre, using a dinner plate as a template. Whilst the bird bath is still in separate parts, remove some of the waste wood: this is slightly easier now than once they have been joined.

3 Cover one side of the butt joints with water-resistant glue. Put plenty on so that it will be squeezed out when they are clamped. Push them together and clamp with sash clamps. These are placed alternatively on the front and the back so that the wood is not distorted (*see* Fig 13.3). When dry, cut a rebate in the underside with a circular saw and clean it up with a rebating plane (*see* Fig 13.4).

Fig 13.4
Cleaning up the rebate on the underside of the bath.

Fig 13.5
Hollowing out the bowl.

4 Turn the piece over and start enlarging the hollow with a 1in (25mm) half-round gouge. Work from the edge towards the centre so that the gouge cuts will radiate out from the middle (*see* Fig 13.5). I liked the look of the patterns left by the gouge, so I decided to leave the bowl with a tooled finish rather than smooth the surface. When you have finished hollowing, clean up the flat top surface with a plane.

Finishing

1 Apply two coats of sealing solution, to penetrate the surface of the wood and provide a barrier against water. The bath can be left like this, but I also applied two coats of polyurethane varnish to enhance its appearance. The manufacturers of the water sealing solution recommend that you leave about one month before doing this.

Fig 13.6
The completed bowl, sealed and varnished.

COUNTRY GARDENS

Gardens are an important habitat for many creatures. Nearly 200 different species of birds have been recorded in British gardens. Country gardens are especially important because of their location and size. In a large garden there is room for mature trees and more scope for plant diversity, which is the key to attracting varied wildlife.

Because of their size, there are usually odd corners in country gardens that are not cultivated and are left for weeds and nettles to grow unhindered. A pond of some description is often a feature. Both of these factors help to make country gardens important for flourishing wildlife.

The projects in this chapter are also suitable for smaller gardens in the suburbs depending on the surrounding environment.

RUSTIC NEST BOX FOR TITS

NESTING BOX FOR KESTRELS

GREAT SPOTTED WOODPECKER

14

Nesting Box for Treecreepers

Treecreepers are small brown birds with curved beaks. They are found in most woods, parks, and gardens with mature trees and are common throughout the UK. Crawling along branches and tree trunks, hunting for insects in the crevices, they look like mice and not birds. They are easily overlooked as they are well camouflaged, but in winter can be seen when they join small flocks of tits and finches moving from garden to garden.

This nest box is designed to resemble the shape of treecreepers' natural nesting holes behind loose bark and in the cracks on mature trees. It is constructed from ½in (12mm) exterior quality plywood.

For the best results it should be situated between 6 and 10ft (2 and 3m) from the ground, on the side of a mature tree.

CUTTING LIST

Back (1)	Plywood	14½ x 6¾ x ½in (368 x 171 x 12mm)
Sides (1)	Plywood	11¾ x 4½ x ½in (298 x 114 x 12mm)
Front (1)	Plywood	12 x 6¾ x ½in (305 x 171 x 12mm)
Lid (1)	Plywood	6¾ x 6 x ½in (171 x 152 x 12mm)
	ALSO REQUIRED:	
Plastic flashing		7½ x 8in (190 x 203mm)
Gate latch (1)		2in (50mm)
Hinge (1)		1½in (38mm)

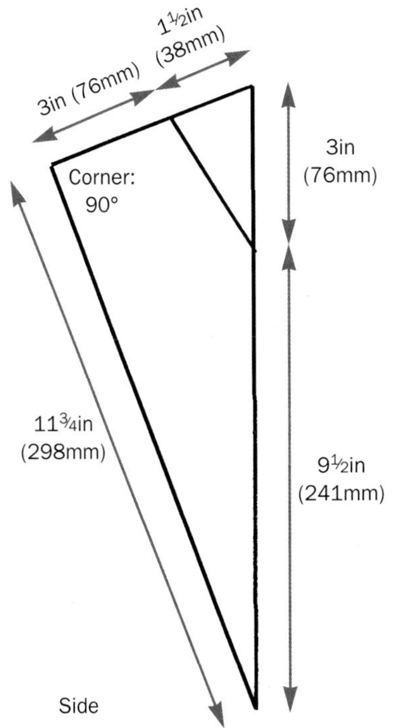

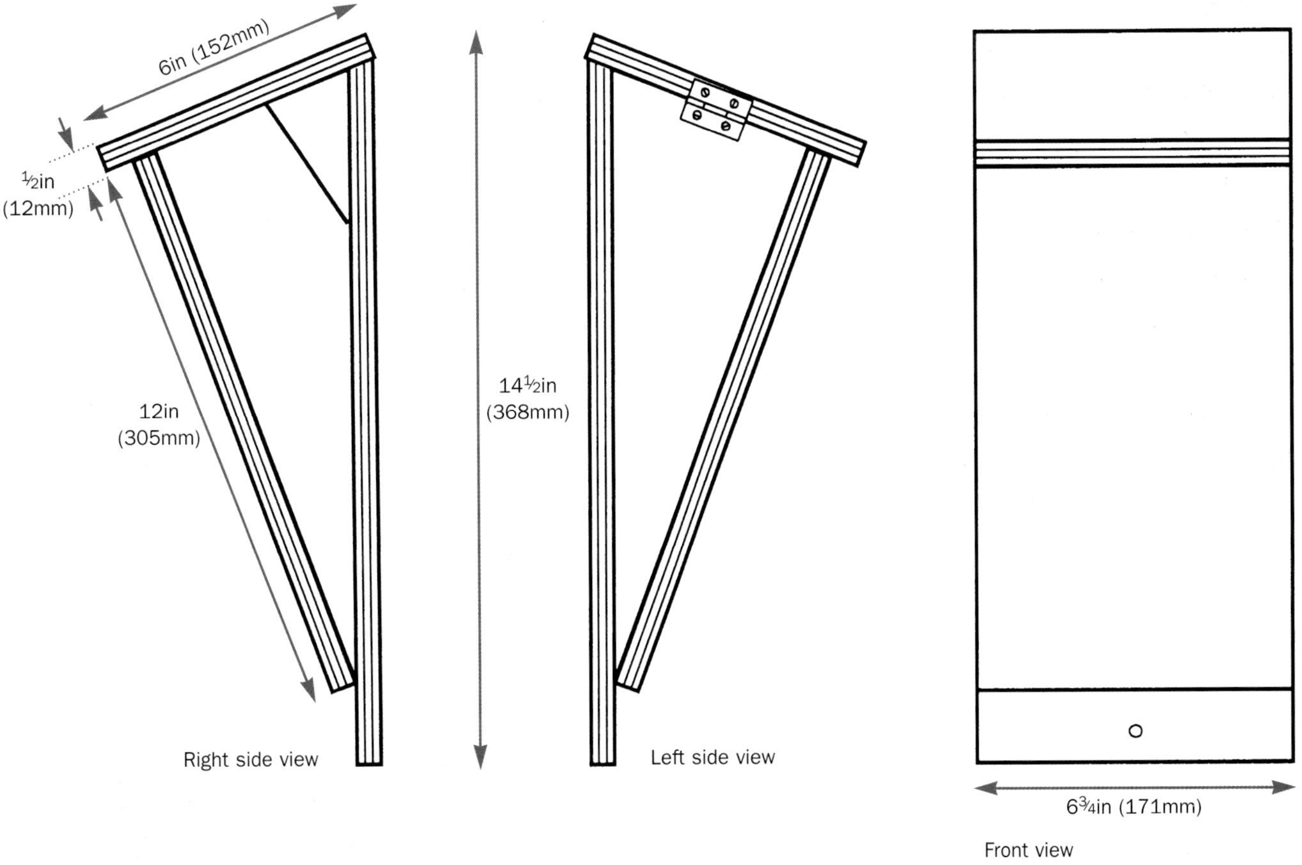

6in (152mm)

½in
(12mm)

12in
(305mm)

Right side view

14½in
(368mm)

Left side view

6¾in (171mm)

Front view

Fig 14.1
Plan with dimensions.

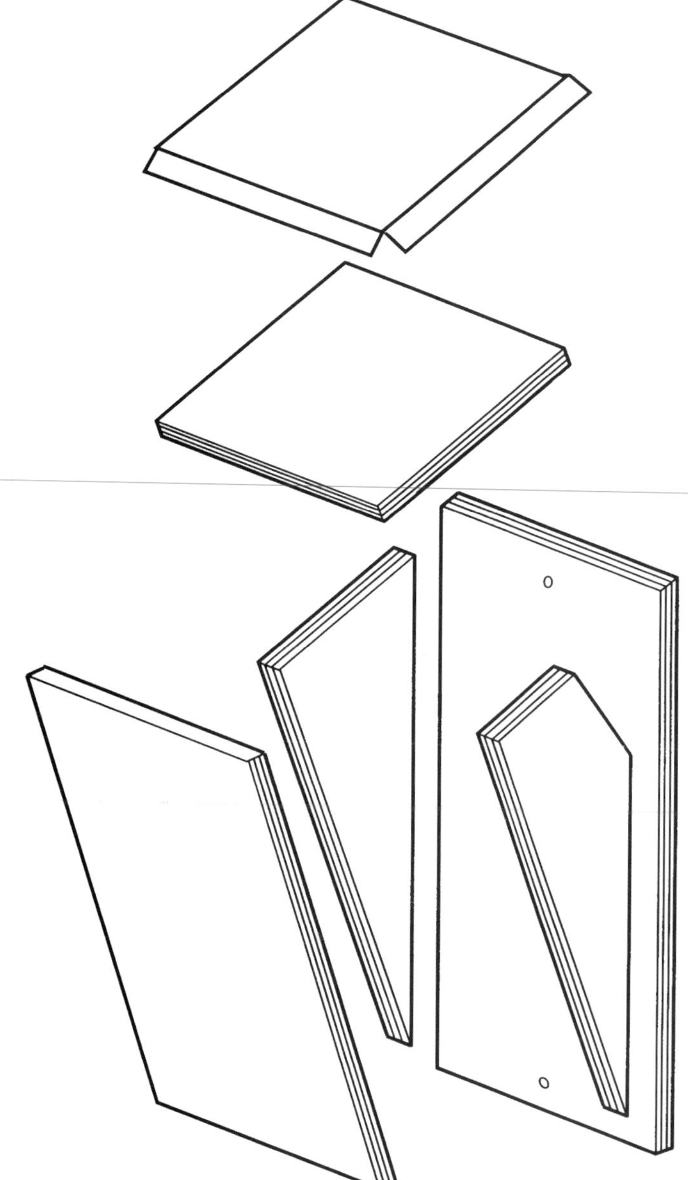

Construction

1 Fix the plywood together using 1in (25mm) oval brads and waterproof glue. To position the ovals accurately, drill small pilot holes in the top piece of ply as a guide. This is particularly important when the brads are fitted close to an edge. (*See* Chapter 2, page 11.)

Cut the two sides from a single piece of ply measuring 11¾ x 4½in (298 x 114mm). Draw a diagonal line between two corners and cut along it to form the two sides. The resulting long diagonal edges are the ones that will be fixed to the back. On one of the sides, cut off the corner adjacent to the right angle to make the access hole for the bird. Smooth the edges with a plane and glasspaper.

2 Using a set square, ruler and pencil, mark out the shape of the back and cut it with a panel saw. Drill a hole at the top and base – these will eventually be used to fix the box to the tree. Note that the top edge of the back is sloped to match the angle at which the sides join to the back. This is so that the lid will sit without leaving any gaps. To find the angle for the top edge of the back, use one of the sides as a template. Hold it against the side of the back and draw along its top edge to mark the profile on the top edge of the back. Mark out and cut the front and the lid. (*See* Fig 14.3.)

Fig 14.2
Construction details.

Fig 14.3
The plywood parts.

Fig 14.4
Presenting the sides to the back.

3 Nail and glue the two sides onto the back and then fit the front by the same method (*see* Fig 14.5). Fit the lid with a 1½in (38mm) hinge to allow access, and then fit the lid to the box (*see* Fig 14.6).

FINISHING

1 Paint the exterior of the box with clear, water-repellent finish.

2 On the top of the lid fit a piece of plastic self-adhesive flashing to keep out the rain, and fix a 2in (50mm) gate latch to hold the lid shut. (*See* Chapter 2, page 19 and Chapter 5, page 34.)

Fig 14.5
Fixing the front on with glue and nails.

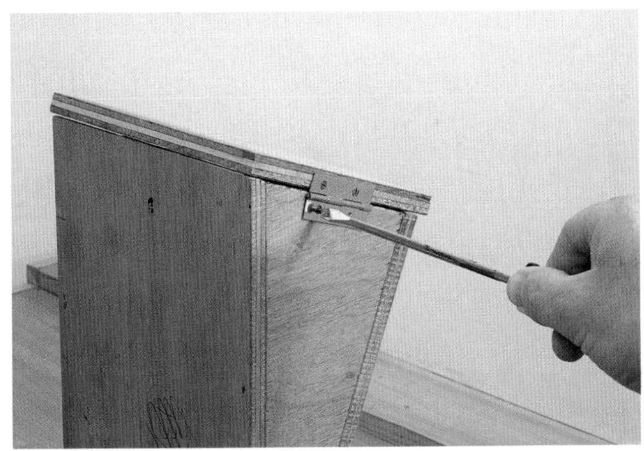

Fig 14.6
Fitting the lid with a brass hinge.

Fig 14.7
Trimming the edges of the plastic flashing.

Fig 14.8
The completed nesting box.

15

Nesting Box for Kestrels

Kestrels are small falcons that feed on mice, voles and beetles. They are commonly seen hovering over the grass verges along motorways and can be seen swooping down on their prey from this hovering vantage point or from a high perch.

They usually nest in hollow trees or on the ledges of cliffs or high buildings, but they take readily to artificial nest boxes. The nest box should be situated at least 20ft (6m) from the ground, in a tree or on the side of a building in a sheltered position. I have finished the box with a batten on the side so that it can be nailed to a tree, but if it is to be situated in the fork of a tree, the batten can be dispensed with and the box simply tied on.

Because kestrels are about the same size as pigeons, it is not unknown for pigeons to take up residence in the boxes intended for kestrels. There is not very much that can be done about this.

This box is made from ¾in (18mm) exterior quality plywood and is joined with waterproof glue and 2in (50mm) oval nails. A perch across the front of the open entrance extends about 6in (152mm) at the sides. I included this for young kestrels to perch on and exercise their wings when preparing for their first flight.

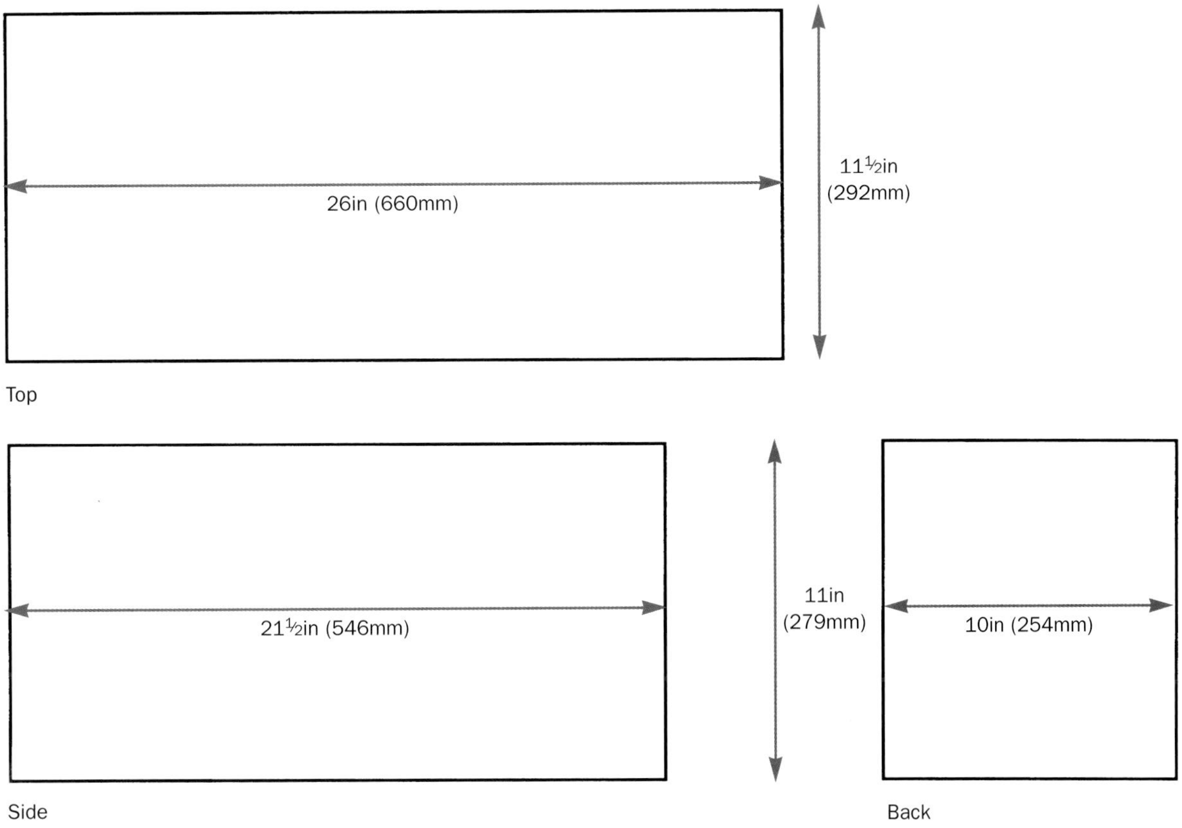

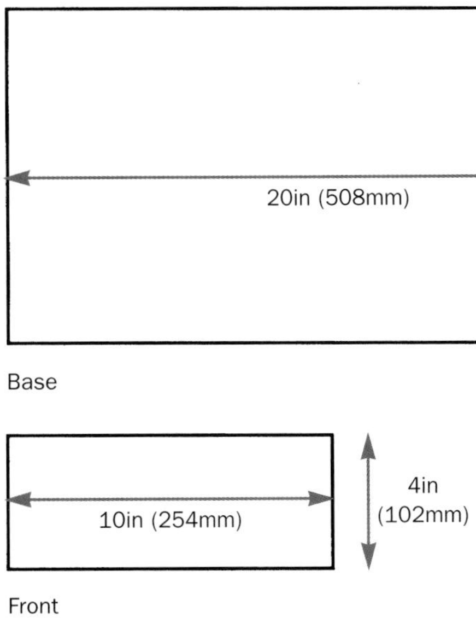

Fig 15.1
Plywood parts with dimensions.

CUTTING LIST

Top (1)	Plywood	26 x 11½ x ¾in (660 x 292 x 18mm)
Sides (2)	Plywood	21½ x 11 x ¾in (546 x 279 x 18mm)
Back (1)	Plywood	11 x 10 x ¾in (279 x 254 x 18mm)
Base (1)	Plywood	20 x 10 x ¾in (508 x 254 x 18mm)
Front (1)	Plywood	10 x 4 x ¾in (254 x 102 x 18mm)
Perch (1)	Ramin doweling	16 x ¾in diameter (406 x 18mm diameter)

ALSO REQUIRED:

Roofing felt	approx. 28 x 14in (711 x 356mm)

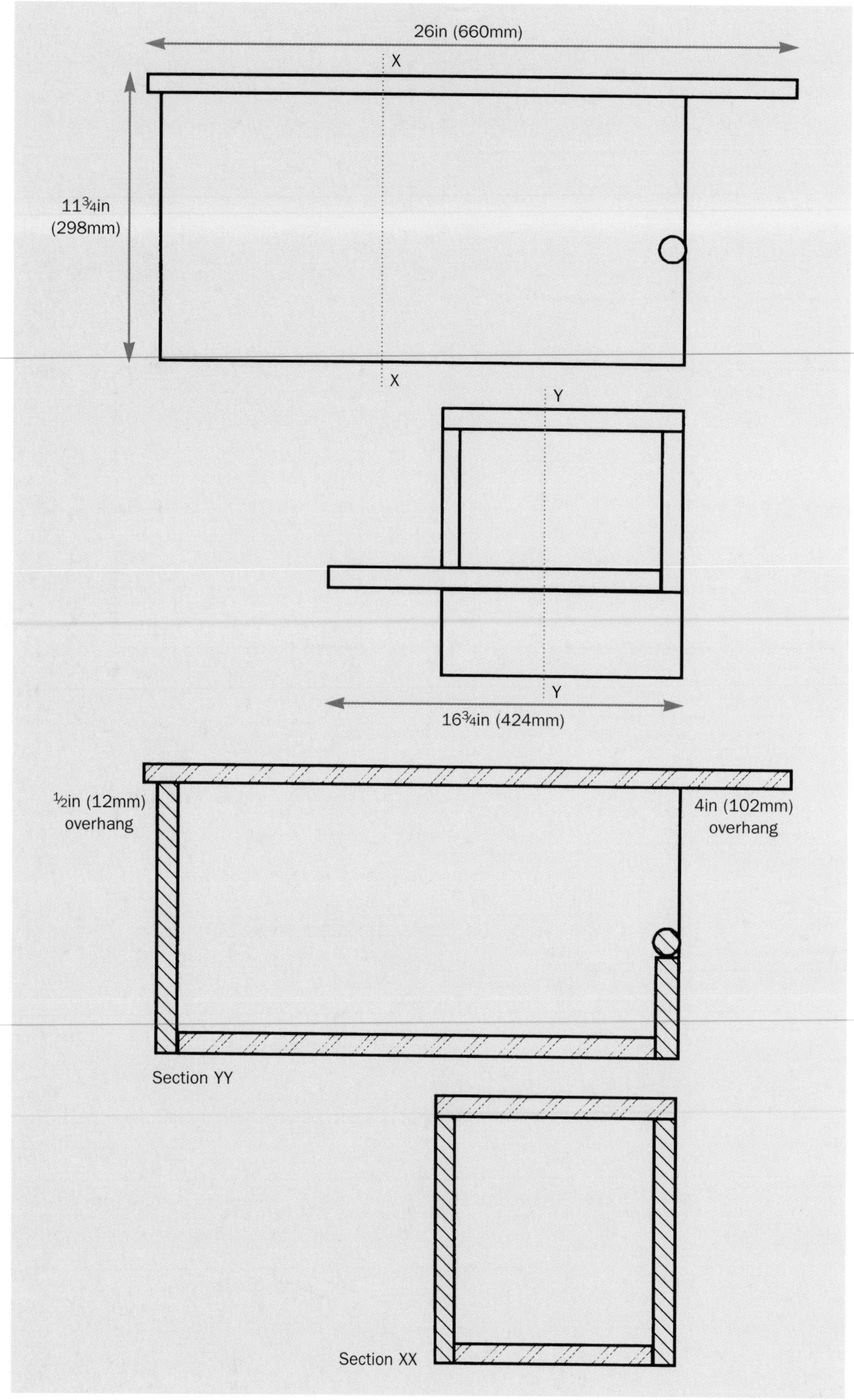

Fig 15.2
Plan with sections.

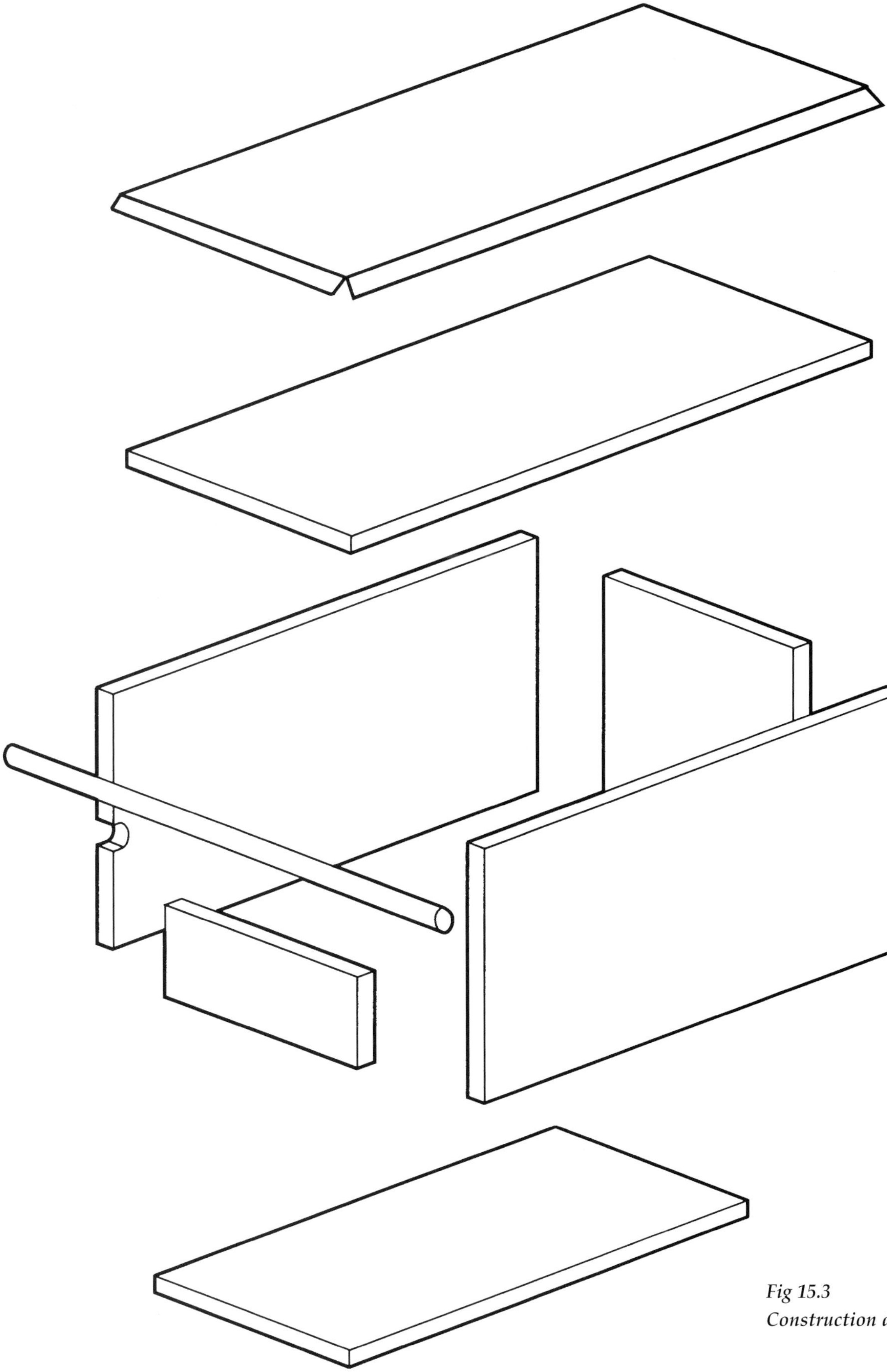

Fig 15.3
Construction details.

Construction

1 Mark the size, shape and position of all the wooden pieces except the perch on a sheet of ¾in (18mm) plywood, using a pencil, square, and long steel ruler. Plane all the edges flat and smooth the corners with glasspaper.

2 Join the base to the back with nails and glue. To make this easier, drill small pilot holes in the top pieces where the nails will be used, to guide them. (*See* Chapter 2, page 11.) After the nails have been hammered home, punch the heads below the surface. Follow this by fixing the sides, top and front into position using the same method. (*See* Figs 15.5 and 15.6.)

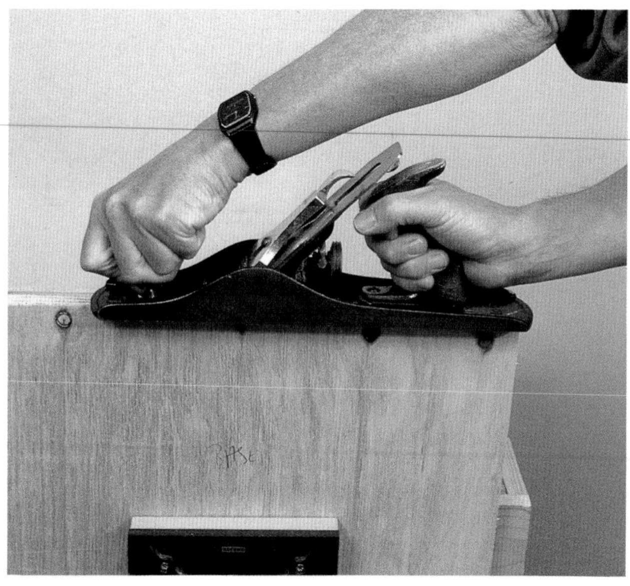

Fig 15.4
Smoothing the edges of the plywood with a jack plane.

Fig 15.5
The partially finished box.

Fig 15.6
Fixing the roof with glue and nails.

3 Cut a piece of ¾in (18mm) doweling for the perch. Make a notch to house this in one of the sides, using a coping saw, and fix the perch in place with nails and glue. (*See* Fig 15.7.)

4 From another piece of thick plywood, cut the batten to fix the box onto a tree or building. Attach this to the sides of the box with screws and glue. Drill holes in the ends of the batten to take the nails that will hold it in place, and drill further holes in the base of the next box for drainage.

***Fig 15.7** (above)*
Cutting a notch for the perch.

FINISHING

1 Paint clear sealing solution on using a soft-bristle brush. To stop the rain seeping through the top, cover it with roofing felt. Mark out the felt using a white pencil and a long steel rule, and cut it with a craft knife. (*See* Chapter 2, page 19.) Hold the felt in position with ½in (12mm) galvanized clout nails.

2 Once the box is positioned, place some wood shavings in the base to encourage the kestrels to use the nest.

***Fig 15.8** (below)*
The nesting box, ready for use.

16

Squirrel-Proof Peanut Feeder

Grey squirrels are frequent visitors to most gardens and can be enchanting with their acrobatic antics. Unfortunately, although cute to look at, they are also rapacious predators and will eat birds' eggs and nestlings. Whilst it is not possible to keep them out of a garden, it is best for the other wildlife if they are not actively encouraged. Given the chance, they will eat all the food that is put out for birds, so I designed this feeder to prevent them.

The feeder consists of two mesh cages made from zinc-coated wire. The inner cage, of smaller mesh, holds the peanuts and the outer cage, of larger mesh, keeps out the squirrels. Holes are cut in the larger mesh big enough to allow smaller birds, such as blue, great, and coal tits to enter, but too small for squirrels and larger, undesirable birds such as starlings and pigeons. Hang the feeder high enough to be out of the reach of cats.

The wooden parts of the feeder are made from ¾in (18mm) exterior quality plywood. Theoretically, the squirrels could eventually chew through this and get to the seed, but I have had feeders made from this material in my garden for several years and the squirrels have never persisted long enough to gain access.

CUTTING LIST

Hexagonal lid (1)	Plywood	4¼ x 3 11/16 x ¾in (108 x 94 x 18mm)
Circular base of lid (1)	Plywood	1 15/16 x ¾in diameter (50 x 18mm diameter)
Hexagonal top (1)	Plywood	7 x 6 1/16 x ¾in (178 x 154 x 18mm)
Hexagonal base (1)	Plywood	7 x 6 1/16 x ¾in (178 x 154 x 18mm)
Circular base of feeder (1)	Plywood	¾ x 1 15/16in diameter (18 x 50mm diameter)

ALSO REQUIRED:

Self-adhesive flashing for lid	approx. 5 x 5in (127 x 127mm)
Self-adhesive flashing for top	approx. 9 x 9in (229 x 229mm)
Wire mesh, ½in (12mm) square	21 x 7½in (533 x 191mm)
Wire mesh, ¼in (6mm)square	6¾ x 6½in (171 x 165mm)
Brass screw eyes (2)	
Fuse wire, 30amp	
Fuse wire, 15amp	

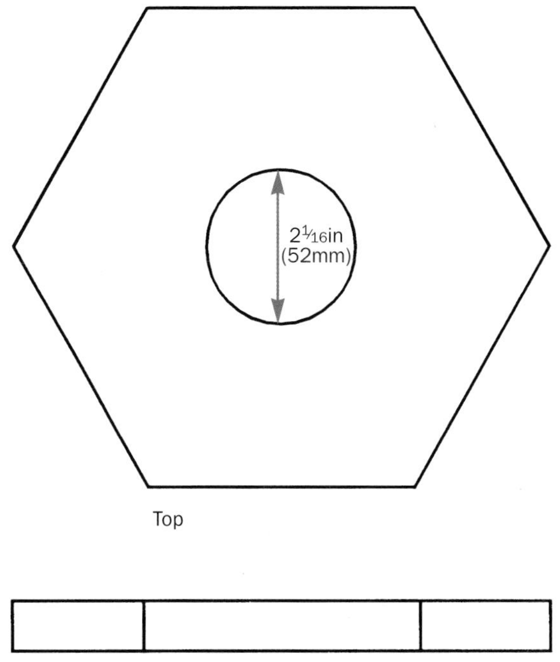

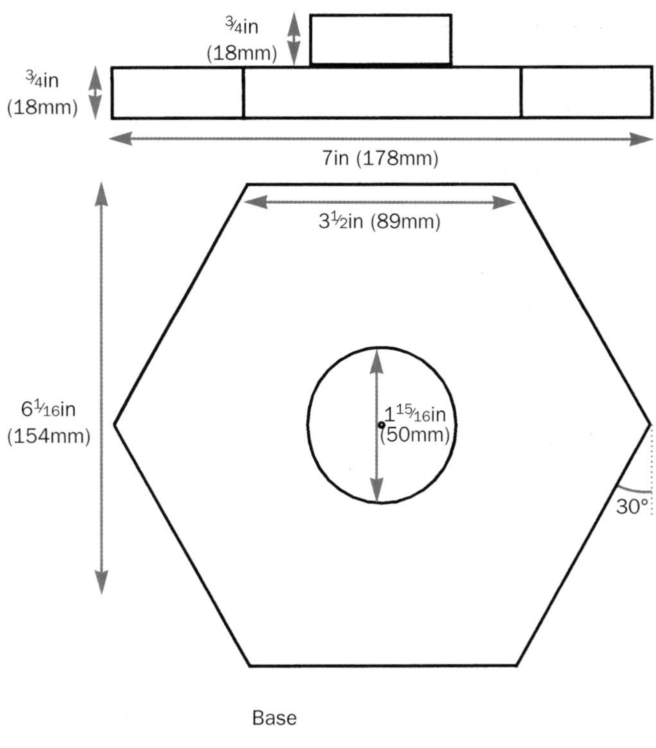

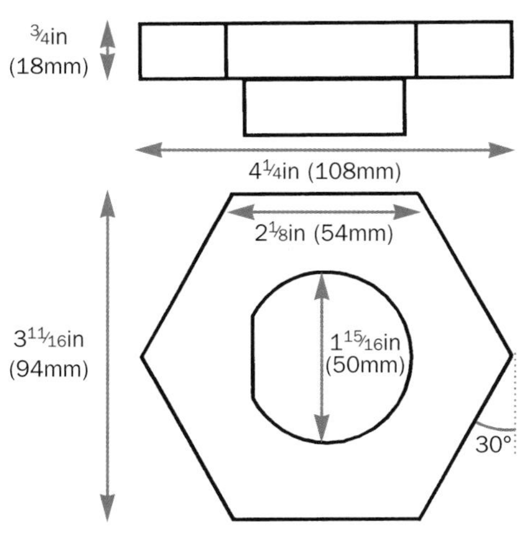

Fig 16.1
All the wooden parts with dimensions.

Fig 16.2 Section with dimensions.

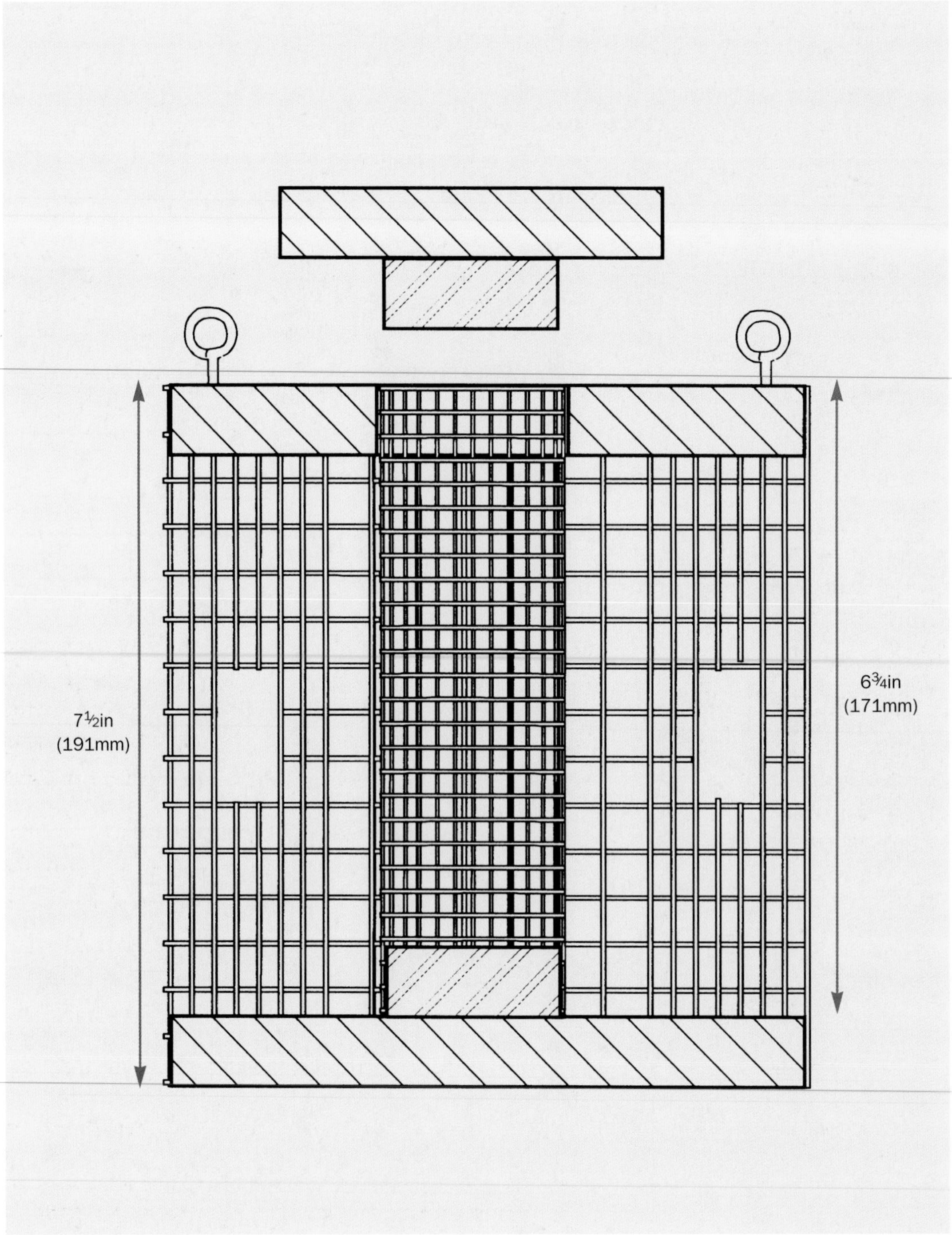

7½in (191mm)

6¾in (171mm)

CONSTRUCTION

1 Using a 30° set square, mark and cut out two large hexagons and one small hexagon from plywood. Round the corners of each one slightly with glasspaper. These pieces are for the top and base of the outer cage and for the top of the lid. Use a 2in (50mm) diameter hole saw to make a hole in the centre of one of the large hexagons and retain the circular cut-out for use later. From a scrap piece of plywood, use the same sized hole saw to cut a second circular piece.

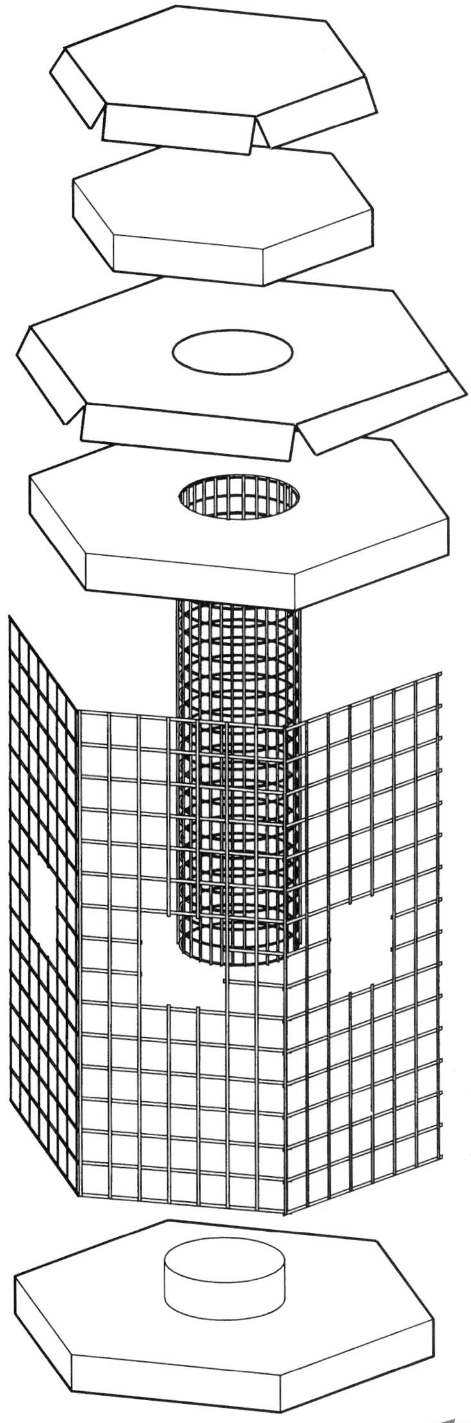

Fig 16.4
The completed wooden parts.

2 To make the outer cage, cut a piece of ½in (12mm) wire mesh, 21 x 7½in (533 x 191mm), using wire cutters. Every 3½in (89mm) along the length of this panel, bend the mesh to form a hexagon using a piece of scrap wood as a former (*see* Fig 16.5). When the mesh forms a complete hexagon, bind the two edges together with 30amp fuse wire. I chose fuse wire for the job because it is flexible, will not rust and is readily available.

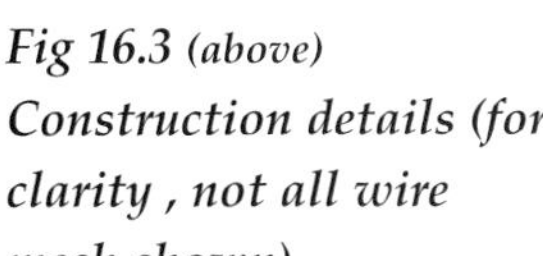

***Fig 16.3** (above)*
Construction details (for clarity , not all wire mesh shown).

Outer mesh ½in (12mm)

21in (533mm)

7½in (191mm)

***Fig 16.5** (right)*
Mesh panel size for outer cage.

Fig 16.6
Bending the outer cage into a hexagonal shape.

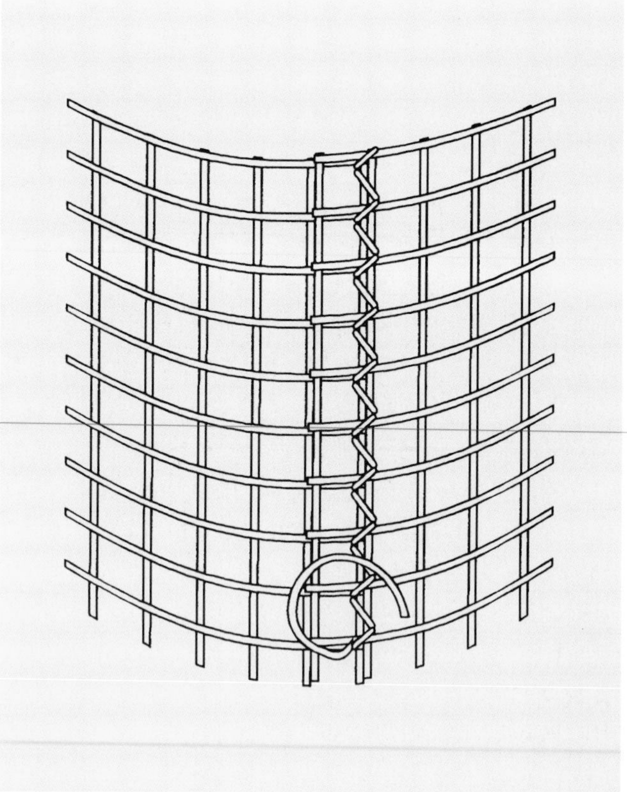

Fig 16.7
Binding the wire mesh for the outer cage.

3 To make the inner cage that holds the peanuts, cut a piece of ¼in (6mm) wire mesh measuring 6½in (165mm) for the circumference and 6¾in (171mm) high. Bend the wire into a cylinder using a rolling pin as a former. Overlap the ends by ¼in (6mm) and bind them together with 15amp fuse wire.

Assembly

1 Take one of the circular pieces that you put aside earlier and ensure that it fits into the end of the wire peanut cylinder. Test also that the other end of the mesh cylinder fits into the circular hole cut into the top hexagon. Adjust the wood if either piece does not fit, using a file. Following this, make sure that the large mesh cage fits around the top and bottom plywood hexagons. If it is too tight, adjust the fit by planing the edges of the plywood.

Glue and screw the circular plywood that fits inside the small mesh cylinder onto the base plywood hexagon (*see* Fig 16.7). Fit the small mesh cylinder onto this and use a stapler to secure it. Fit the large mesh cage around the base and staple this also. Put the top hexagon inside the large mesh cage with the small mesh cylinder fitted into the hole in its centre. Staple around the outside of the top to secure it. It is not necessary to staple the top of the small mesh cylinder if it fits tightly into the hole.

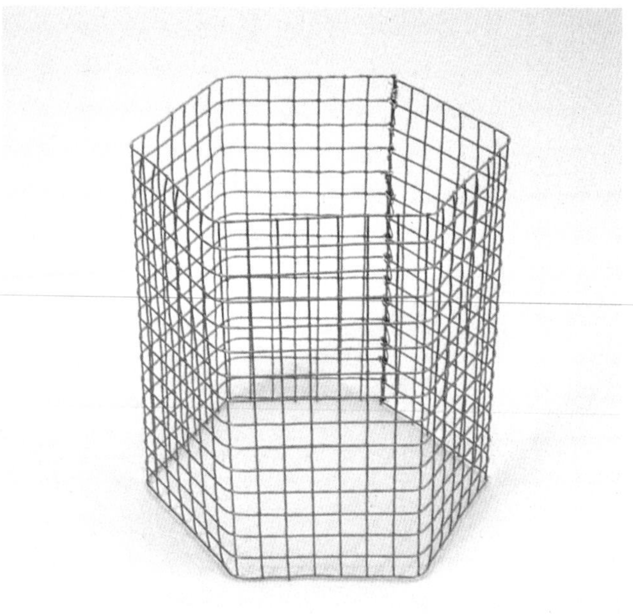

Fig 16.8
The hexagonal outer cage before the access holes are cut.

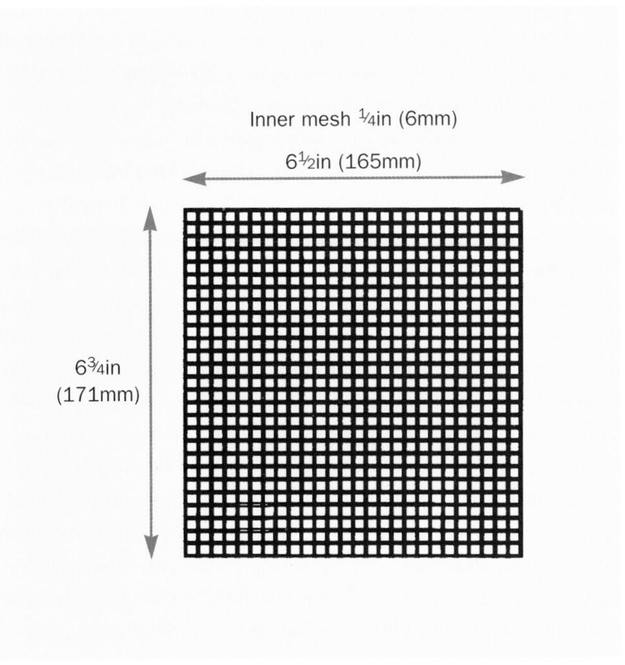

Fig 16.9
Mesh panel size for the inner cage.

Fig 16.11
The base of the feeder.

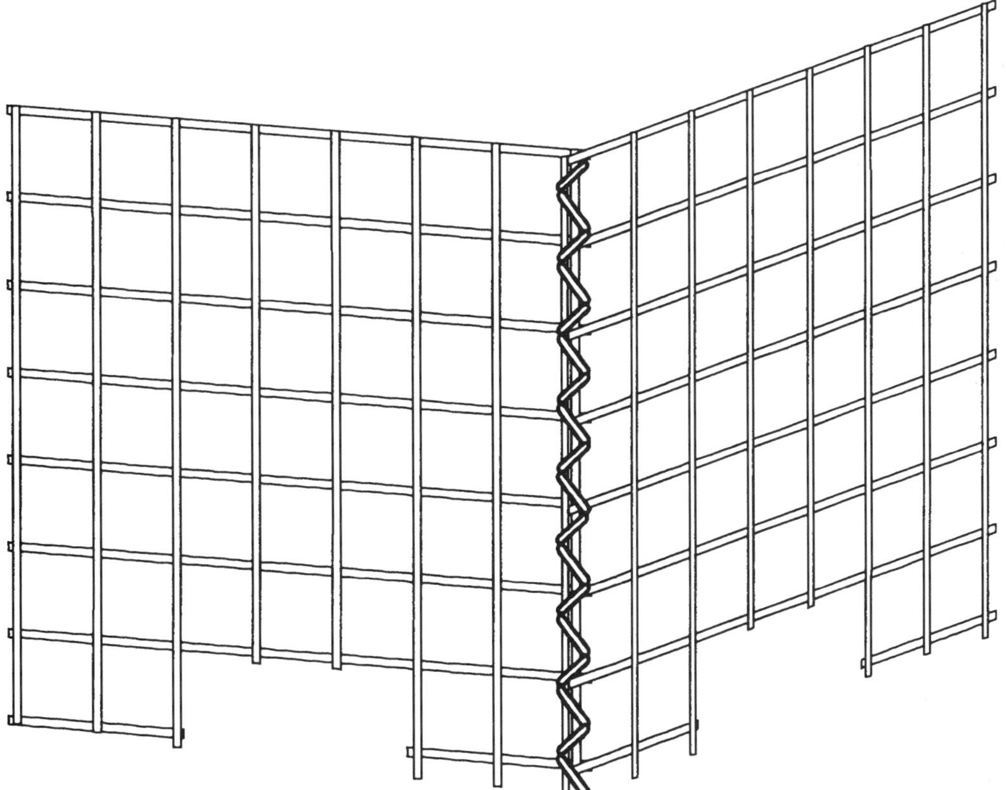

Fig 16.10
Binding the wire mesh for the inner cage.

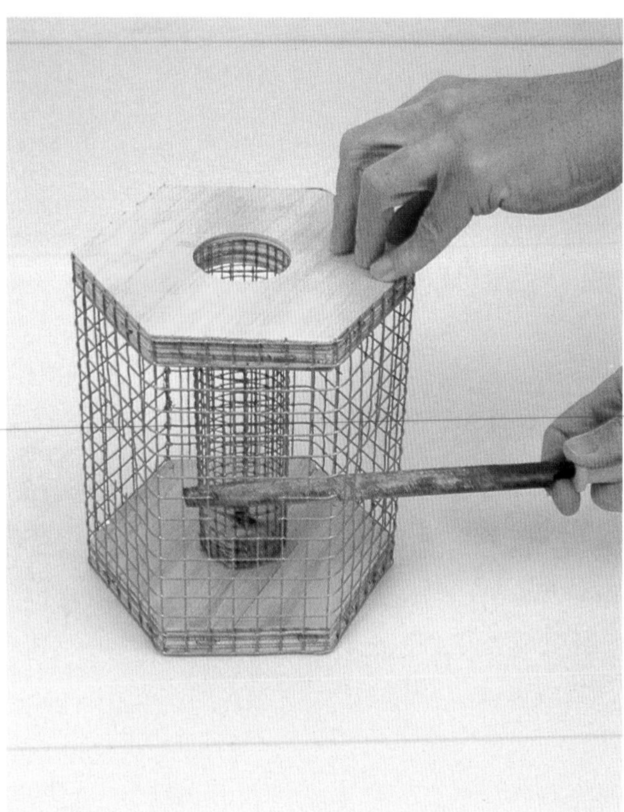

Fig 16.12
Filing off any ends on the wire.

2 Use wire cutters to make the holes in the large mesh cage. File the ends of the wire to remove any sharp edges (*see* Fig 16.12), although they would probably not be a problem as birds habitually perch in bushes and shrubs that are covered in thorns without any ill effects.

3 Test the other piece of circular plywood to ensure that it fits inside the top of the small mesh cylinder. I found that it was necessary for a small flat section to be filed on the edge to accommodate the overlap and wire binding at the top of the cylinder.

Use a screw and glue to fix the circular plywood to the underside of the small hexagon to form a lid. If the lid is a reasonably tight fit it will not be necessary to fix a catch onto it in order to hold it in place.

Finishing

1 Paint all the wooden parts with water-repellent sealer.

2 Make and fit the waterproof covering for the top. To do this cut a length of self-adhesive flashing from a roll and lay it sticky side up. Turn the feeder upside down and place it on the sticky side of the flashing. Use a craft knife to cut out a hexagon that is ¾in (18mm) larger all around than the top. This is easily done if a piece of scrap wood ¾in (18mm) thick is held against the top and used as a straightedge to guide the knife. Cut notches at the corner so that the flashing can be bent around the top and stuck to the edges: press the flashing down so that it sticks securely.

Use a craft knife to cut a hole in the centre of the top so that the lid can fit in. Use the same procedure to cover the lid with flashing.

3 Fit two brass screw eyes to the top of the lid so that the feeder can be hung in a tree. I fitted a length of brass chain because squirrels would chew through string: wire would be equally suitable.

Fig 16.13
Feeder with lid and wire in place.

17

Rustic Nest Box for Tits

There is no evidence to suggest that blue tits and great tits prefer their nest boxes to look like a natural hole in a tree, however, as I like the idea of having natural looking nest boxes I made this one from a cherry log that I saved when the tree was cleared from a friend's garden.

The type of tree that the log comes from is not important as long as the dimensions are approximately the same. It should be about 14in (356mm) long and about 7in (179mm) in diameter. The roof is made from the same material so ensure that you have additional pieces from which to cut these parts.

The nest box should be sited in a sheltered position on a tree or building, 8–10ft (2.5–3m) from the ground.

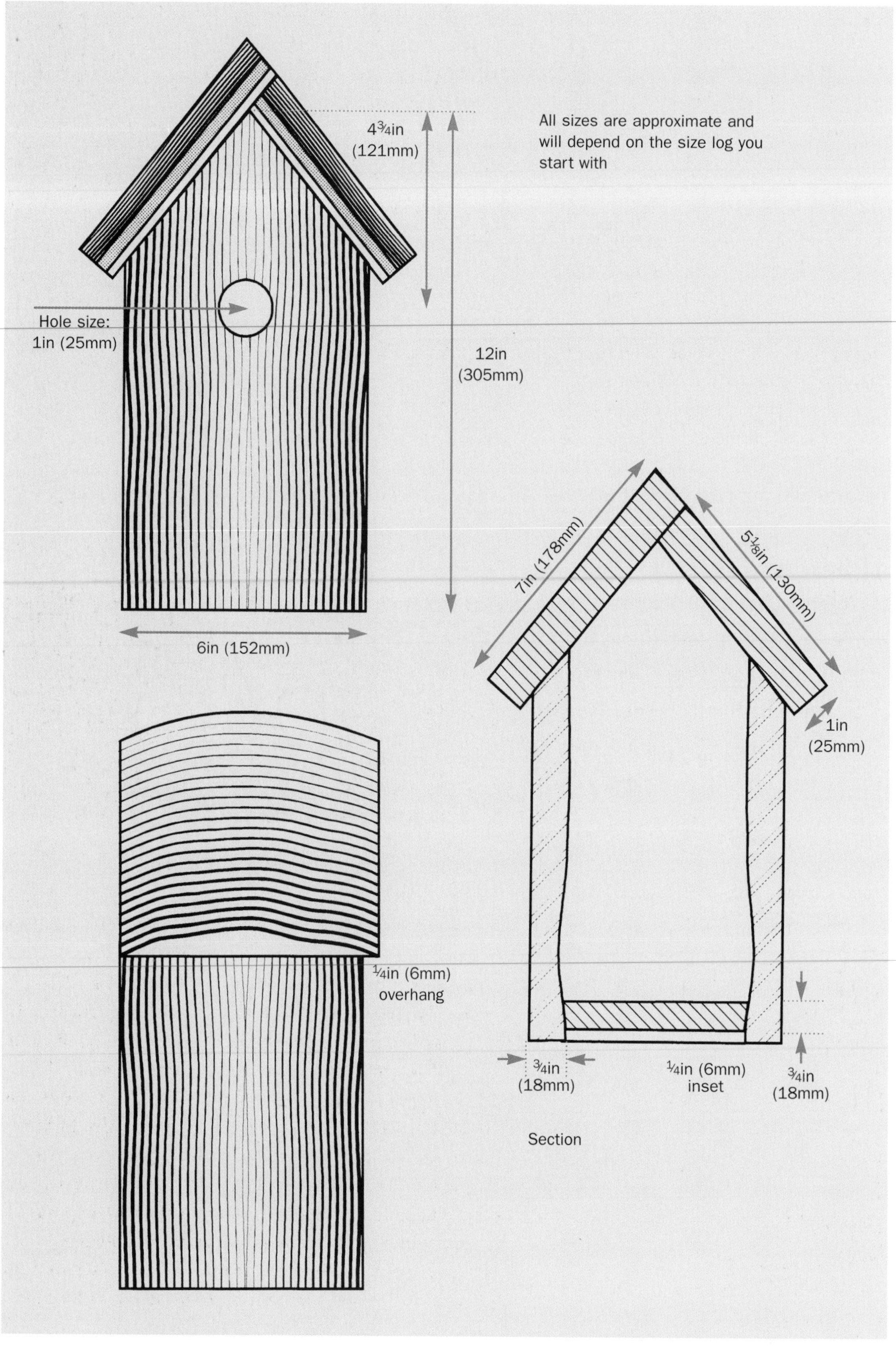

4¾in
(121mm)

All sizes are approximate and
will depend on the size log you
start with

Hole size:
1in (25mm)

12in
(305mm)

6in (152mm)

7in (178mm)

5⅛in (130mm)

1in
(25mm)

¼in (6mm)
overhang

¾in
(18mm)

¼in (6mm)
inset

¾in
(18mm)

Section

Fig 17.1
Plan with dimensions.

Construction

Hollowed Body

1 Cut the log to the correct length and plane a flat area on the back so that it will fit flush against the surface it is eventually fixed to (*see* Fig 17.3). Using a white pencil, so that it will show up on the bark, mark the lines where the log will be sawn to form the roof slope, and cut along these lines with a panel saw.

2 The next stage is to remove the waste wood from the centre of the log leaving a wall thickness of approximately ¾in (18mm). In both ends of the log, using a 1in (25mm) spade bit in a power drill, make a series of holes ¾in (18mm) in from the edge, to the maximum depth the bit will allow. This can be a bit laborious, but eventually the holes from both ends will meet and the wood from the centre can be removed in a plug. The rest of the waste can be removed with a 1in (25mm) half-round gouge (*see* Fig 17.4). Unless all of the drilled holes meet up edge to edge, the 'plug' will not come out cleanly, so it may be necessary to use a little brute force, and a mallet and chisel, to remove it. Do not make the insides smooth as rough walls will help the chicks climb out of the nest box when they fledge. However, at the base of the log make the insides smooth as a wooden plug is fitted here to make a floor for the nest box.

Fig 17.3
Planing a flat on the back of the log.

Fig 17.4
Hollowing out the centre.

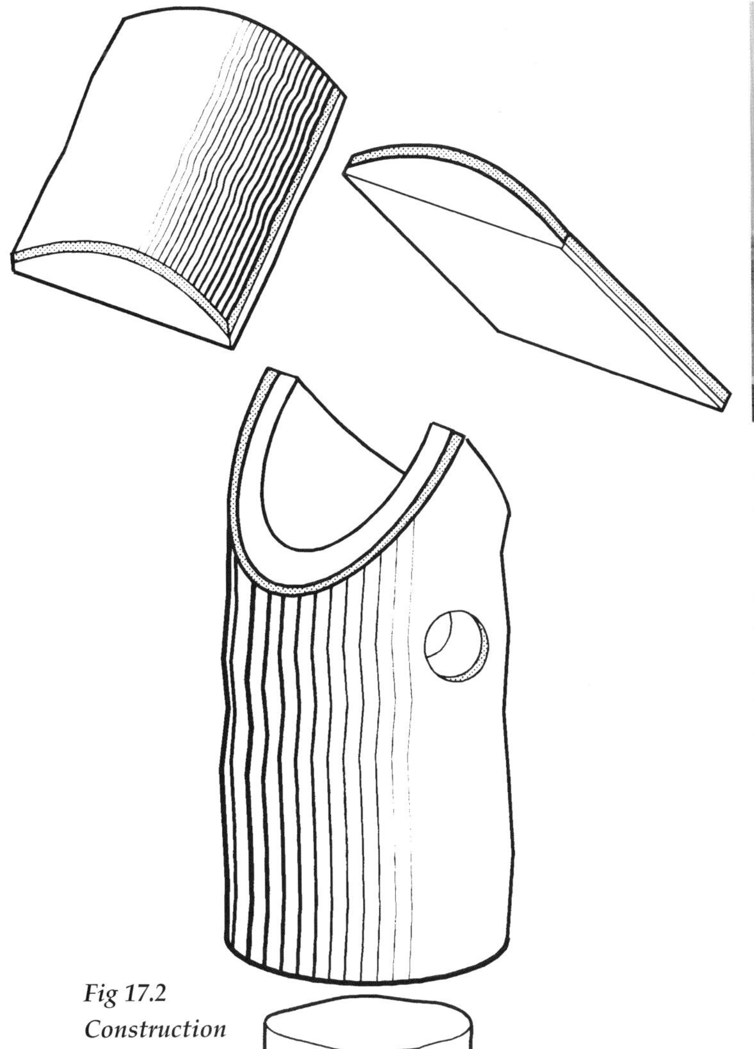

Fig 17.2
Construction details.

If the walls of the log are badly cracked, force some glue into them and clamp until the glue is set – this will make it structurally sound. Cut a 1in (25mm) access hole in the front with a hole saw.

3 Make the plug for the base from a piece of hardwood board about ¾in (18mm) thick. To get the correct shape, stand the base of the log on the board, reach inside and draw around the inside edge with a pencil. You either need small hands for this or the help of somebody who has. When the wood has been marked, cut the shape out with a coping saw, a little oversized, and fit it into the base of the log. It might be necessary to adjust the size of the plug with a rasp to get a good fit. When this is satisfactory glue it into place.

ROOF

1 The two roof sections are made from a piece of cherry wood about 1in (25mm) thick, with the bark still in place. Cut one side to the correct size (*see* Fig 17.5) and nail and glue it into place. I find it helps me to nail accurately if guide holes are drilled first.

Fig 17.5
Testing to see that one of the roof pieces fits accurately.

To get the shape of the top edge of the second piece marked accurately, hold it in place and draw around the edge of the first part (*see* Fig 17.6). Cut the second part to size and fix it in place.

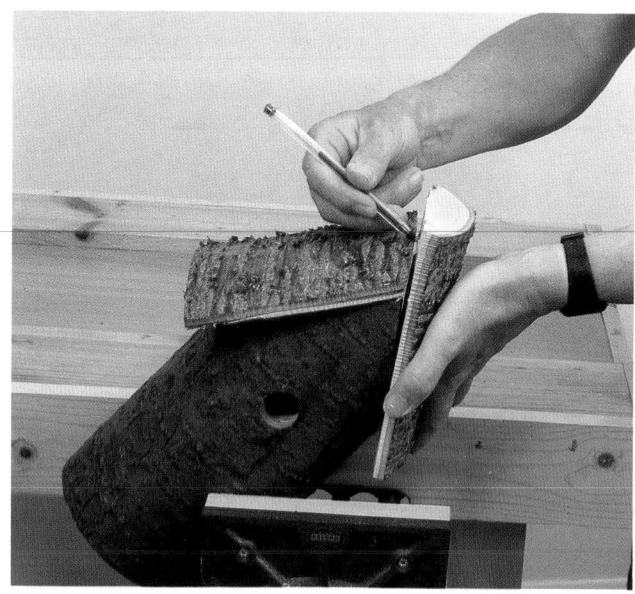

Fig 17.6
Marking the position to cut the second roof panel.

FIXING

1 The nest box is fixed to a tree with a single screw. To accommodate this, drill a hole in the back that is in line with the access hole in the front. Put the screw into the hole via the front access hole using a pair of long-nosed pliers, and screw it up. This is a bit tricky and might need a couple of attempts. It is not important if it is not held tightly – the birds will not mind if it swings around slightly as long as it does not drop off.

Fig 17.7
The assembled nest box.

GARDENS NEAR PONDS OR LAKES

If you have a pond in or near your garden it greatly increases the variety of wildlife that will be attracted to it. Even the smallest pond will encourage frogs and dragonflies and, if you are fortunate, ducks as well.

The pond in my garden is only 6 x 4ft (1,829 x 1,219mm), but a pair of wild mallard ducks have raised a family of 10 ducklings on it.

MALLARD

DUCK BARREL

WADER DECOY

18

Decoy Duck

A garden situated near a lake or river is likely to have a large population of ducks in the vicinity, so a pair of them might take up residence in your pond without any encouragement, but you could speed up their residency by luring them with a decoy. The word 'decoy' comes from the Dutch *'de Kooi'* meaning 'the cage'. They were originally used for hunting, but will serve equally well in attracting ducks to your garden.

It is not necessary for a decoy to be an exact replica, but it must convey the duck's character by its size, colours, and feather patterns.

I used a section from an old pine gate post, but almost any wood will suffice: you don't need to obtain a block of lime or other premium carving wood as this is a working model and not intended for ornamental purposes. This follows traditional decoy carving practice. The early carvers in the USA, where the modern duck carving hobby began, used any materials they could obtain cheaply, including redundant pine telegraph posts.

Ensure that any material you use is well seasoned. To help avoid any major cracks, hollow out the block. This is a traditional method and was practised by the original decoy makers. Wood dries out quicker on the outside than on the inside, so in thick pieces of wood there is more stress built up between the dry outside and the still-wet inside than in thin pieces. This means that thick pieces are more likely to crack. Hollowing out the centre means that the wood has a thinner section than the original solid piece, and is thus more stable. Hollowing also helps the duck to float on the surface in a natural way.

When the decoy is finished, a small weight is hung beneath it, to make it float upright. If you intend to use it in a large pond or lake, it should also be fitted with a longer cord and a large weight, to stop it drifting away.

The head is made separately from the body for this decoy because an all-in-one carving would require a larger piece of wood.

CUTTING LIST

Body (1)	Pine	13½ x 3¾ x 6½in (343 x 95 x 165mm)
Base of body (1)	Pine	11 x 1½ x 6½in (279 x 38 x 165mm)
Head (1)	Pine	6 x 5¾ x 2½in (152 x 146 x 63mm)
ALSO REQUIRED:		
Brass screw eye (1)		
Lead fishing weight (1)	4oz (110g)	

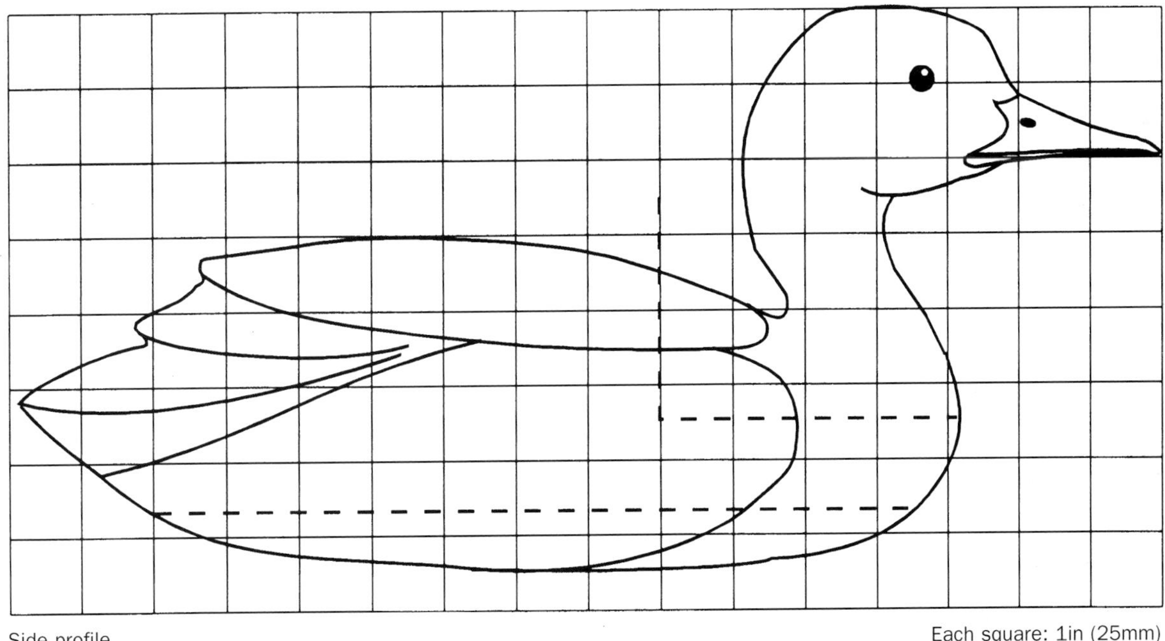

Fig 18.1 Side profile.

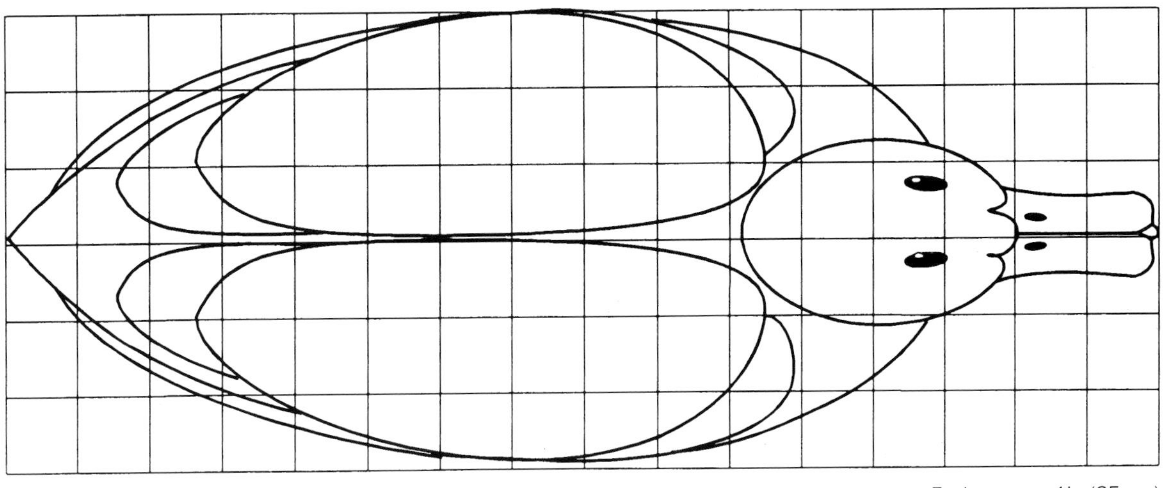

Fig 18.2 Plan profile.

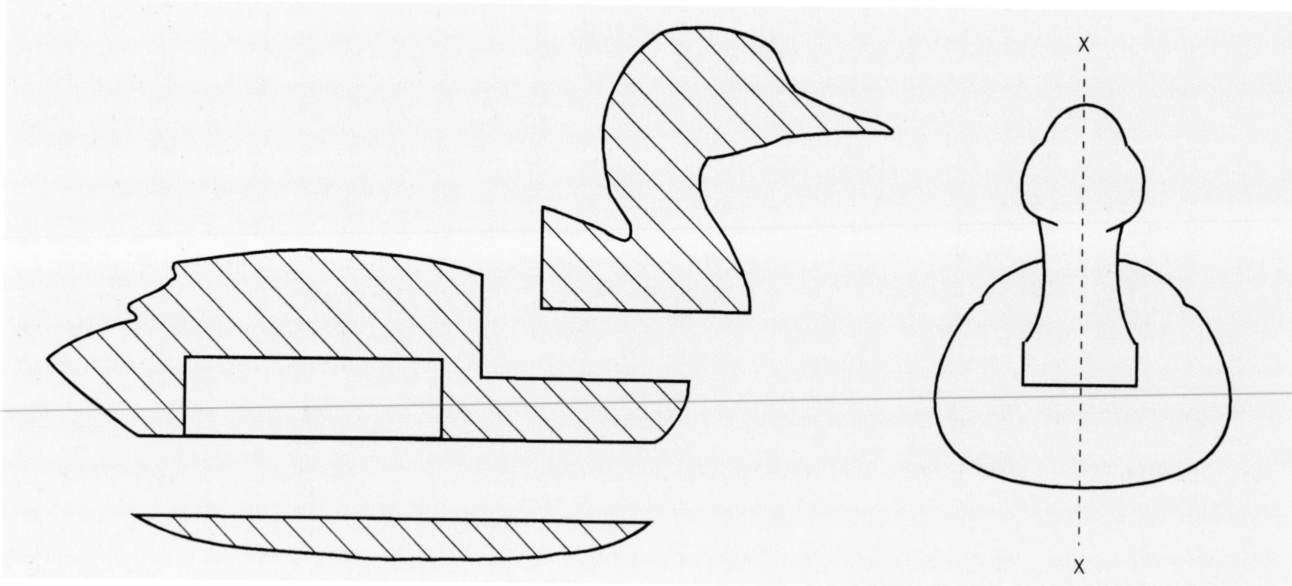

Fig 18.3
Sections for jointing.

Carving

THE BLANK

1 Make a cardboard template for the side profile of the duck shape from Fig 18.1. On a piece of pine large enough for the body, not including the base or the head, draw the side profile by tracing around the template. (The shape required is indicated by the broken line in Fig 18.1.) Plane the bottom of this piece of wood flat so that the base can be stuck on later, after the centre has been hollowed out. Cut around the side profile with a band saw.

Using Fig 18.2 as a guide, draw the plan profile on the top of the body you have formed, and cut around this with a band saw. Mark the area to be hollowed out on the underside, ensuring that approximately 1in (25mm) thickness is left all around. Do not go too near the front of the body where the joint to house the head will be made (*see* Fig 18.3). Drill out the waste wood in the hollow to a depth of 1½in (38mm), using a 1in (25mm) spade bit.

2 Select a suitable piece of wood for the base (indicated on Fig 18.1), and plane a flat surface on one side where it will join the underside of the duck.

Fig 18.4
Preparing to stick the base to the body.

Cut the base on a band saw so that it has a similar shape to the duck's underside, and glue the two parts together. Apply ample waterproof glue to both surfaces so that there is plenty of 'squeeze out' when the two halves are clamped together.

3 Whilst this is drying, obtain a piece of wood for the head and mark out the shape from the cardboard templates. Cut around the profile with a band saw then, with a hand saw, cut rebates in the neck area about ⅜in (9mm) deep, to make the neck and the joint where the neck fits the body narrower than the head.

Fig 18.5
Testing the joint between the head and the body for fit.

4 Remove the clamps from the body and, using the base of the neck as a guide, mark the position and width of the joint to house the head. To form this housing use a tenon saw to cut as far down the sides as possible, drill out some of the waste wood, and clean out the rest of the recess with a chisel.

Try the head in the body frequently to check for the accuracy of the fit as the chiselling proceeds. When the fit is satisfactory, put the head to one side whilst the initial carving of the body proceeds. This is because the head might get in the way in the early stages of the shaping when large lumps of wood will be removed with a gouge.

REFINING THE HEAD AND BODY

1 Draw a guideline around the centre of the profile to help keep the carving symmetrical when rounding the shape (*see* Fig 18.8). This is a very useful guideline and should be continually redrawn as it gets carved away.

Using a combination of large rasp and 1in (25mm) gouge, start to round off all the corners, stopping occasionally to see that the proportions look correct and that not too much wood is being removed. At this stage the body should begin to resemble a duck.

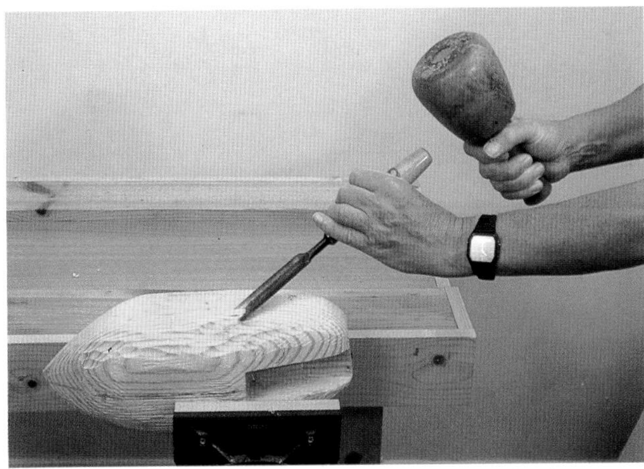

Fig 18.6
Using a 1in (25mm) gouge to rough out the body shape.

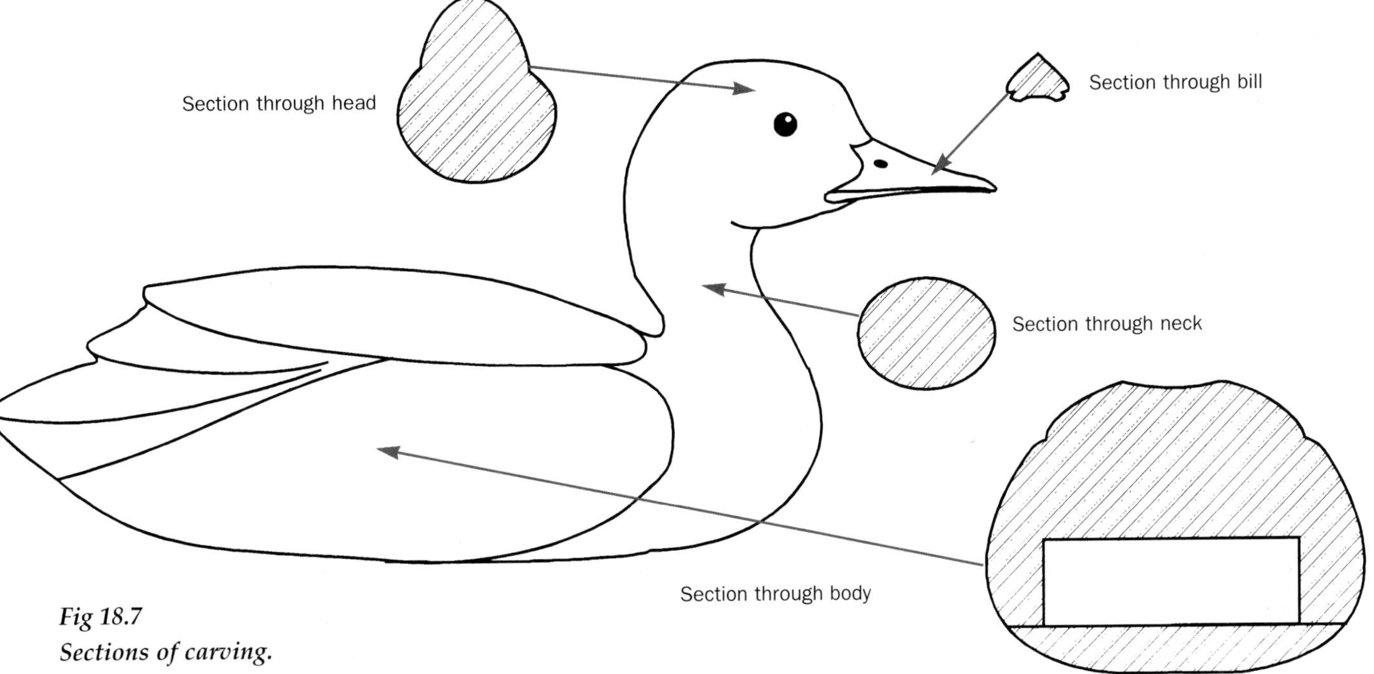

Fig 18.7
Sections of carving.

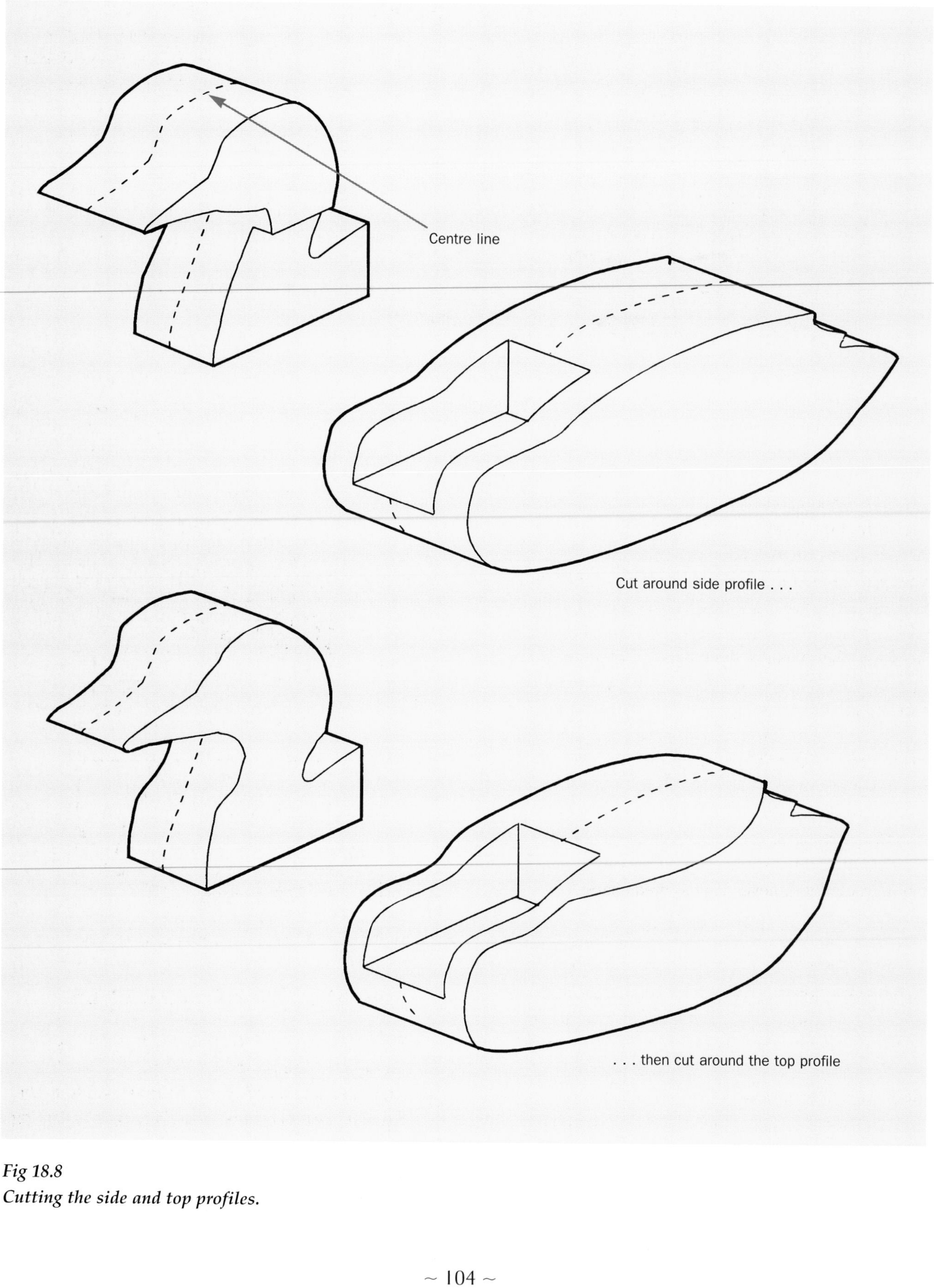

Centre line

Cut around side profile . . .

. . . then cut around the top profile

Fig 18.8
Cutting the side and top profiles.

Fig 18.9 (left)
After the head is glued into place, the positions of the wings are marked.

2 Stop working on the body, mark a centre line around the head, and bring it to the same roughly carved state as the body. Stick the head to the body with waterproof glue. When the glue has set, smooth the join between the neck and the body.

3 Draw the shapes of the wings on the body (*see* Fig 18.9), and form a slight hollow along these lines using a ½in (12mm) gouge. Next, mark the position of the tail feathers and, using a combination of chisels and rotary rasp, rough out their shape. Most of the remaining carving is done with a rotary rasp fixed to a drill with a flexible drive. If the centre line is removed as carving proceeds, redraw it. When shaping the wings and the tail I continually rework all around the body so that it gradually achieves the required shape.

4 As the body shape nears completion, work on the head to bring it to the same state. Start this by rounding the head and neck with a ½in (12mm) gouge, carefully removing small chips and continually checking from all angles to ensure that not too much is being removed. For a carving of this size, a ½in (12mm) chisel is suitable for most of the initial shaping.

Having done this, draw the outline of the beak and the front of the head as seen from above (*see* Fig 18.2) onto the wood and cut it out with a coping saw. Use a chisel to refine the shape.

Fig 18.10 (below)
Front profile.

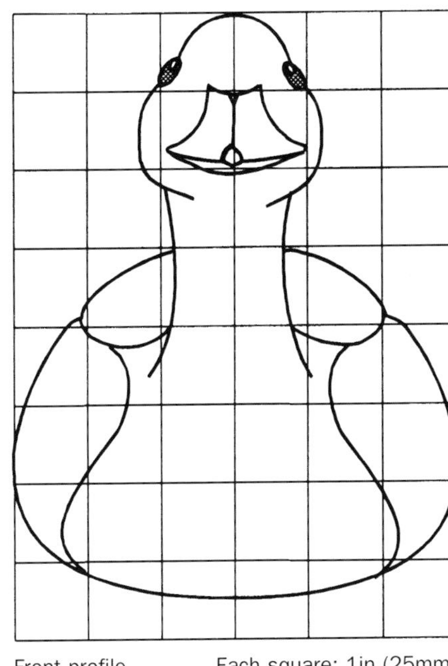

POSITIONING THE EYES

1 The next part to be tackled, and one of the most important, is the positioning of the eyes. Mark them on with a pencil and check their position from the side, top and front, to ensure that it is correct. Following this, use a small gouge to form the hollows above the cheeks in which the eyes nestle. These hollows are clearly shown in Fig 18.10.

2 When the hollows are correctly carved, mark the position of the eyes in pencil again, and check from all angles. Cut out the hollow for the eyes with a 3⁄8in (9mm) round gauge. Make the initial cuts downwards, with the chisel held upright on the wood, all around the outline of the eye. Next, make a slanting cut so that when it meets the first cut it removes a series of chips, which leaves the eyeball standing proud of the surface (*see* Fig 18.11). Round off and smooth the edges of the eyes with glasspaper.

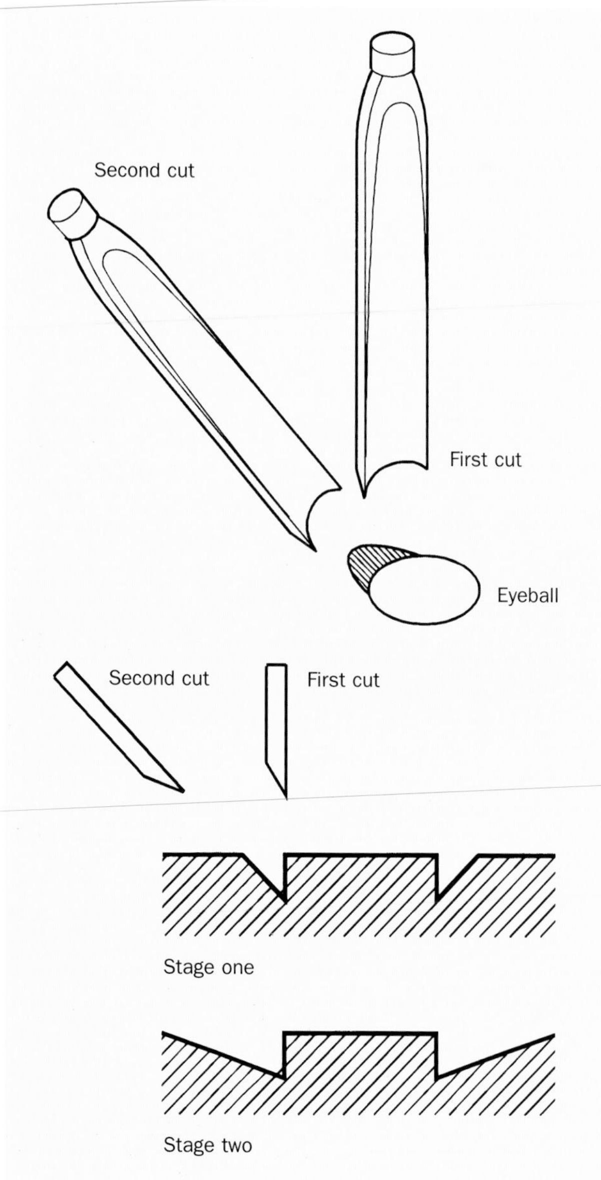

Fig 18.11
Forming the eyes.

REFINING THE BEAK

1 With the eyes finished, the beak is worked on again, so that a section through it looks like Fig 18.4. When this is done, rework the whole of the head with a shallow, 1⁄2in (12mm) fishtail gouge to refine and smooth the shape. Remove all the gouge marks on the rest of the head and the body with a sander (*see* Fig 18.12).

2 To complete, use a waterproof filler to fill any holes and gaps, and smooth the whole duck with glasspaper.

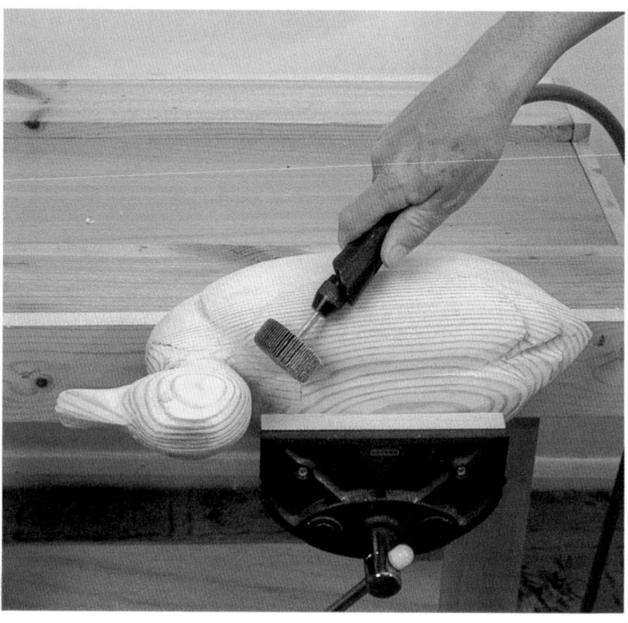

Fig 18.12
Sanding away the gouge marks.

PAINTING

1 To provide a ground for painting, apply a coat of white acrylic primer. When the primer is dry, mark the position of the main colour areas with pencil before starting to paint. (For general guidance, *see* Chapter 2, page 20.) For this decoy, use best quality artists' sable brushes, ranging from No. 0 to No. 6.

To get the colours as accurate as possible, I visited the mallard ducks on a nearby canal, taking my watercolours to make a few colour swatches for later reference, when painting the carving in the workshop.

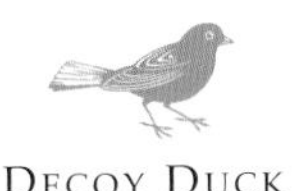

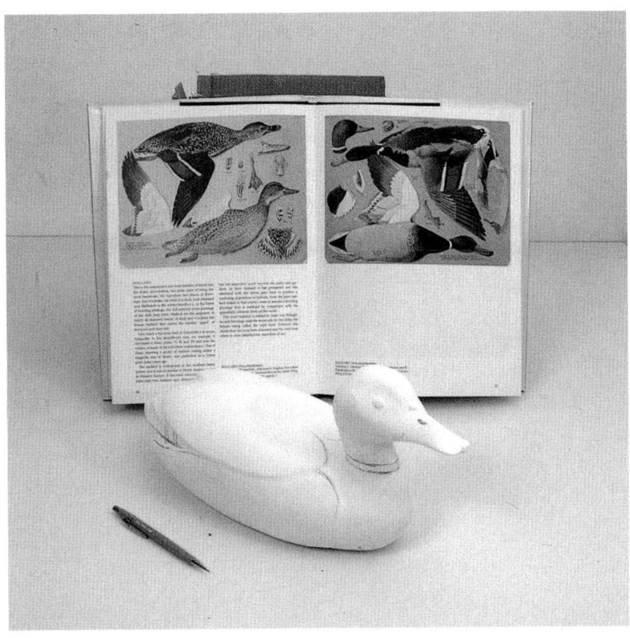

Fig 18.13
Using a book for reference, to get the position of the coloured areas.

MAIN COLOUR MIXES
Breast
Wings and sides
Light tone for head
Beak
Wing flashes
Tail
Head

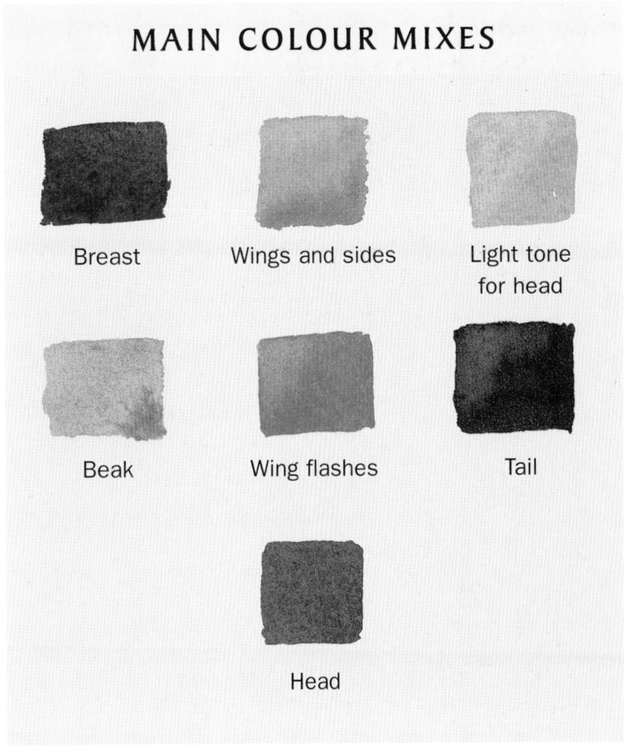

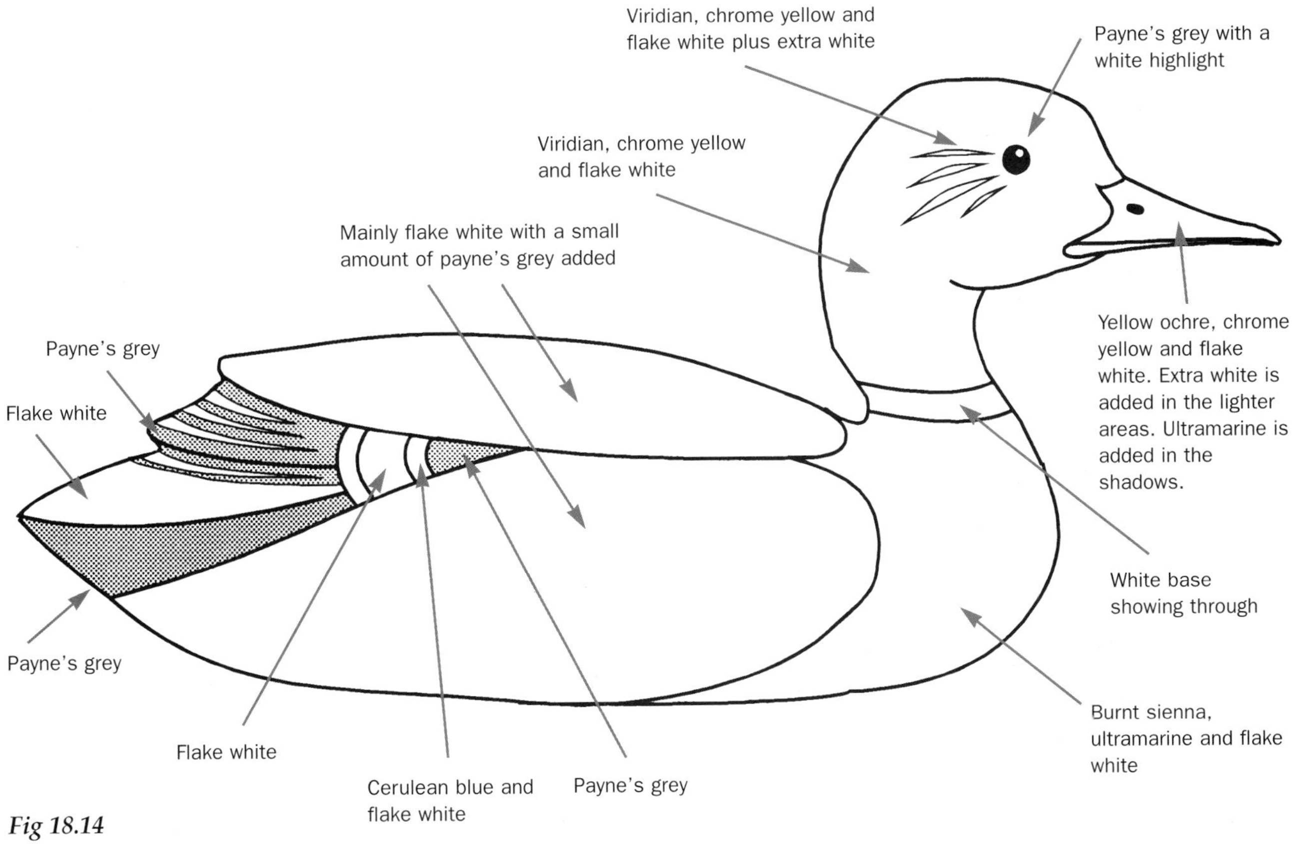

Viridian, chrome yellow and flake white plus extra white
Payne's grey with a white highlight
Viridian, chrome yellow and flake white
Mainly flake white with a small amount of payne's grey added
Payne's grey
Flake white
Yellow ochre, chrome yellow and flake white. Extra white is added in the lighter areas. Ultramarine is added in the shadows.
White base showing through
Payne's grey
Burnt sienna, ultramarine and flake white
Flake white
Cerulean blue and flake white
Payne's grey

Fig 18.14
Painting scheme.

MALLARD AND CHICKS

2 For the mallard breast colour, that is the area below the white ring on the neck, use a mixture of burnt sienna, ultramarine and flake white, and for the head, a mixture of viridian, chrome yellow and flake white. Lighten this tone for the patches around the eyes. For the white neck band, allow the white ground to show through. Make the beak colour by mixing yellow ochre, chrome yellow and flake white, adding extra white for the highlights and, to give a green tone to the shadows, mixing in some ultramarine. Paint the nostrils with ultramarine and burnt umber.

The mixture for the tail is ultramarine, payne's grey and flake white, and for the wings and body sides, payne's grey and flake white. The top wings are a slightly lighter shade of grey than the sides so the mix for these areas will need a little more white. The flashes on the wings are flake white and cerulean blue.

Finishing

1 Give the entire duck several coats of matt acrylic varnish. Matt varnish is simply gloss varnish with particles added to dull it down, so it is important to stir it well before use. The consequences of not stirring are that the varnish might be glossier than expected. When this is done, apply two additional coats of gloss varnish to the beak and the eyes.

2 When the varnishing is complete, fix a brass screw eye to the underside of the duck and attach a 4oz (110g) lead fishing weight to it with a short length of nylon cord.

Fig 18.15 The decoy with weight attached.

19

Wader Decoy

Oystercatchers are large, strikingly coloured wading birds that, in common with other waders, can be seen at the seaside and along the edges of river estuaries. They are attracted to these areas because they feed on the small worms and crustaceans that live in the mud and amongst the rocks.

Decoys have been used for centuries to lure birds within range of hunters' guns, but there is no reason why they should not be used for benign purposes. Although waders are occasionally found in inland waterways and reservoirs, it is unlikely that you will have much success in getting them to visit your garden if you don't live near the coast.

Until a couple of years ago it would not have occurred to me to recommend attempting to get waders to visit a garden, but on a winter visit to the coast recently, I saw several oystercatchers foraging on the grass verges beside a fairly busy road, and in a large garden several miles from the sea. Because of this, I decided to make a decoy oystercatcher. If you are fortunate enough to have a garden that backs onto the coast or an estuary, place them on the foreshore.

It is not important which wood you use, as it will be painted. I chose to recycle a piece of pine that had once supported the roof of an old cottage. As this particular joist was not as thick as the design called for, I stuck two pieces together to make up the correct size.

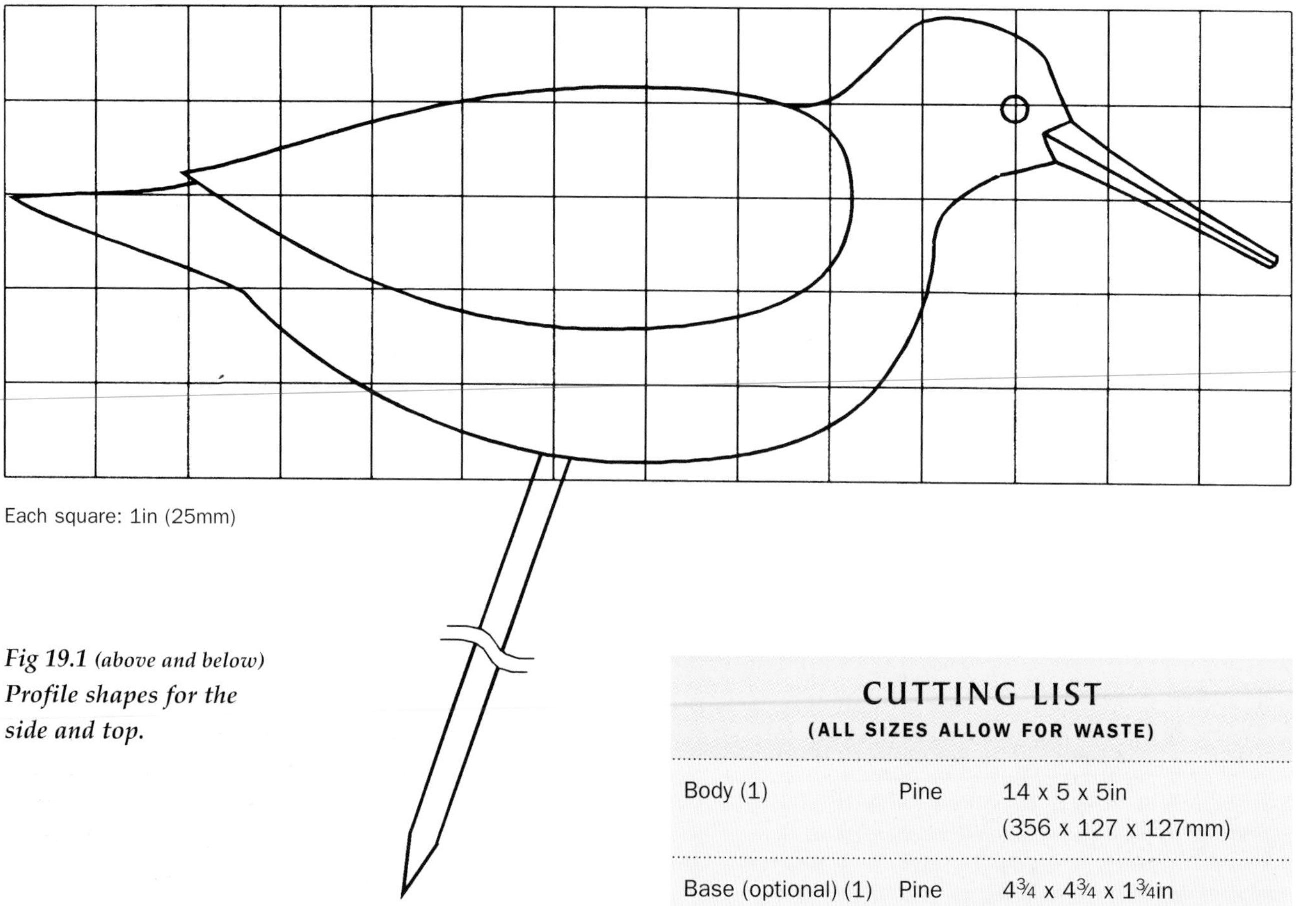

Each square: 1in (25mm)

***Fig 19.1** (above and below) Profile shapes for the side and top.*

CUTTING LIST
(ALL SIZES ALLOW FOR WASTE)

Body (1)	Pine	14 x 5 x 5in (356 x 127 x 127mm)
Base (optional) (1)	Pine	$4\frac{3}{4}$ x $4\frac{3}{4}$ x $1\frac{3}{4}$in (121 x 121 x 44mm)
Leg (1)	Dowel	9 x $\frac{3}{8}$in diameter (229 x 9mm diameter)

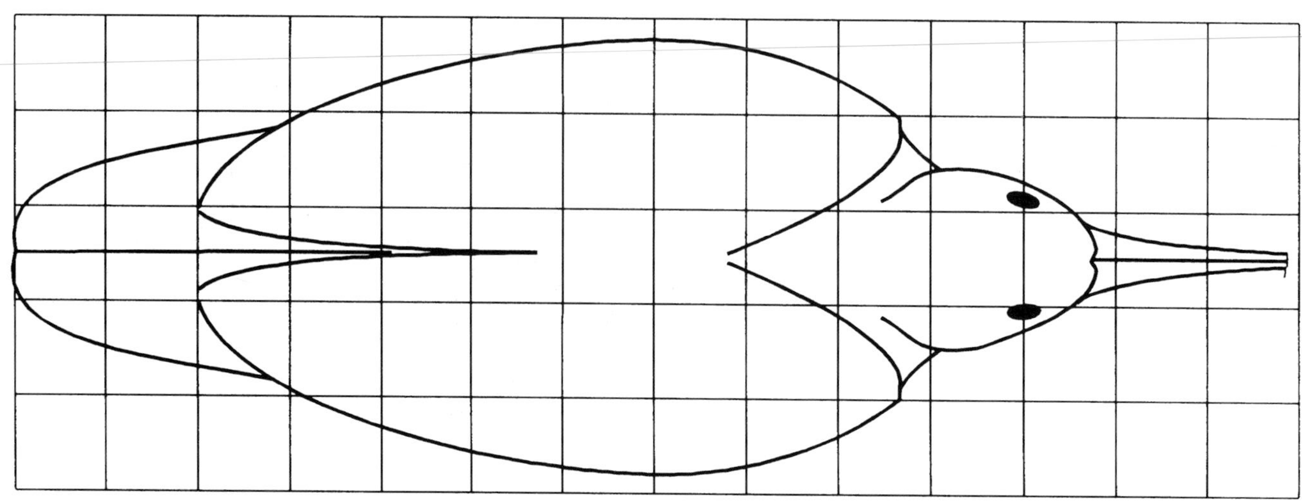

Each square: 1in (25mm)

Carving

THE BLANK

1 If your piece of timber has a sawn or rough finish, clean up the sides with a plane then transfer the squared-up profile to it (*see* Fig 19.2). Position the shape on the wood to get the grain on the beak running as close to horizontal as possible. Cut out the shape with a band saw, allowing about 1/16in (1.5mm) for error (*see* Fig 19.3). Do this for both the side and the top profile. One

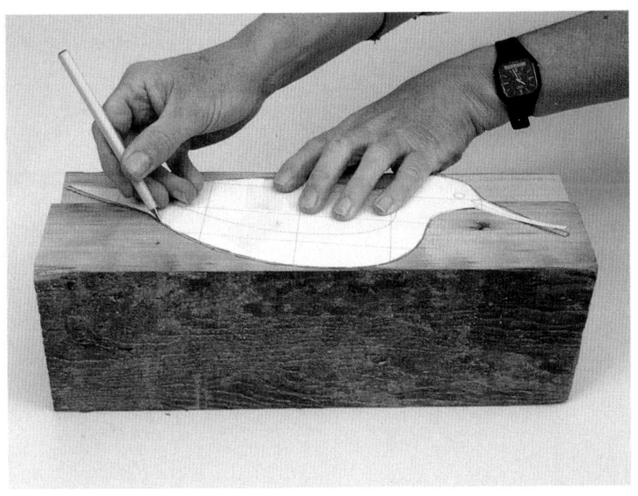

Fig 19.2
Marking the shape from a cardboard template.

Fig 19.3
After the side profile is cut.

problem is that as you cut around the side profiles, the top drawing is cut off and so can't be used as a guide. To cope with this, you can either attempt to redraw the profile, or stick the parts that have been removed back into place temporarily with a few spots of adhesive.

2 These initial cuts give a block-like shape. Draw a centre line along the length of this to guide the carving (*see* Fig 19.4).

Fig 19.4
After the top profile is cut.

OYSTERCATCHER

REFINING THE SHAPE

1 Starting on the square edges and moving around the body, remove waste wood first with a 1in (25mm) half-round gouge (*see* Fig 19.6) and then with a rotary rasp mounted on a flexible shaft on a power drill. Both the gouge and the rasp remove large amounts of wood quickly, but I find the rasp is easier to control, if it is used to cut along the grain at a slow speed.

Do not worry about carving details at this stage, but concentrate on getting the overall shape accurate. It helps if lines are drawn on the blank to indicate the shoulders and wing edges and the position of the eyes.

2 Using a gouge, carve the slight hollow between the wings near the shoulder, then mark out and cut the position of the wing tips near the tail. The idea is to gradually work all over the decoy to refine the shape.

Fig 19.6
Roughing out the shape with a chisel.

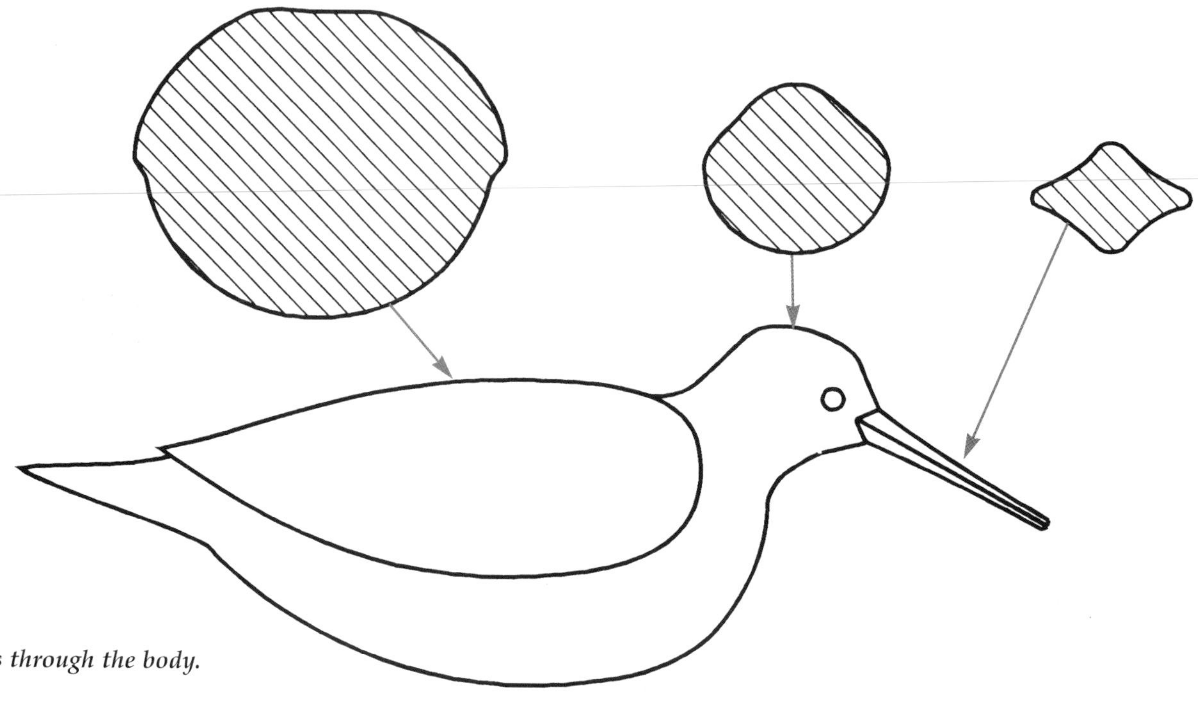

Fig 19.5
Sections through the body.

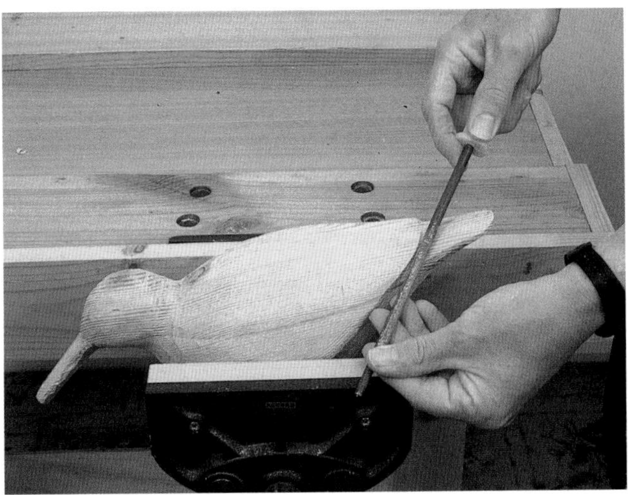

Fig 19.7
Detailing the ends of the wings with a file.

When I start a carving I remove large amounts of wood quickly, but as I proceed, I spend less time carving and more time looking, to ensure that not too much wood is removed.

3 Round the head with a rasp and carve a hollow following the pencil lines that indicate the bottom edges of the wing (*see* Fig 19.7). This hollow should be very shallow at the front edge near the shoulder, where the white breast feathers overlap the wings. Continue refining the shape of the decoy until the head, tail and body look almost finished, before starting work on the beak (*see* Fig 19.8).

4 Although oystercatchers have a thin beak, I left it slightly thicker on my model. This is because decoys have to be robust and stand up to hard use. However, if the model is to be used for display purposes, it should be made thinner. Use a very sharp chisel or a craft knife to work on the beak.

5 With the body and beak shapes refined, correct any holes or mistakes with cellulose filler and smooth the entire model using several grades of glasspaper.

6 Drill a hole in the underside of the body, and make a spike from ⅜in (9mm) ramin dowel to fit. Note that the dowel is set in the decoy at an angle so that when it is pushed vertically into the ground, the decoy will assume a characteristic position.

BASE

1 I made a wooden base for my decoy to hold it upright when it was stored. A base is also useful for holding whilst the decoy is painted. If it is to be displayed, the base should be planed and varnished.

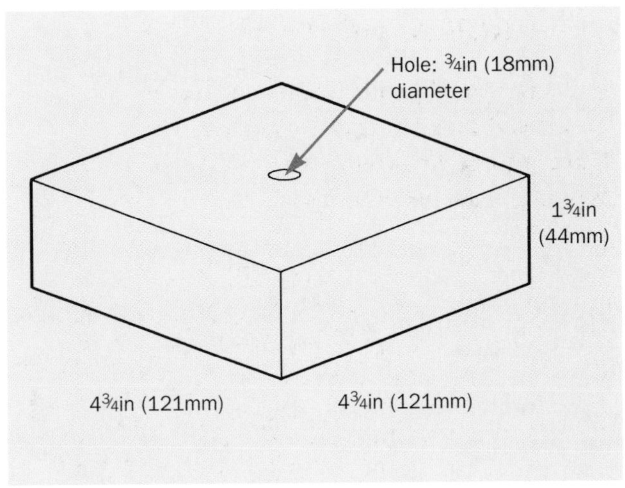

Fig 19.9 (above)
Optional base.

Fig 19.8 (right)
The body with the fine details on the beak left to carve.

Painting

1 For this model I chose acrylic paints simply because I enjoy using both oils and acrylics and like to have a change now and again. Start by painting the model with two coats of white acrylic primer. When this is dry, indicate the areas to be painted using a pencil. Pay particular attention to the position of the eyes. (*See* Chapter 2, page 20.)

MAIN COLOUR MIXES

Eyes and beak
Body
Legs

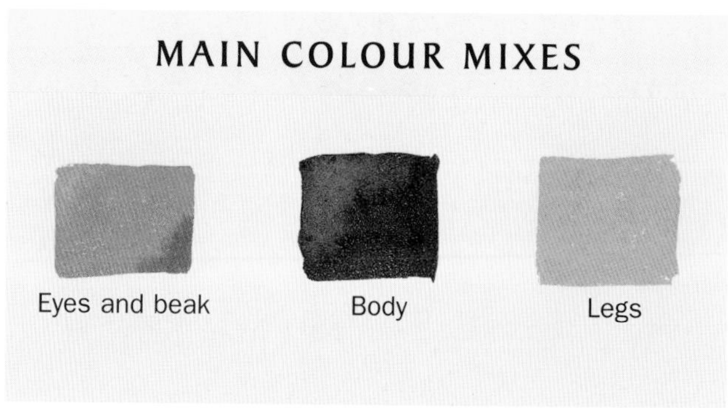

Fig 19.10
Painting scheme.

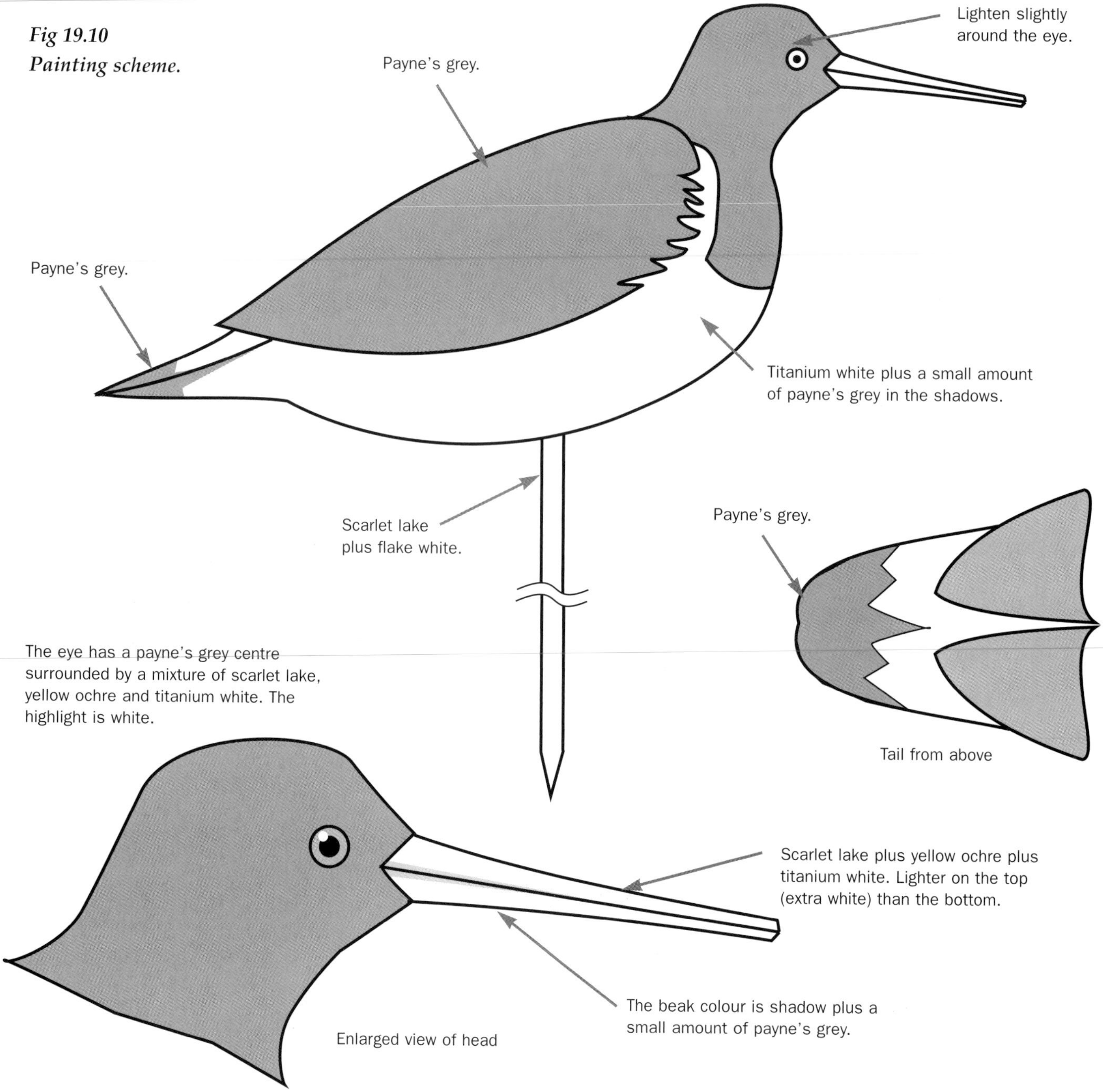

Lighten slightly around the eye.
Payne's grey.
Payne's grey.
Titanium white plus a small amount of payne's grey in the shadows.
Scarlet lake plus flake white.
Payne's grey.
Tail from above
The eye has a payne's grey centre surrounded by a mixture of scarlet lake, yellow ochre and titanium white. The highlight is white.
Scarlet lake plus yellow ochre plus titanium white. Lighter on the top (extra white) than the bottom.
The beak colour is shadow plus a small amount of payne's grey.
Enlarged view of head

Fig 19.11
Blocking in the large areas of black on the wings.

2 Apply the paint fairly thickly in the direction of the feathers so that the brush strokes show and add texture. Using payne's grey and a No. 2 brush, follow the pencil outlines around the eyes and the area where the beak meets the head. Using a No. 6 sable brush, paint the edges of the wings and the black areas of the neck and tail. When this is done, block in the main areas of black with a large brush.

Paint the area of white on the breast and underside of the bird with titanium white, adding just a touch of payne's grey for the shadow areas under the wings at the tail and under the body. Add a little white paint to the payne's grey around the eyes and lighten the surrounding area.

For the eyes paint a payne's grey centre surrounded by a mixture of scarlet lake, yellow ochre and flake white. Add fine detailing with a No. 0 sable brush and finally, add a small white highlight to make them sparkle.

Paint the beak with the same red mixture as the eyes. Make the top of the beak a lighter colour than the underside by adding a little white, and put in the two small nostrils by adding a touch of payne's grey. Finally, paint the dowel with a mixture of scarlet lake and titanium white.

Finishing

1 Finish the job by applying several coats of matt acrylic varnish.

Fig 19.12
The completed wader.

Duck Barrel

Given the correct conditions, a number of water birds take readily to nest boxes. These include mallard ducks, mandarin ducks and moorhens. This box is intended for mallards or domesticated ducks. It needs to be located in a 'safe' position to avoid predators, inside a fenced enclosure – on an island in the centre of a pond is ideal. I made a stand to keep it clear of the ground and a ramp to provide easy access for the ducklings.

I found purchasing a barrel by far the most difficult part of this project. In the end I obtained one – which was just about to be cut in half to make plant containers – from a garden centre. It is made of oak and, by the smell of the inside, once contained brandy. It is best to avoid using a barrel that has a strong odour. The diameter at its widest part is 24in (610mm), which is slightly large. A barrel with a largest diameter of about 20in (508mm) would be ideal.

CUTTING LIST

Side rails (2)	Pine	20½ x 4 x 1¾in (521 x 102 x 44mm)
Front rail (1)	Pine	20 x 4 x 1¾in (508 x 102 x 44mm)
Back rail (1)	Pine	20 x 4 x 1¾in (508 x 102 x 44mm)
Wedges (4)	Pine	6 x 4 x 1¾in (152 x 102 x 44mm)
Ramp (1)	Plywood	18 x 5 x ¾in (457 x 127 x 18mm)

ALSO REQUIRED:

Barrel (1)	24in (610mm) max. diameter

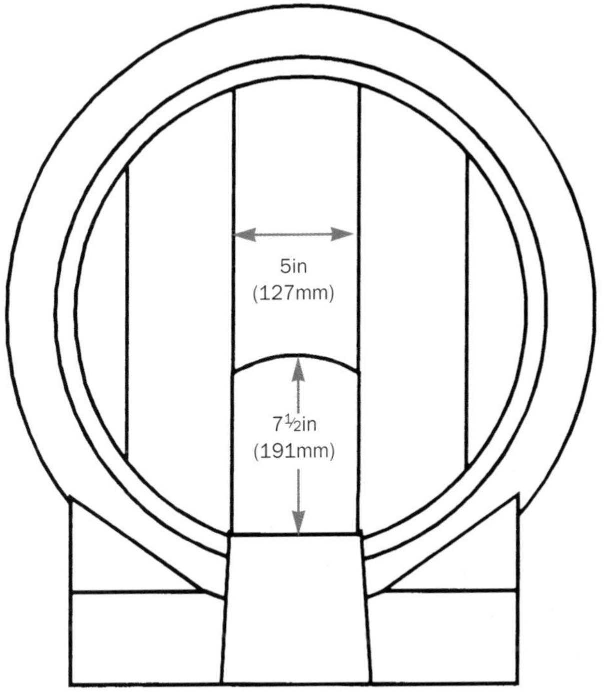

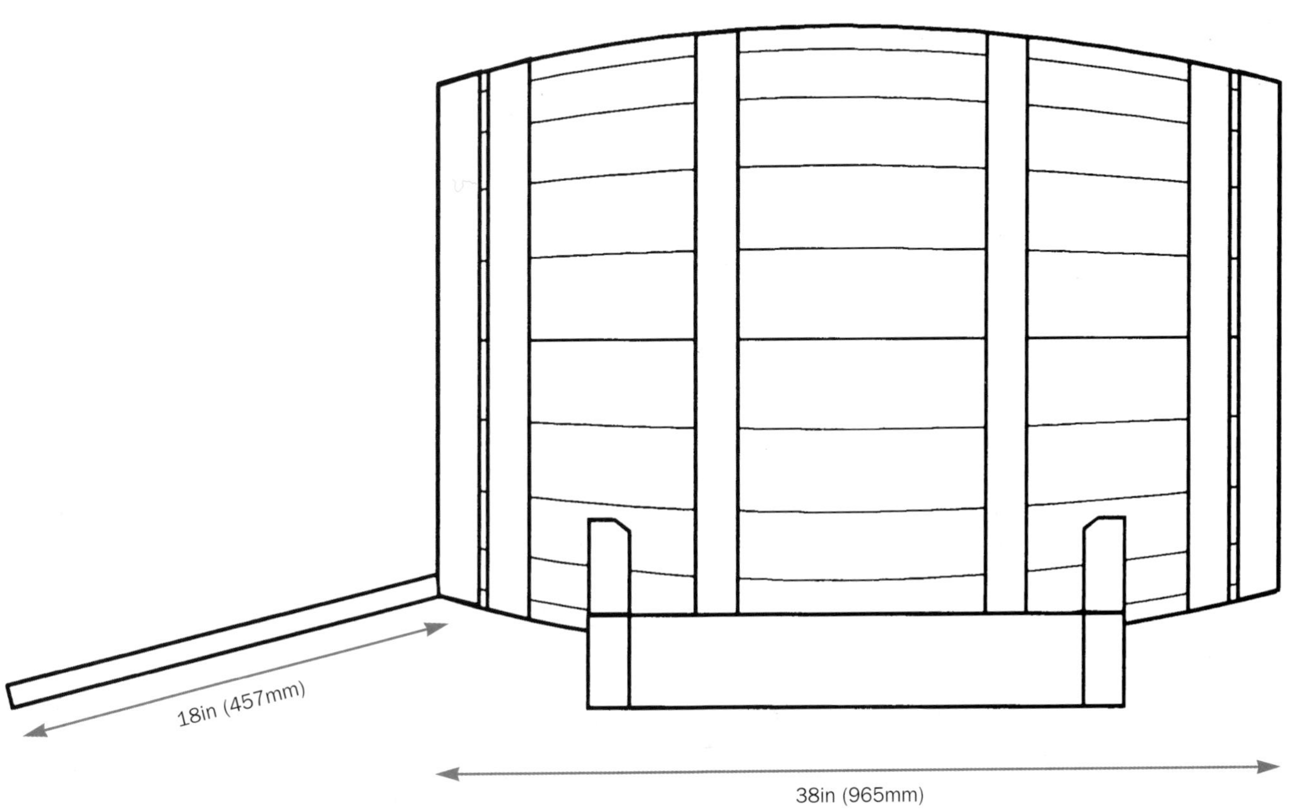

Fig 20.1
Barrel plan with dimensions.

CONSTRUCTION

BARREL

1 If the barrel is second-hand then the first job is to clean up the outside. Do this with a wire brush fitted to a power drill and follow up by cutting out the entrance hole with a jigsaw.

Fig 20.2
Using a wire brush on a power drill to clean the barrel.

2 Treat all the wooden parts with coloured wood preserver. When this is dry, mask around the outside edges of the metal hoops with masking tape and paint the hoops with matt black paint. Paint for use on wrought iron is ideal for this job. Fix the ramp to the front of the barrel with a couple of nails.

BASE AND RAMP

1 I made the stand from sawn pine with a section size of 4 x 1¾in (102 x 44mm). All of the dimensions in the drawings are for a barrel the same size that I made: they need to be altered in proportion for barrels of a different size.

From a length of sawn pine, cut the four rails. Take the front rail and present it to the barrel to estimate the radius of the curve that needs to be cut in the top edge. Draw this shape on the rail and cut it with a jigsaw. Hold the shape against the barrel to test for accuracy of fit and adjust it with a half-round rasp if required. Use this piece as a template to mark out the back rail, and cut out the back rail in the same way.

Fig 20.3
A jigsaw is ideal for cutting the entrance.

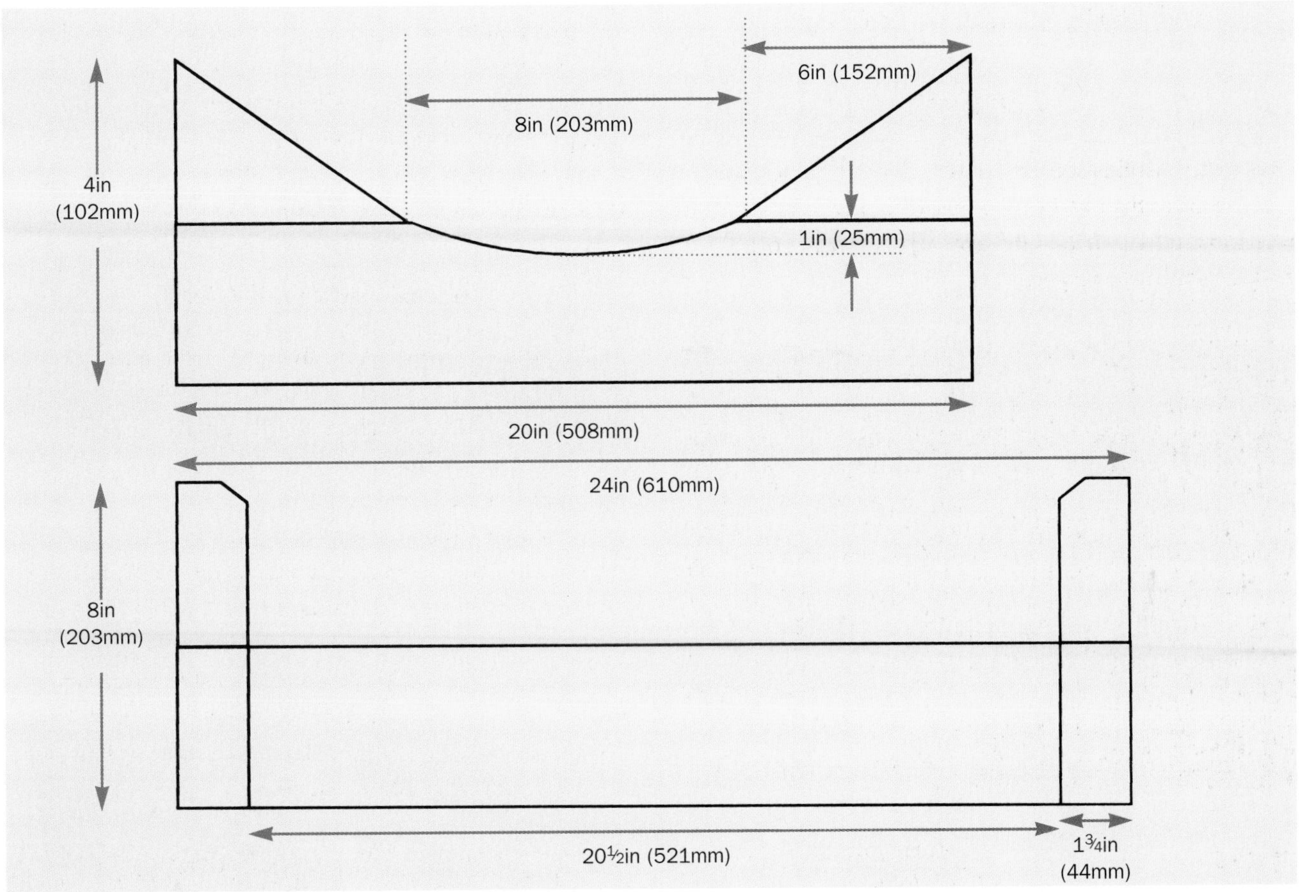

6in (152mm)
8in (203mm)
4in (102mm)
1in (25mm)
20in (508mm)
24in (610mm)
8in (203mm)
20½in (521mm)
1¾in (44mm)

Fig 20.4
Base plan with dimensions.

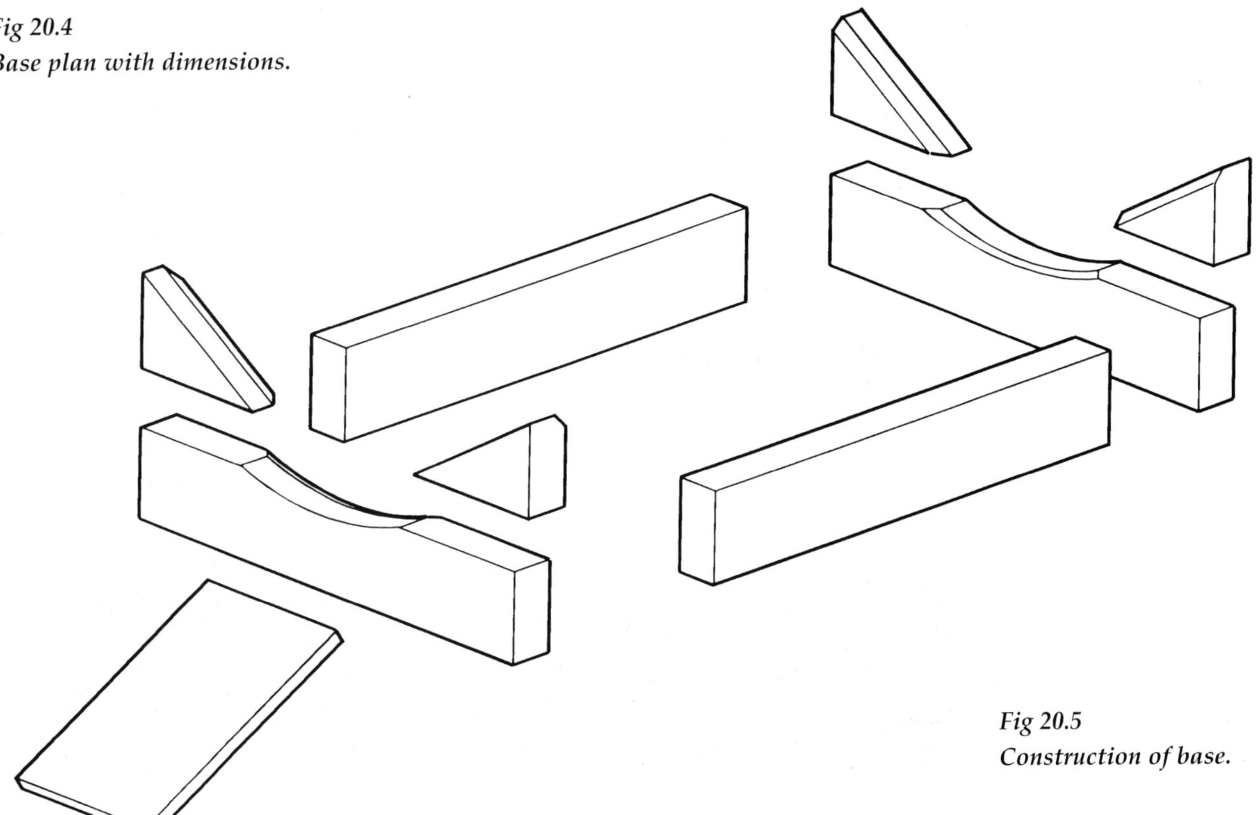

Fig 20.5
Construction of base.

Fig 20.6
Nailed butt joints are used for the corners.

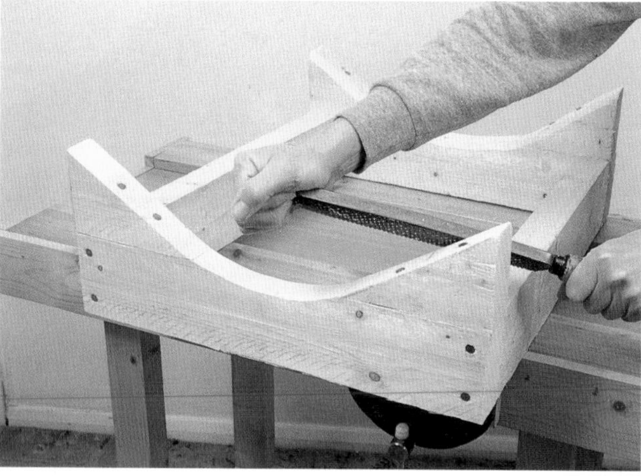

Fig 20.7
Using a rasp to chamfer the inside edges of the stand.

2 Join the four corners of the base using nailed butt joints (*see* Chapter 2, page 14). Glue them with water-resistant adhesive and nail them with 4in (100mm) wire nails.

3 Cut the four wedges to size and fix them to the frame with nails and glue. Using a rasp, chamfer the inside edges of the front and back rail (*see* Fig 20.7) so that the cask will sit securely against it. When you nail the wedges on, set the nails to one side so that they are not in the way when you cut the chamfer. Cut the ramp from a piece of ¾in (18mm) plywood.

Fig 20.8
After completion, the stand is treated with coloured wood preserver.

Finishing

1 Finish both the ramp and the stand with coloured wood preserver.

Fig 20.9
Barrel, stand and ramp.

Domestic Animals and Birds

Keeping birds and domestic animals for food goes back as far as recorded history, and birds such as fighting cocks and peacocks were kept for entertainment and ornamental purposes. A similar trend continues today. Budgerigars, canaries, doves, rabbits and many other animals are all kept as pets to entertain their owners.

WALL-MOUNTED DOVECOTE

GARDEN AVIARY

GUINEA-PIG HUTCH

21

Wall-Mounted Dovecote

Many traditional stone- and brick-built cotes can be found scattered around the countryside, some of them dating back to Norman times. The name 'dove' originally covered a variety of doves and pigeons all of which were kept to provide food. Today, white doves are usually kept to enhance a garden and my dovecote is meant for this purpose.

The cote must be situated out of the reach of predators such as cats and foxes. Very often they are mounted on a tall pole, but I made mine so that it could be attached to the side of a house or outbuilding. They should be set about 8–10ft (2½–3½m) from the ground. My cote is designed for a maximum of six pairs of doves. There are no partitions on the roosting shelves because the birds will sort out their own areas. The front rests on the shelves and is held on with a couple of bolts so that it can be completely removed for cleaning purposes. The roosting shelves are extended so that they protrude at the front to make it easy for the birds to take off and land.

I used ¾in (18mm) exterior quality plywood, and the complete cote can be made from an 8 x 4ft (2,438 x 1,219mm) sheet with some left over. All of the parts are joined together with 2in (50mm) oval nails and waterproof glue, as described in Chapter 2.

CUTTING LIST

Back (1)	Plywood	34 x 24 x ¾in (864 x 610 x 18mm)
Front (1)	Plywood	34 x 24 x ¾in (864 x 610 x 18mm)
Shelves (2)	Plywood	34 x 16 x ¾in (864 x 406 x 18mm)
Short roof panel (1)	Plywood	20¼ x 14 x ¾in (514 x 356 x 18mm)
Long roof panel (1)	Plywood	21⅜ x 14 x ¾in (543 x 356 x 18mm)
Short roof support (1)	Plywood	18⅛ x 1⅛ x ¾in (460 x 28 x 18mm)
Long roof support (1)	Plywood	19¼ x 1⅛ x ¾in (489 x 28 x 18mm)
Sides (2)	Plywood	17 x 12¾ x ¾in (432 x 324 x 18mm)
ALSO REQUIRED:		
Bolts (2)		4in (100mm)

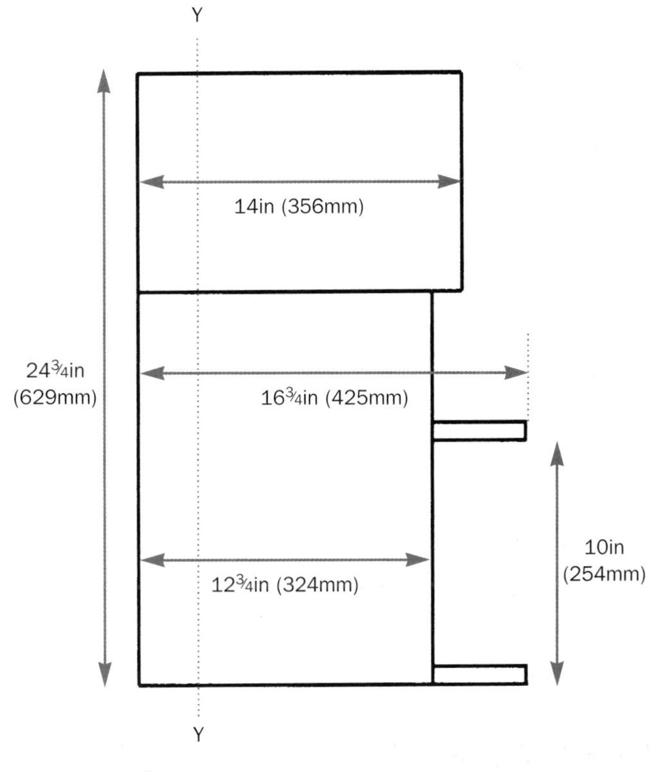

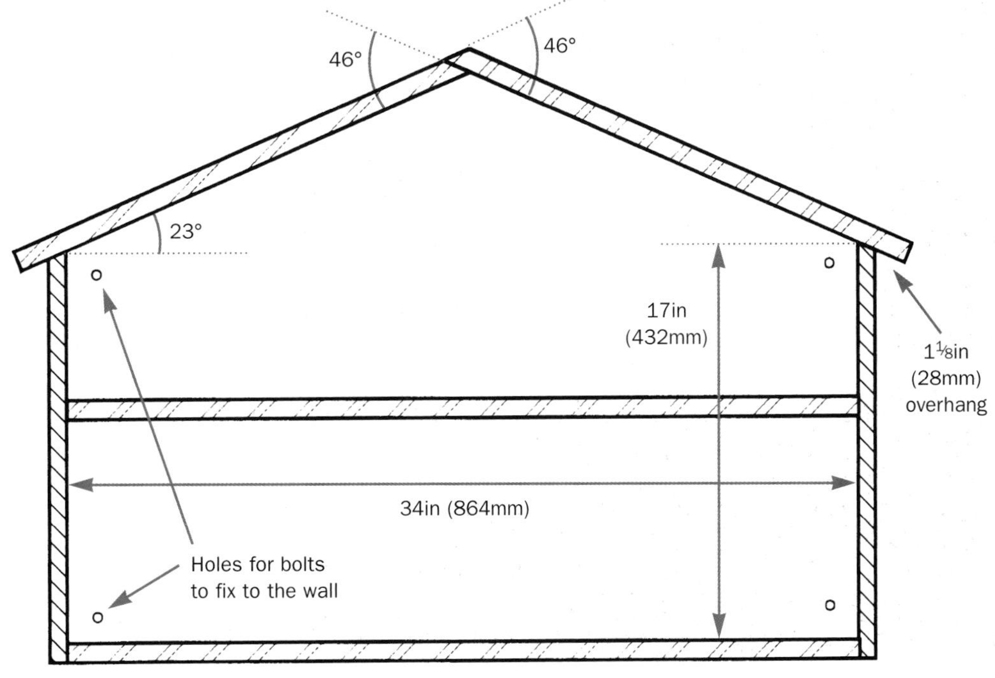

Fig 21.1
Side view with section and dimensions.

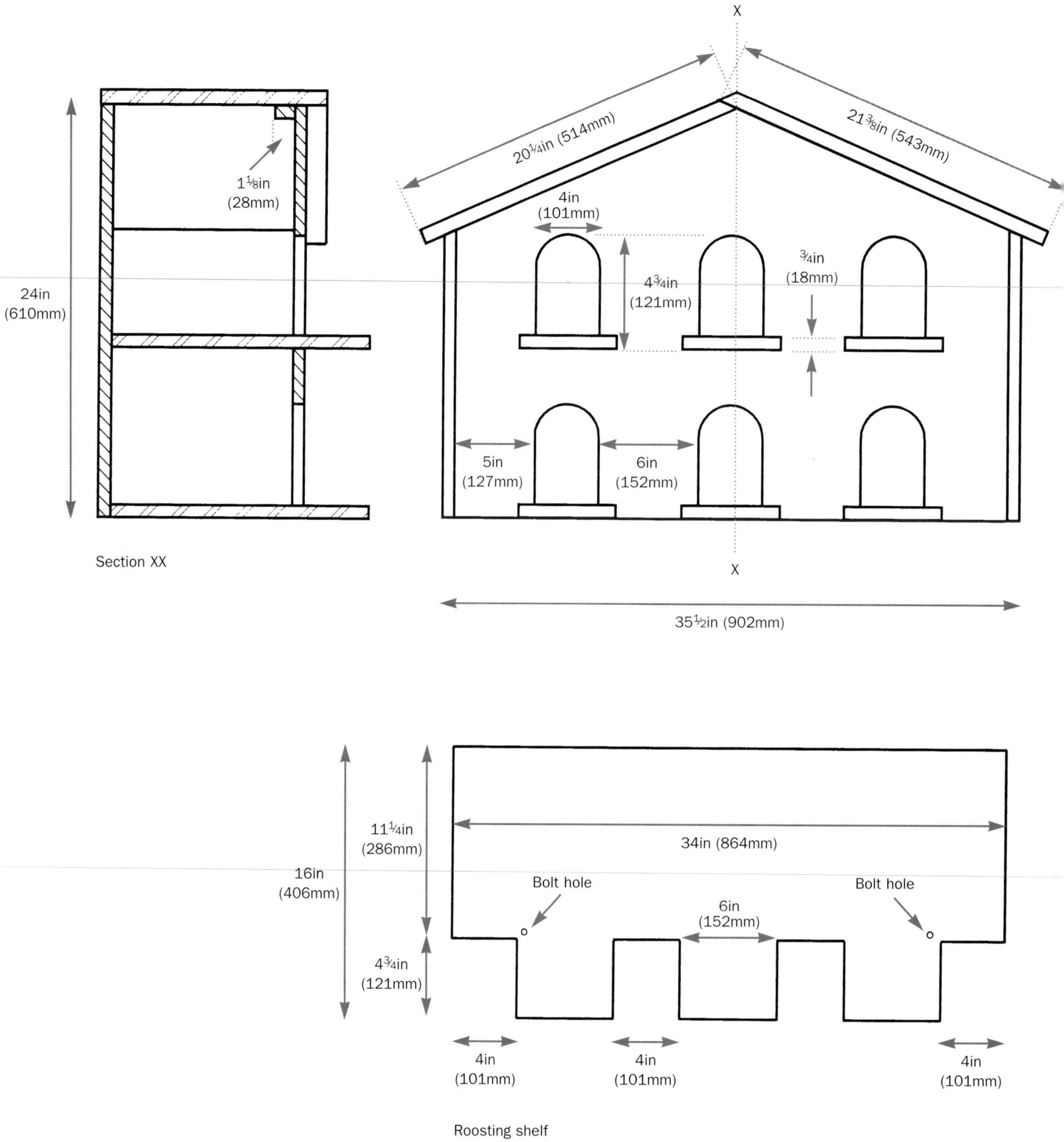

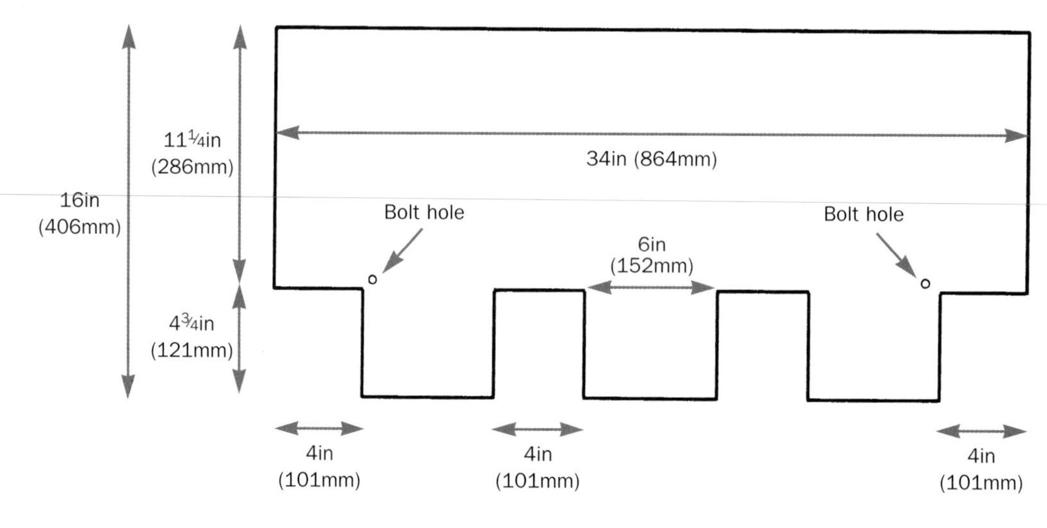

Fig 21.2
Front view, sections and plan of shelves with dimensions.

Fig 21.3
Location of bolts and roof supports.

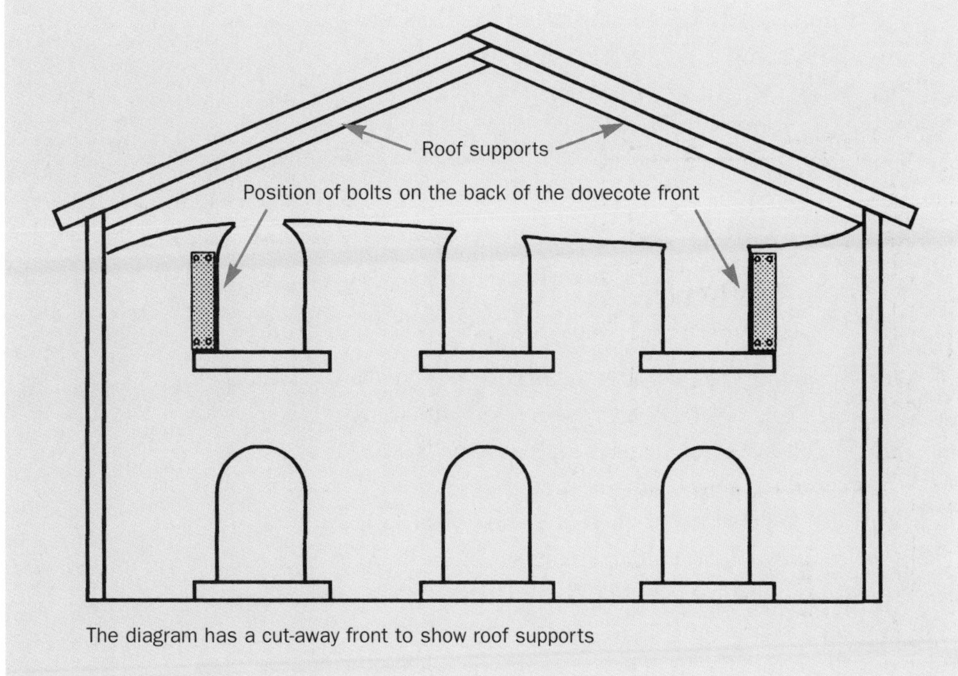

CONSTRUCTION

1 Plan the position of all the pieces on the plywood sheet so that waste is kept to a minimum. Using a long steel rule, a square and a pencil, mark out the back and cut it out using a panel saw. When you cut across the grain of the outside layer of ply, it tends to splinter on the back side away from the saw. To prevent this, I scribe along the line with a marking knife before cutting.

2 Use the back as a template to mark out the shape for the front and cut this out in the same way. Smooth all of the edges with a plane and glasspaper. Mark the position and shape of the entrances and the slots below them that will accommodate the fronts of the roosting shelves. To get a rounded top I used a 4in (100mm) paint tin as a template (*see* Fig 21.4). Use a jigsaw to cut out the entrances (*see* Fig 21.5) and smooth the edges with a half-round file and glasspaper.

Fig 21.4
Using a paint pot as a template to mark the curved shape for the entrances.

Fig 21.5
Cutting the entrances with a jigsaw.

3 Cut two pieces of plywood to size for the sides and use a power saw to cut the top edges to an angle of 23° upon which the roof will sit. Using a rip and jigsaw, cut out the two roosting shelves. After the edges have been smoothed, use exterior grade cellulose filler to fill any gaps and holes.

Assembly

1 Start by joining the two sides to the back with nails and glue. Next, fit the two shelves and join them to the sides and back. To get the nails to fit into the centre of the shelves when you nail them through from the back, measure the position of the shelves and draw lines where the centres will be, on the outside of the back. When the lower shelf has been nailed into place, fit the front in position temporarily and use this to position the middle shelf, so that the front of the shelf is held in place by the front panel, whilst the middle shelf is nailed in place. When the shelves are firmly in place, remove the front to make any adjustments required to the front panel. This will ensure that it slides into place easily.

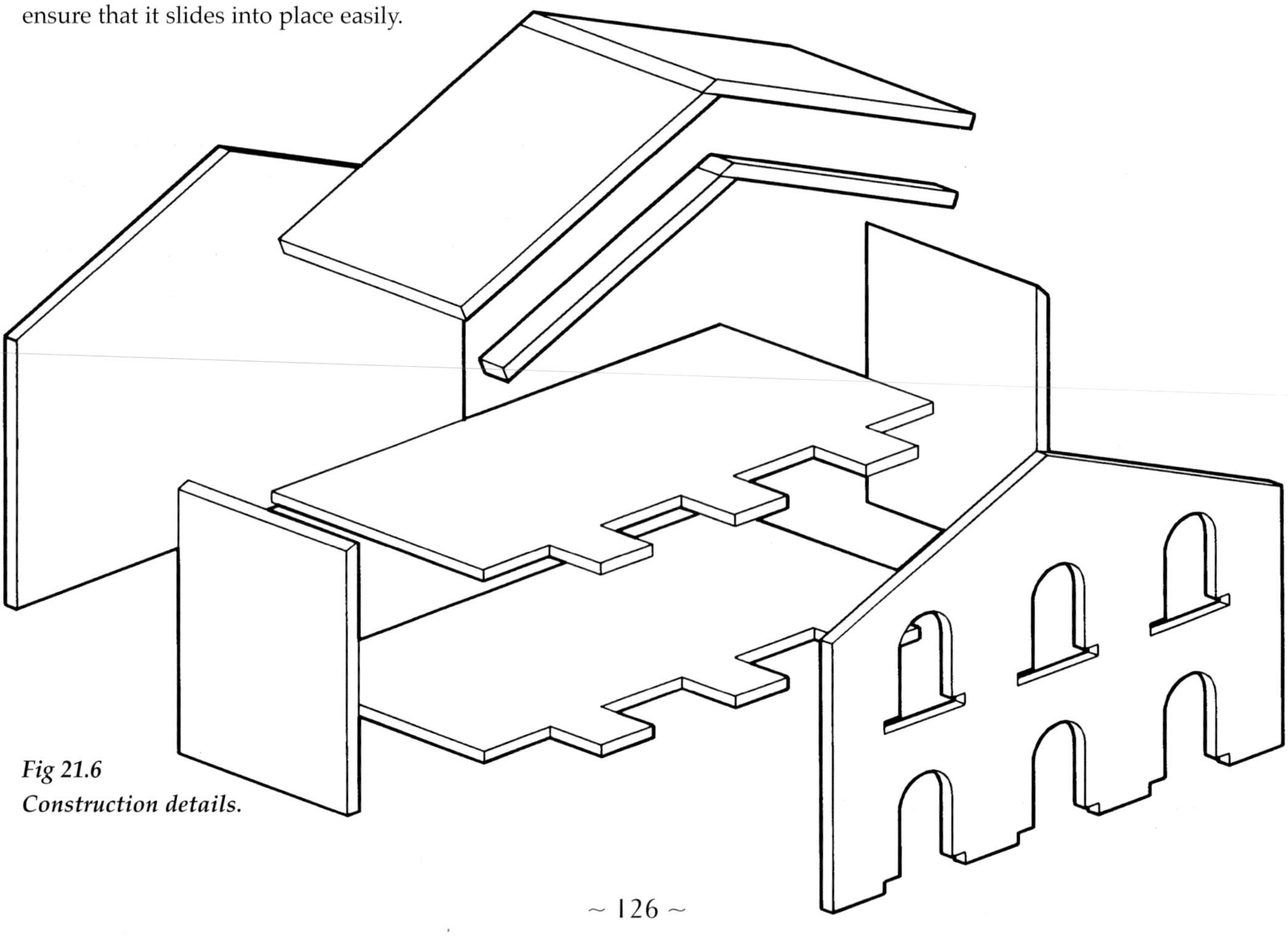

Fig 21.7
The back fixed to the two sides.

Fig 21.6
Construction details.

Fig 21.8
The two roosting shelves are fixed with nails.

2 Before fitting the roof panels, fit the two bolts that lock it into place to the back of the front panel (*see* Fig 21.9). Once the bolts are fitted, put the front panel into position and mark where the bolts will lock into the middle shelf. Remove the front and drill holes in the middle shelf for the bolts to slide into. It is easier to drill these holes without the roof panel in place. (*See* Fig 21.10.)

Fig 21.9
The position of the bolts on the back of the front.

Fig 21.10
Ensuring that the front fits the rest of the assembly.

Make the roof panels and cut the ends to the correct angle with a power saw before nailing them into place. Follow this by cutting the two strips of plywood that support the roof and the front panel. Drill four holes in the corner of the back panel for the screws that will fix the dovecote to the wall (see Chapter 2, page 9).

FINISHING

1 As I wanted the dovecote to look decorative, I finished it with white gloss paint. Fill any holes and gaps with weatherproof cellulose filler and then smooth the surface with glasspaper. Apply a coat of priming paint first and then white undercoat. Rub this down with fine glasspaper before applying the white gloss paint.

22

Garden Aviary

This design is modular so that the aviary can be enlarged by putting extra panels in the flight area, and so that it is easy to take apart for transport. I made it 6½ft (2m) high to allow most people to stand in it without stooping.

I included a shelter (made from exterior quality plywood, which has good insulation properties) and a window so that the interior is not too dark: this might discourage the birds from entering. The larger door in the shelter provides access for cleaning.

The flight cage does not have a floor as the aviary is designed to be bolted to a concrete base or placed directly onto the lawn. The advantage of the second method is that the aviary can be moved around the garden so that one area does not get over-used. Site the aviary in a sheltered area of the garden, but not under a tree as the leaves will collect on the wire mesh in the autumn.

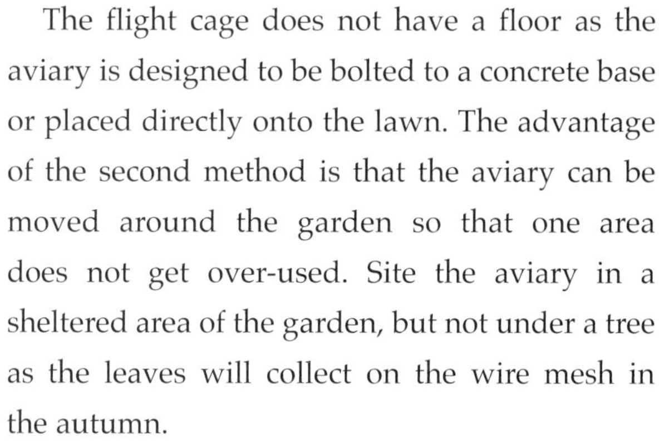

To encourage the birds to breed, nest boxes or ledges should be provided, however, as different birds have different requirements, it is best to buy these from a dealer, to suit which birds you keep.

Perches made from hardwood dowel are required for the shelter and the flight area. For the flight area I used sawn pine, which is reasonably cheap and easy to obtain, and finished it with creosote to provide protection against damp and rot.

CUTTING LIST

PANEL A

Sides (2)	Sawn pine	78 x 1⅞ x 1⅞in (1,981 x 48 x 48mm)
Central door post (1)	Sawn pine	75¼ x 2 x ⅞in (1,911 x 51 x 22mm)
Door stop (1)	Sawn pine	74½ x ⅞ x ⅞in (1,892 x 22 x 22mm)
Cross pieces for top and base (2)	Sawn pine	48 x 1⅞ x 1⅞in (1,219 x 48 x 48mm)
Short cross piece (1)	Sawn pine	14¼ x 2 x ⅞in (362 x 51 x 22mm)

DOOR

Cross pieces (3)	Sawn pine	29⅞ x 2 x ⅞in (759 x 51 x 22mm)
Upright pieces (2)	Sawn pine	74½ x 2 x ⅞in (1,892 x 51 x 22mm)

ALSO REQUIRED:

Galvanized wire mesh, ½in (12mm) square	approx. 16.5yd (15m)
Butt hinges (3)	2in (50mm)
Door bolt (1)	4½in (112mm)

PANELS B

Long vertical sides (2)	Sawn pine	78 x 2 x ⅞in (1,981 x 51 x 22mm)
Short vertical sides (2)	Sawn pine	35⅛ x 2 x ⅞in (892 x 51 x 22mm)
Middle vertical pieces (2)	Sawn pine	42 x 2 x ⅞in (1,067 x 51 x 22mm)
Top horizontal pieces (2)	Sawn pine	18 x 2 x ⅞in (457 x 51 x 22mm)
Middle horizontal pieces (2)	Sawn pine	35½ x 2 x ⅞in (902 x 51 x 22mm)
Base horizontal pieces (2)	Sawn pine	34¼ x 2 x ⅞in (870 x 51 x 22mm)

PANELS C

Vertical pieces (4)	Sawn pine	78 x 2 x ⅞in (1,981 x 51 x 22mm)
Horizontal pieces top and base (4)	Sawn pine	34¼ x 2 x ⅞in (870 x 51 x 22mm)
Horizontal middle pieces (4)	Sawn pine	35 x 2 x ⅞in (889 x 51 x 22mm)

PANEL D

Vertical pieces (3)	Sawn pine	36 x 1⅞ x 1⅞in (914 x 48 x 48mm)
Horizontal pieces (2)	Sawn pine	48 x 1⅞ x 1⅞in (1,219 x 48 x 48mm)

continued over...

CUTTING LIST *continued*

ROOF PANEL		
Cross pieces (3)	Sawn pine	48 x 2 x ⅞in (1,219 x 51 x 22mm)
Side pieces (2)	Sawn pine	57⅝ x 2 x ⅞in (1,464 x 51 22mm)
SHELTER		
Front (1)	Plywood	48 x 43 x ¾in (1,219 x 1,092 x 18mm)
Large door (1)	Plywood	27⅛ x 19⅞ x ¾in (689 x 505 x 18mm)
Sides (2)	Plywood	43 x 16¾ x ¾in (1,092 x 625 x 18mm)
Base (1)	Plywood	46½ x 16¾ x ¾in (1,181 x 425 x 18mm)
Back (1)	Plywood	48 x 36¾ x ¾in (1,219 x 933 x 18mm)
Top (1)	Plywood	48 x 22 x ¾in (1,219 x 559 x 18mm)
Vertical door stops (2)	Pine	25½ x 22 x ⅞in (648 x 51 x 22mm)
Horizontal door stop (1)	Pine	22 x 2 x ⅞in (559 x 51 x 22mm)
Runners for small door (2)	Pine	23½ x 1 x 1in (597 x 25 x 25mm)
Small door (1)	Plywood	12 x 7¼ x 3/16in (305 x 190 x 4mm)
Small door handle (1)	Pine	6 x ¾ x ¾in (152 x 18 x 18mm)
Vertical inside window edging (2)	Plywood	15 x 1 x ¼in (381 x 25 x 6mm)
Horizontal inside window edging (2)	Plywood	11 x 1 x ¼in (279 x 25 x 6mm)
Vertical outside window edging (2)	Pine	14 x ½ x ½in (356 x 12 x 12mm)
Horizontal outside window edging (2)	Pine	10 x ½ x ½in (254 x 12 x 12mm)
Perches (2)	Ramin	17½ x ⅜in diameter (446 x 9mm diameter)
Window (1)	Perspex	14 x 10 x ⅛in (356 x 254 x 3mm)
ALSO REQUIRED:		
Butt hinges (2)		2in (50mm)
Gate latch (1)		2½in (64mm)
Roofing felt		approx. 50 x 24in (1,270 x 610mm)

Fig 22.1
Side view of flight cage, plan with dimensions.

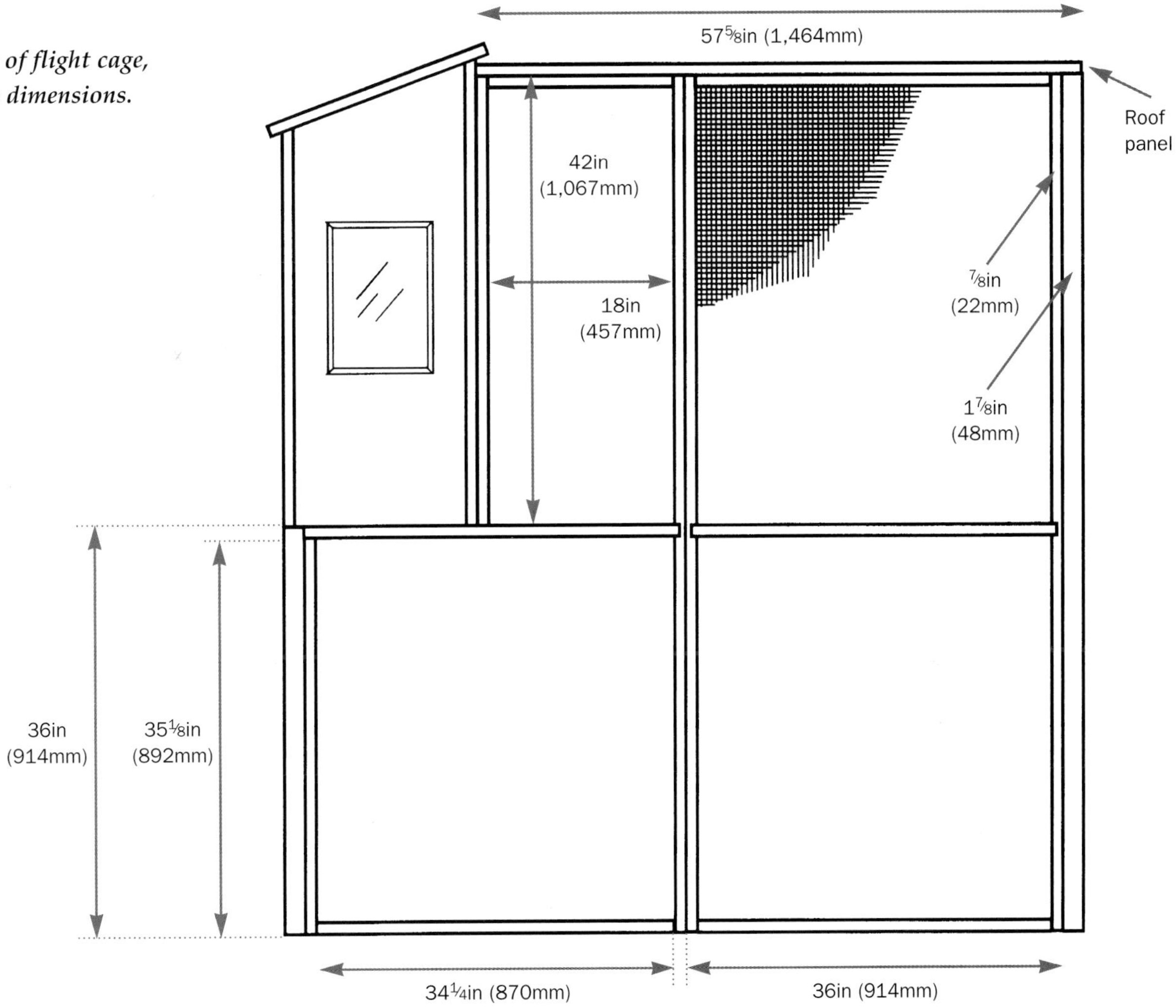

57⅝in (1,464mm)
Roof panel
42in (1,067mm)
18in (457mm)
⅞in (22mm)
1⅞in (48mm)
36in (914mm)
35⅛in (892mm)
34¼in (870mm)
36in (914mm)

Fig 22.2
Top view of flight cage roof, with dimensions.

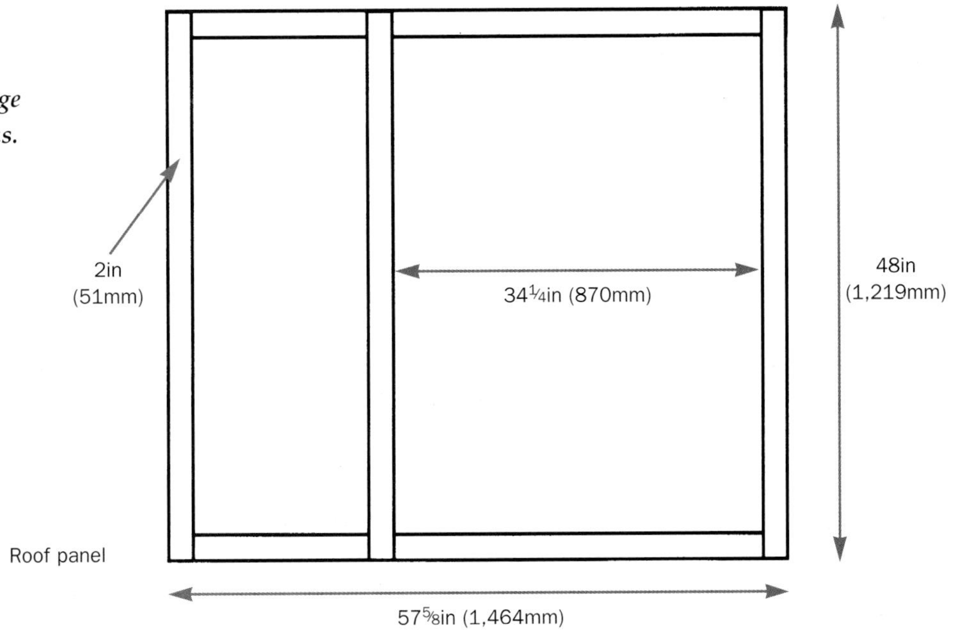

2in (51mm)
34¼in (870mm)
48in (1,219mm)
Roof panel
57⅝in (1,464mm)

Construction of Aviary

END PANEL A

1 The end panels are made from sawn timber with a section size of 1⅞ x 1⅞in (47 x 47mm): this was the nearest standard size to 2in (50mm) square that my local DIY store stocked.

Cut the sides, top and base of the panel to length and make halving joints at their ends (*see* Fig 22.4). As the joints will eventually be glued and screwed, drill the screw holes now. The screws are not only for strength, but also to hold the joint closed whilst the glue dries.

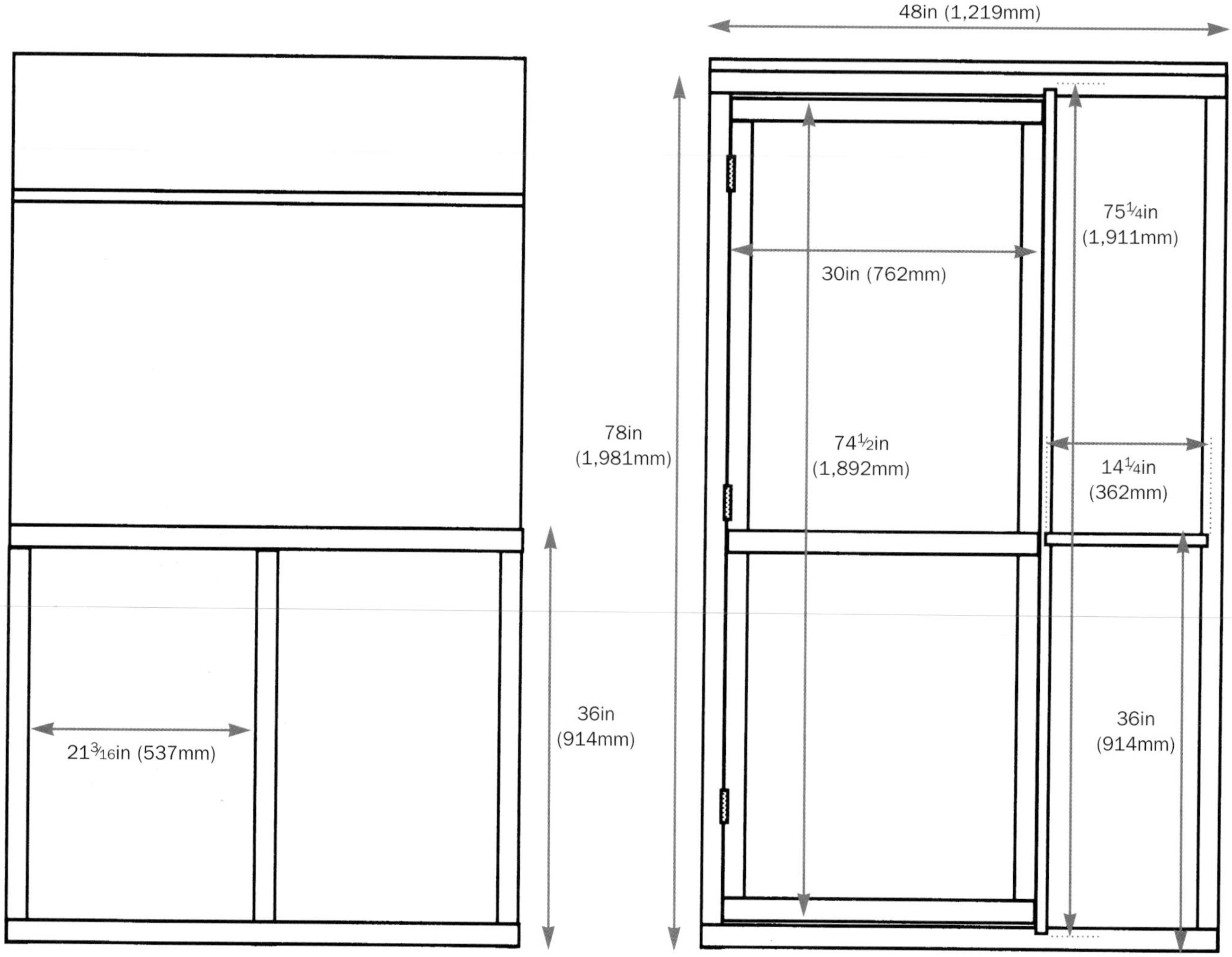

48in (1,219mm)
75¼in (1,911mm)
30in (762mm)
78in (1,981mm)
74½in (1,892mm)
14¼in (362mm)
36in (914mm)
21 3/16in (537mm)
36in (914mm)

Fig 22.3
Front and back view of flight cage, with dimensions.

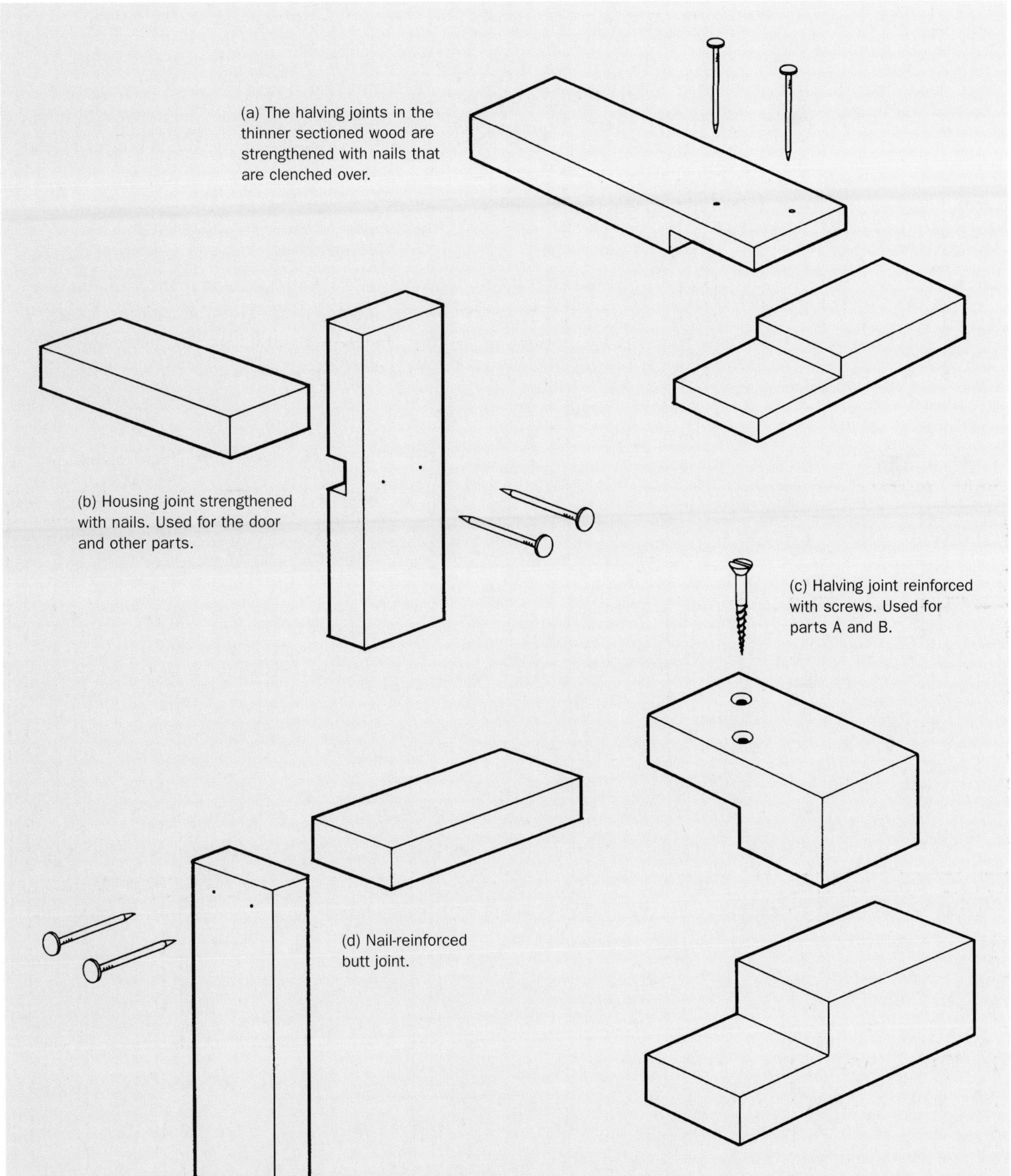

(a) The halving joints in the thinner sectioned wood are strengthened with nails that are clenched over.

(b) Housing joint strengthened with nails. Used for the door and other parts.

(c) Halving joint reinforced with screws. Used for parts A and B.

(d) Nail-reinforced butt joint.

Fig 22.4
Joints used for the aviary.

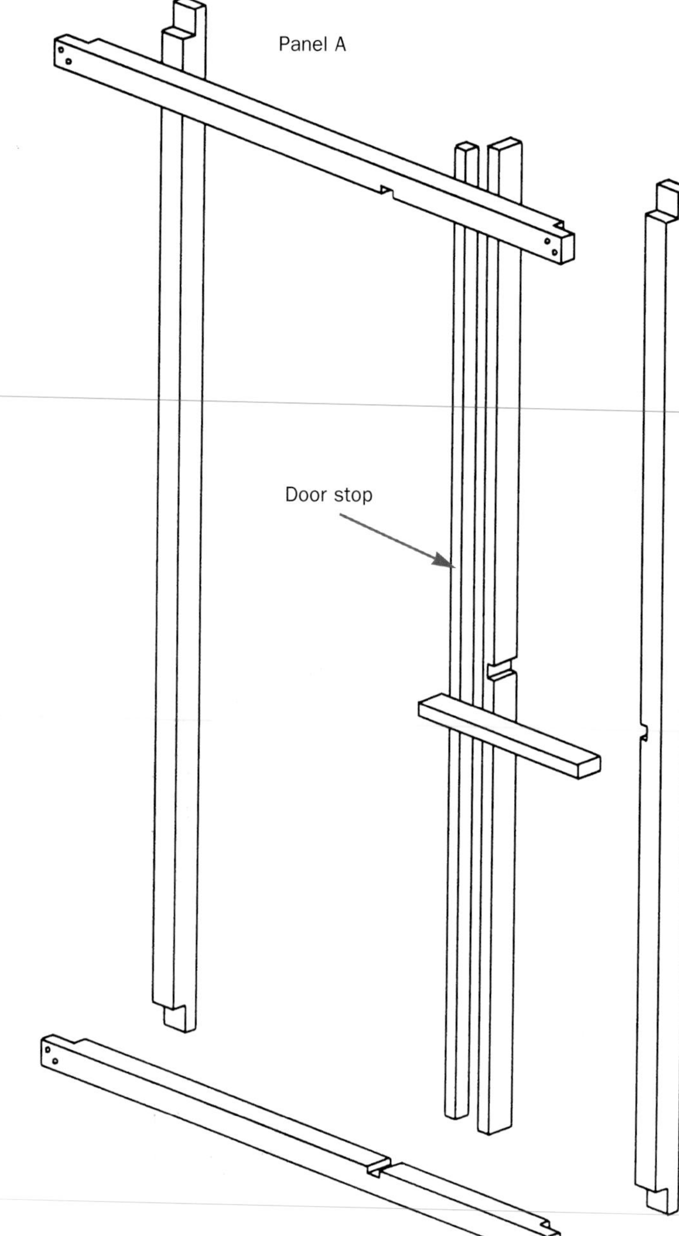

Fig 22.5
Construction of panel A.

Make the housing joints for the central door post, which is cut from ⅞ x 1⅞in (22 x 48mm) sawn pine, in the top and base pieces, and then make the two housing joints for the short cross piece that fits between this post and the left-hand side. Glue all the housing joints and strengthen them with a single 2in (50mm) oval nail. For a door stop, glue and nail a timber strip to the inside back edge of the central door post.

SIDE PANELS B

1 Cut the lengths required from some ⅞ x 2in (22 x 51mm) sawn pine. Choose the straightest pieces for the uprights, which are the longest lengths. Make a halving joint in the long side to house one end of the horizontal cross piece.

2 Join the base to the long upright with a nailed butt joint, then fix the central horizontal cross piece to the long upright with glue and nails. Nail and glue the lower short side to the assembled pieces. Join the short top piece to the middle vertical piece, again with nails and glue, and fix this assembly to the rest of the structure.

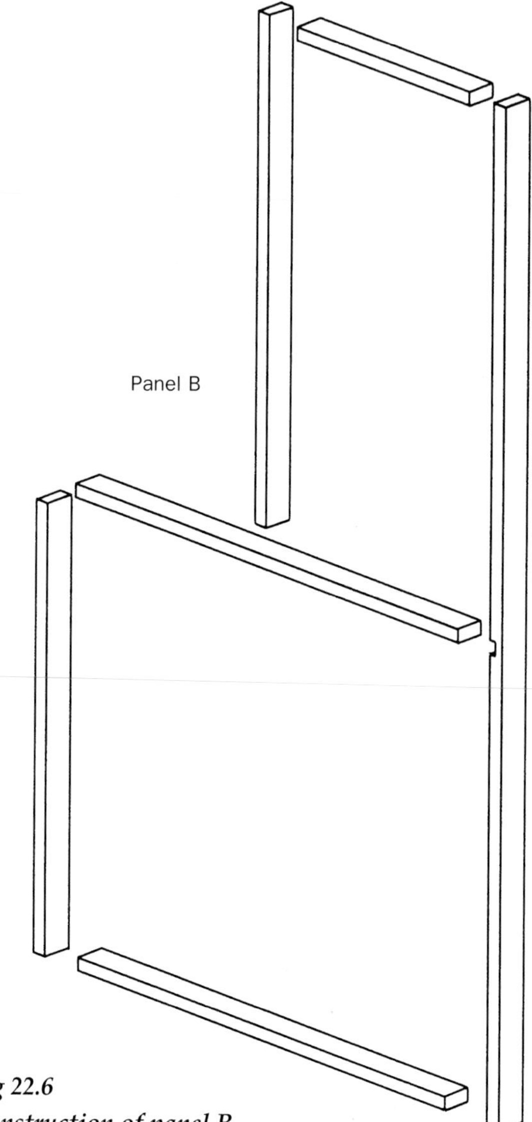

Fig 22.6
Construction of panel B.

Fig 22.7
Strengthening the housing joint with a nail.

SIDE PANELS C

1 Saw the pieces of wood to length and cut housing joints in both uprights for the central cross piece. Use nails and glued butt joints to join the top and base pieces. Drill pilot holes for the nails to avoid splitting the wood and to keep the nails upright.

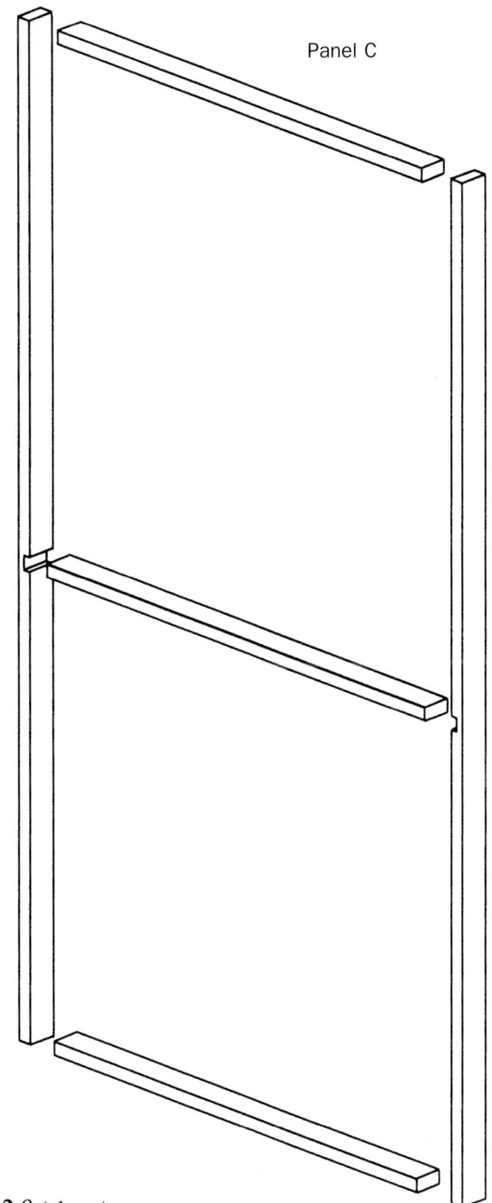

Fig 22.8 (above)
Construction of panel C.

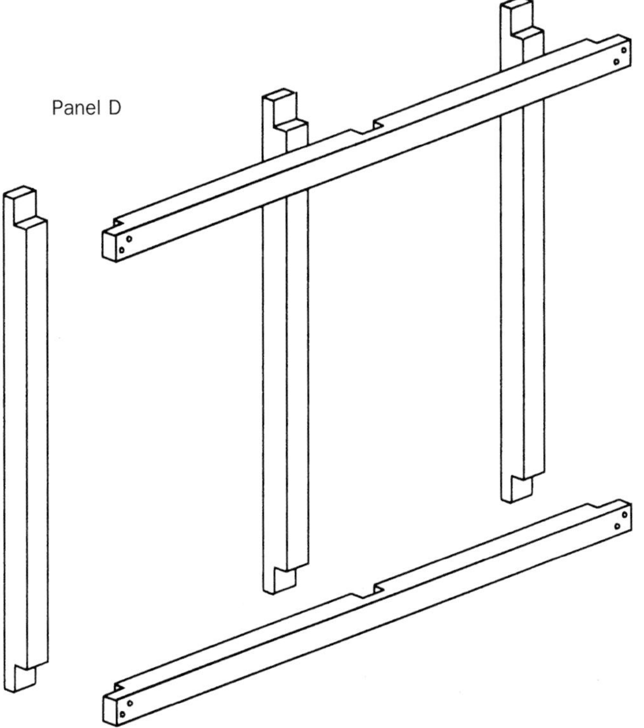

END PANEL D

1 Make this panel from the thicker square-sectioned pine, using halving joints at all the corners and where the middle upright member joins the top and bottom pieces.

Fig 22.9 (left)
Construction of panel D.

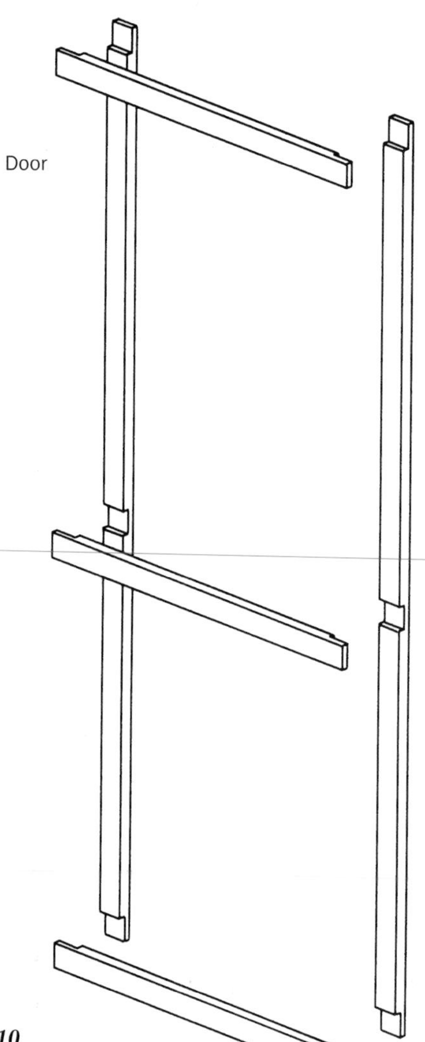

Fig 22.10
Construction of door.

DOOR AND ROOF PANEL

1 For the door, saw the appropriate length of wood for the upright and the three cross pieces and make halving joints at the ends and also in the centres. Strengthen these joints with clenched-over nails (*see* Chapter 2, page 18). Hang the door on panel A with three 2in (50mm) butt hinges and fit a bolt to keep the door closed.

2 The roof panel is a different size, but is made in exactly the same way as the door.

FINISHING OF AVIARY

1 Paint all the wood parts with creosote, and check that the panels are square before covering them with ½in (12mm) galvanized mesh (*see* Fig 22.12). Use tin snips to cut the mesh to size and fix it to the frame with a stapler. The mesh is on the inside of the flight cage when it is assembled.

Fig 22.12
Fixing the wire mesh with a stapler.

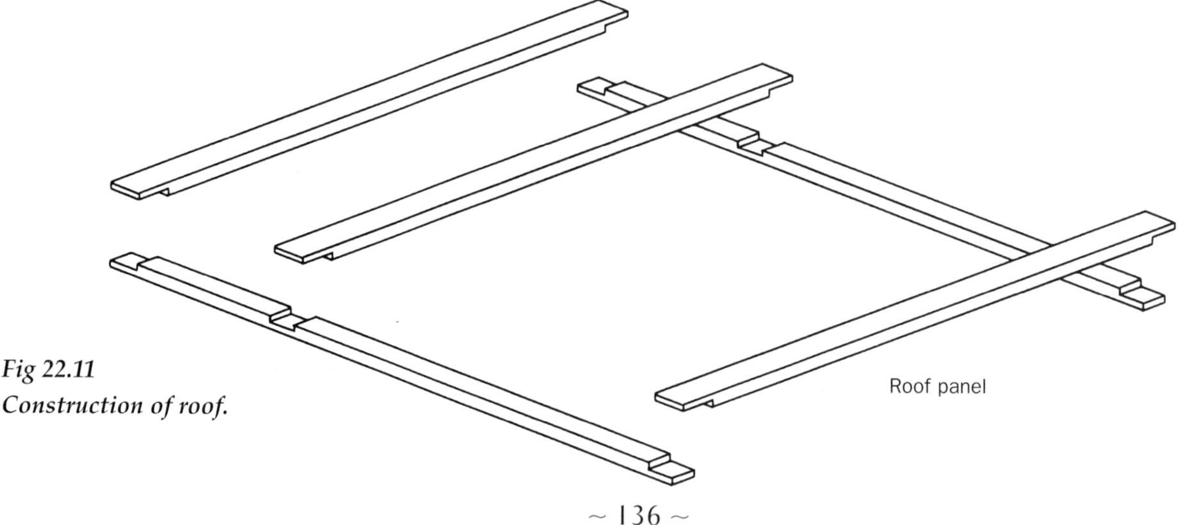

Fig 22.11
Construction of roof.

Construction of Shelter

Front

1 Cut the front to size and form a 20° rebate on the top edge with a power saw. Smooth the edges with a plane. Mark the position of both doors and cut them out with a jigsaw. To do this, begin by drilling holes in the corners of the door areas to give the saw a start. Finish the inside edges with a file and glasspaper.

19⅞in (505mm)
27⅛in
(689mm)

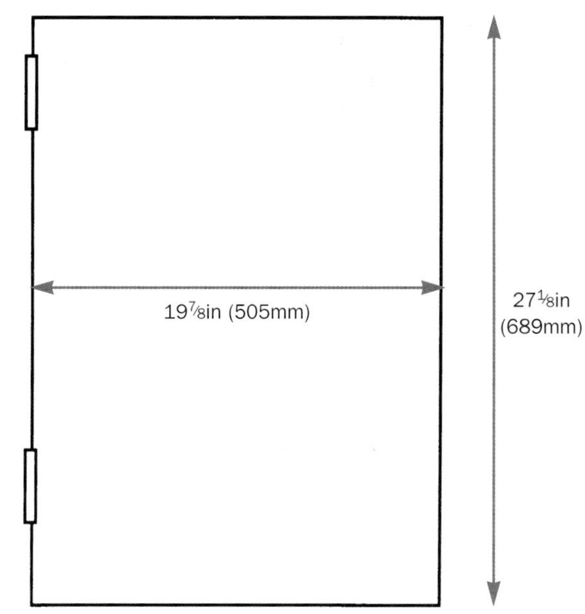

Fig 22.13
Front of shelter, plan with dimensions.

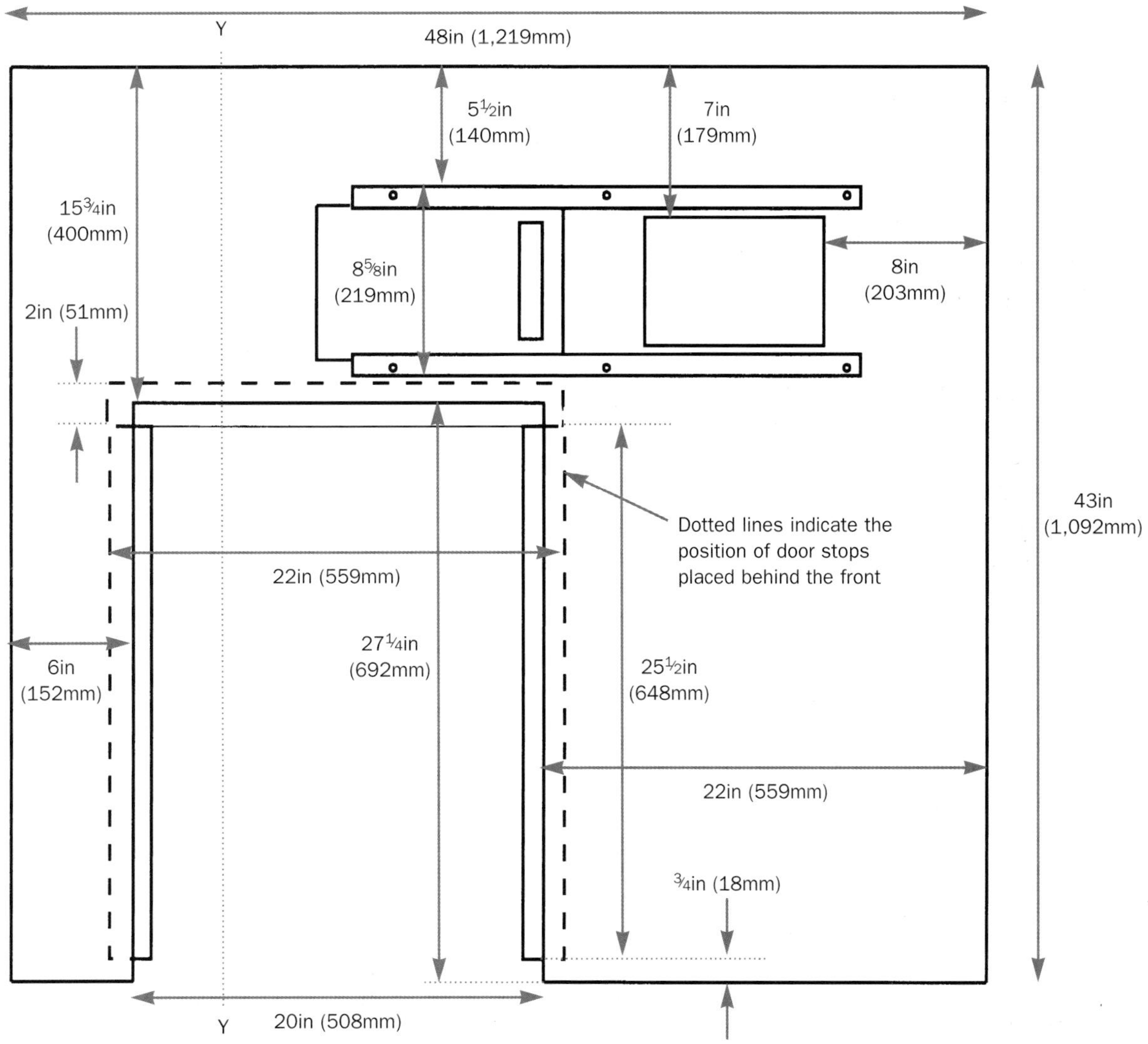

48in (1,219mm)
Y
5½in
(140mm)
7in
(179mm)
15¾in
(400mm)
8⅝in
(219mm)
8in
(203mm)
2in (51mm)
43in
(1,092mm)
Dotted lines indicate the
position of door stops
placed behind the front
22in (559mm)
6in
(152mm)
27¼in
(692mm)
25½in
(648mm)
22in (559mm)
¾in (18mm)
Y
20in (508mm)

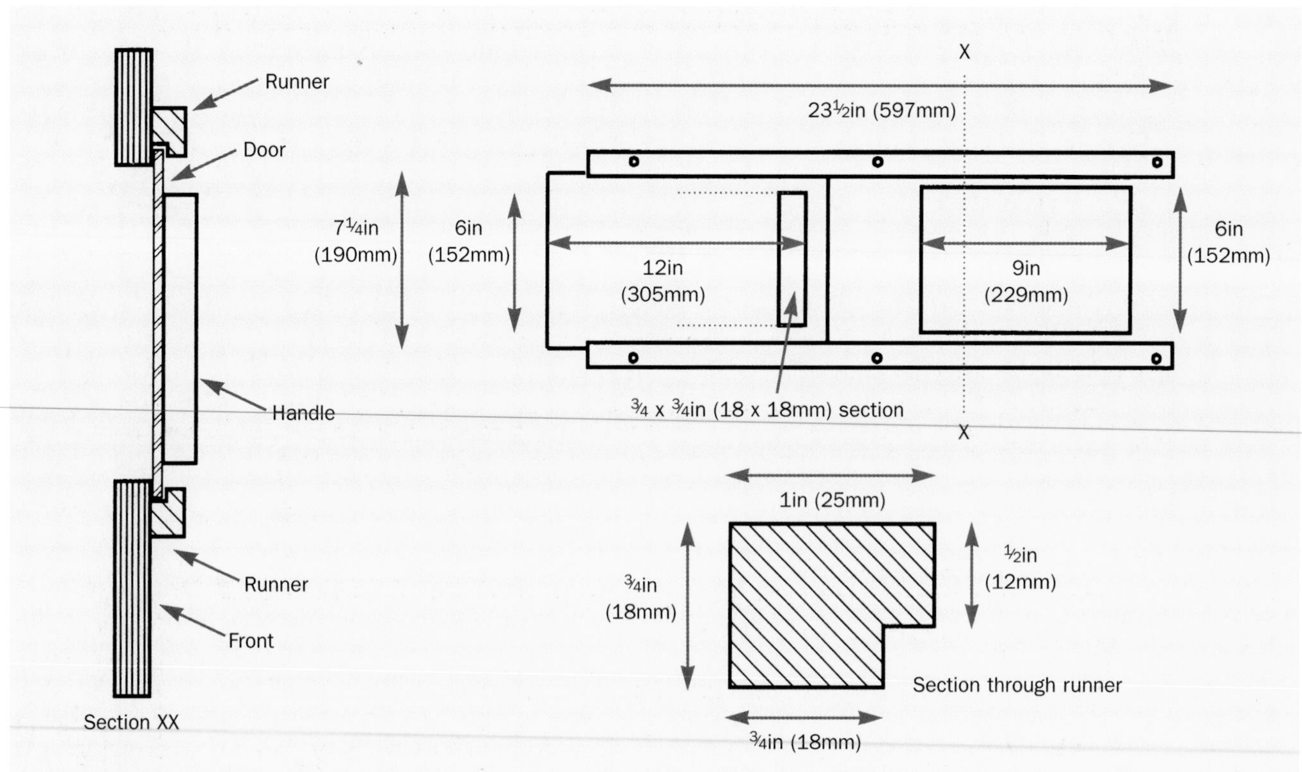

Fig 22.14
Front of shelter, access door for birds, plan with dimensions.

2 Mark and saw the piece of plywood for the large door and, because it is easier at this stage, cut the hinge recesses in the door and the front of the shelter. Fit the hinge to the door, but do not fit the door to the front yet. Fit the piece of wood that serves both as a door stop and draught strip, around the insides of the large door on the back of the front.

3 The purpose of the small opening is to provide access for the birds. It is fitted with a sliding door so that they can be secured inside the shelter if necessary.

To make the sliding door, form a groove ¼ x ¼in (6 x 6mm), using a rebating plane, in two pieces of 1 x 1in (25 x 25mm) pine. Glue and screw these runners to the front, at the top and bottom of the small opening. Make and fit a sliding door from a piece of 3⁄16in (4mm) plywood and stick a piece of square-sectioned pine to the front for a handle. Fit the larger door to the front. (*See* Fig 22.15.)

Fig 22.15
The front of the shelter.

SIDES

1 The two sides have an identical shape, but one of them has an opening cut in it for a window. Mark out one of the sides, cut it out with a panel saw and smooth the edges with a plane. Using this side as a template, mark out the second side and cut it out in the same way. Draw the shape and position of the window

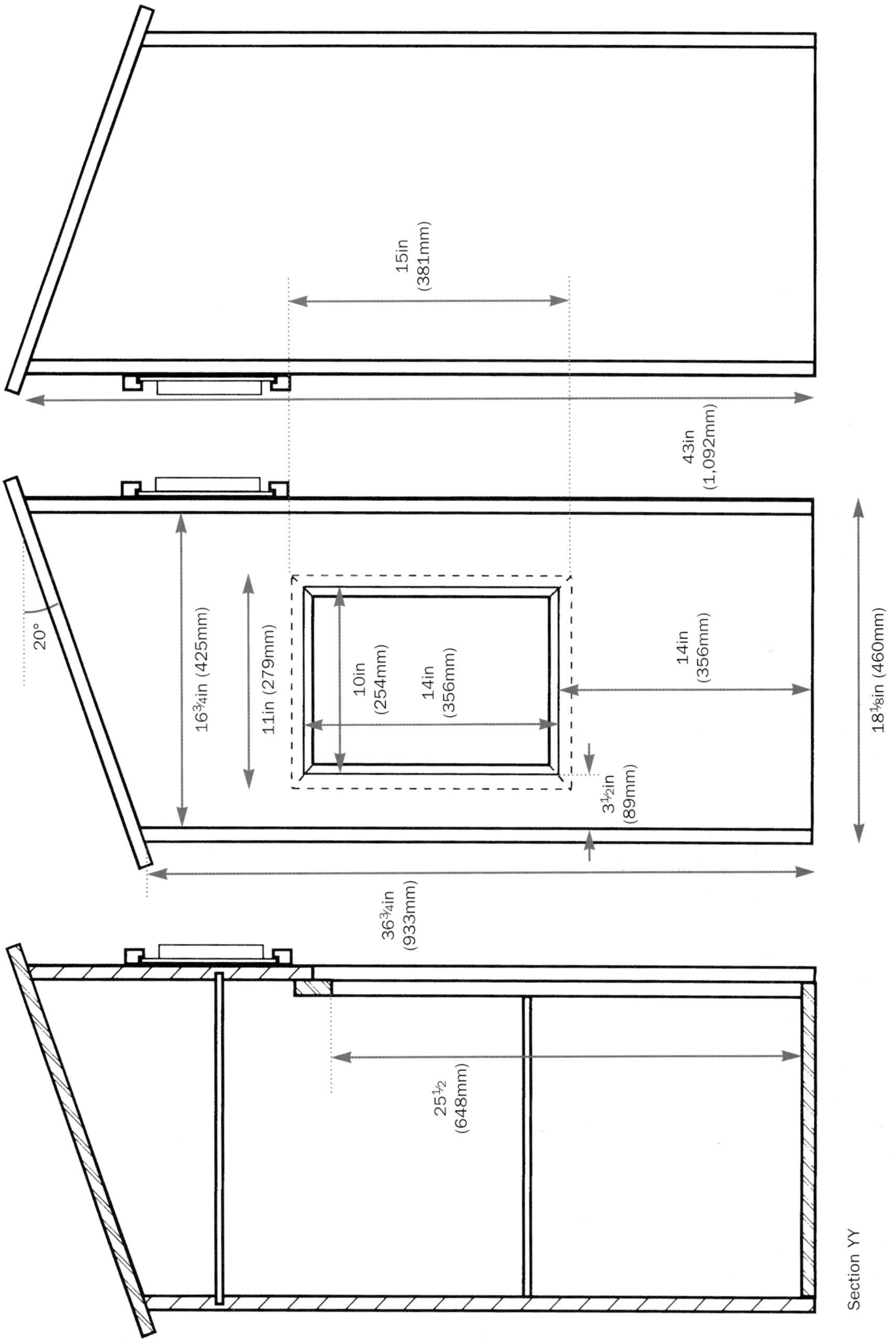

Fig 22.16
Side view of shelter, plan and section with dimensions.

on one of the sides. Before cutting the hole for the window with a jigsaw, drill a hole in one of the corners with a ⅜in (9mm) drill bit to provide an entry point for the saw. Cut around the shape and smooth the edges with a file and glasspaper.

Fig 22.17
Smoothing the inside edge of the window hole.

2 For safety reasons I chose ⅛in (3mm) thick Perspex to glaze the window. Perspex is easily cut with a wood saw and safer to use than glass, particularly when putting nails into the wood next to it, as it doesn't shatter. To hold the Perspex in place, glue and pin plywood pieces with mitred corners around the edge of the window hole, on the inside, but do not fix the Perspex in place at this stage. Cut the mitred pine that will eventually hold the Perspex in place from the outside, and put it to one side until it is required.

BASE, BACK AND TOP

1 Cut out the base, back, and top of the shelter, and slope the top edge of the back with a 20° bevel to match the slope of the roof.

***Fig 22.18** (below)*
Top, base and back of shelter, plan with dimensions.

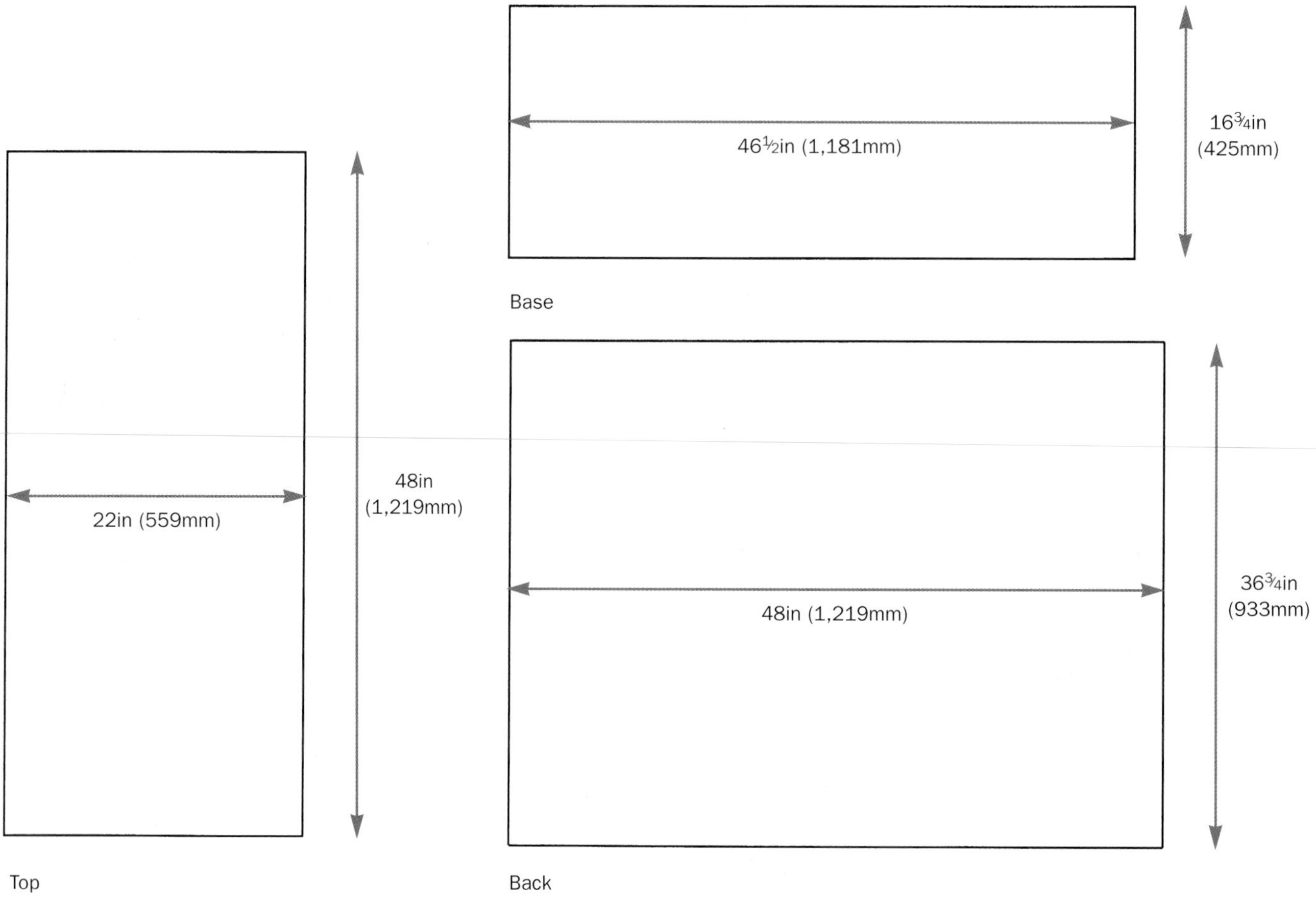

46½in (1,181mm)
16¾in (425mm)
Base

22in (559mm)
48in (1,219mm)
Top

48in (1,219mm)
36¾in (933mm)
Back

Assembly of Shelter

1 Start assembling the shelter by fixing the back to the two sides with glue and 2in (50mm) oval nails. Fix in the base and then the front.

2 Before fitting the top, drill holes on the inside of the front and the back so that perches, made from ⅜in (9mm) hardwood dowel, can be fixed to the inside. The position and number of these perches is arbitrary. Do not drill the holes completely through the wood, but stop at a depth of ½in (12mm). After cutting the perches to the correct length, which is 1in (25mm) longer than the width of the shelter, fit them into place by bending and pushing them into the holes.

3 Nail and glue the top into place and fit the door.

Fig 22.19
Construction of shelter.

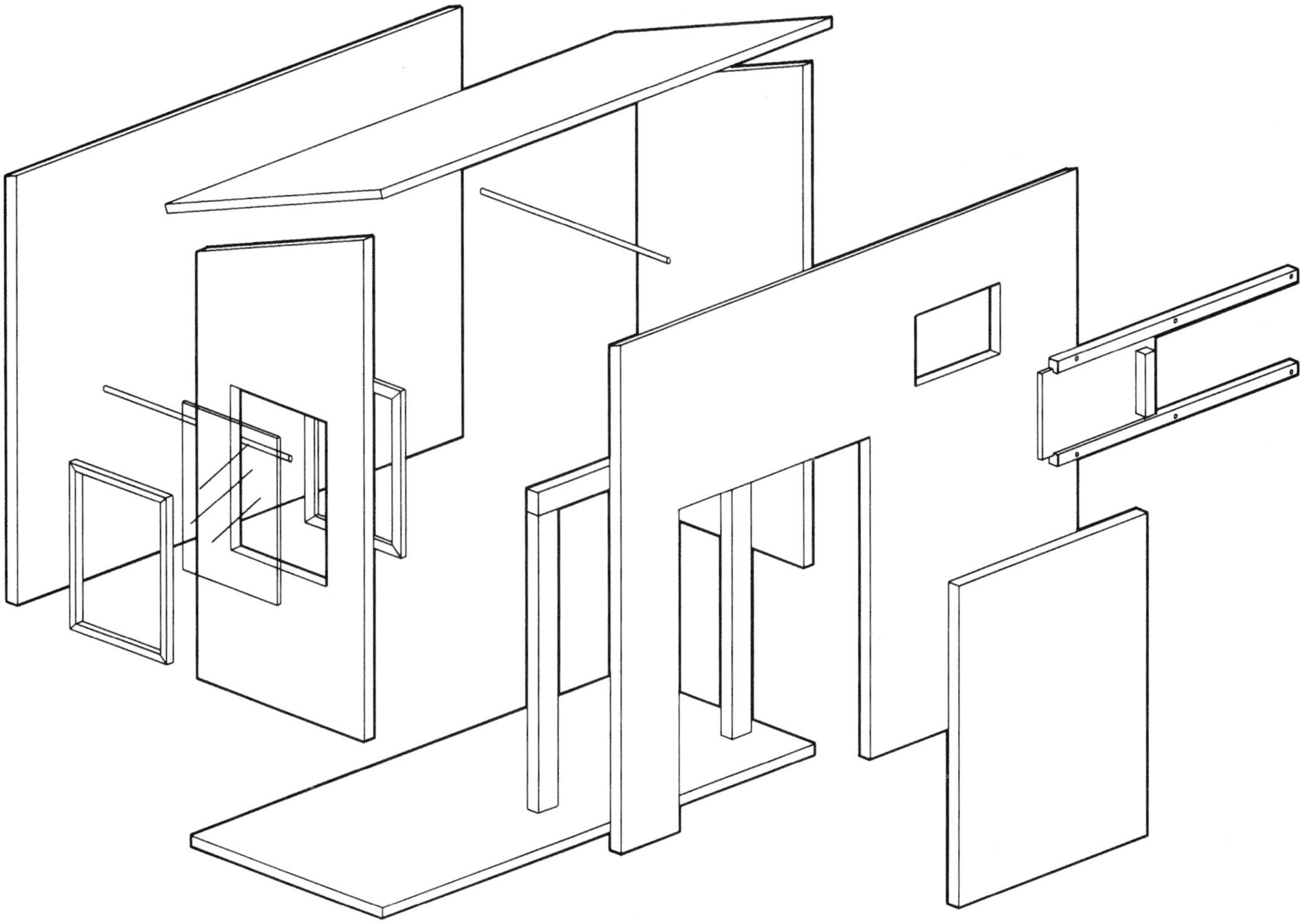

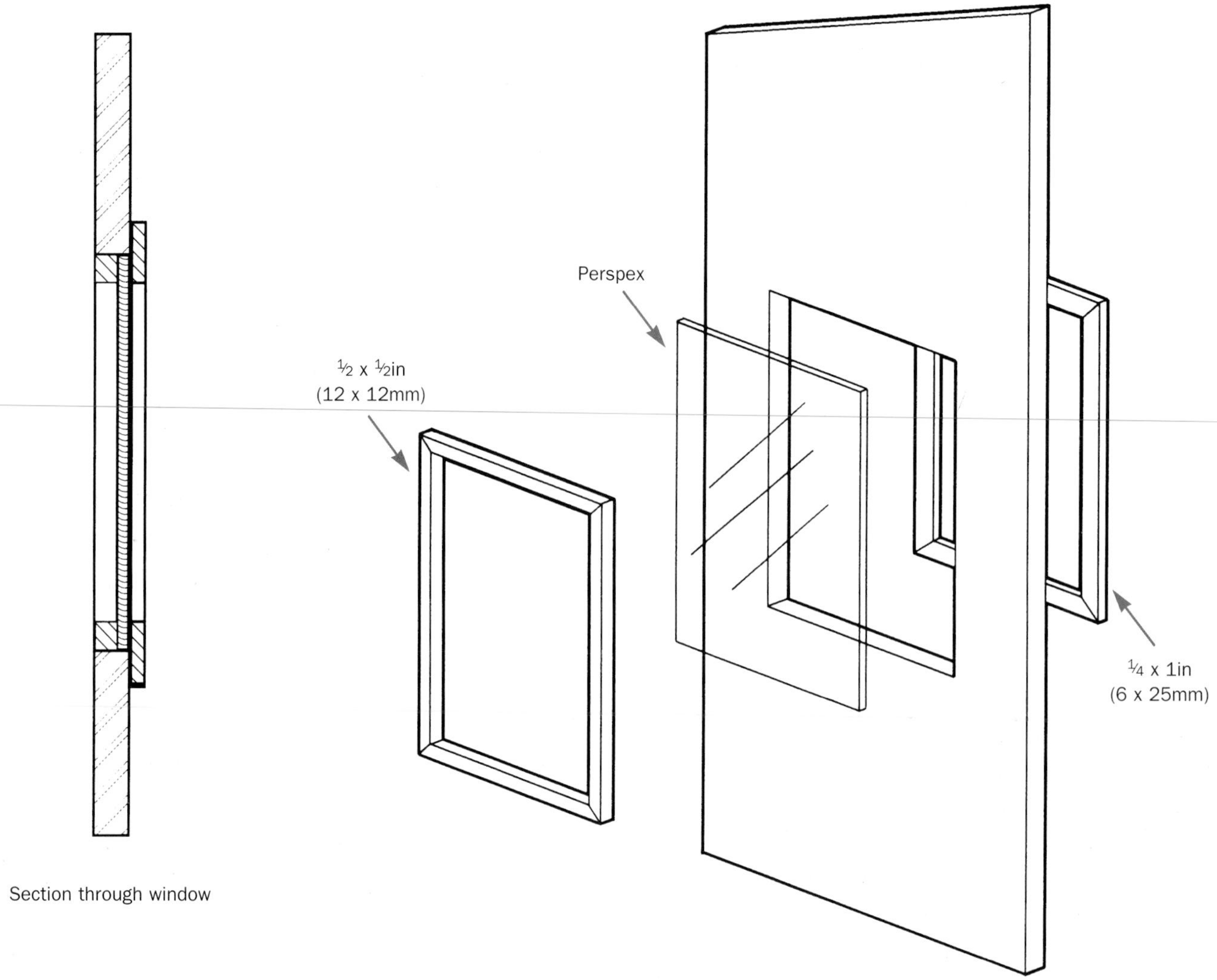

Perspex

½ x ½in
(12 x 12mm)

¼ x 1in
(6 x 25mm)

Section through window

Fig 22.20
Details of window construction.

Finishing of Shelter

1 Paint the entire outside of the shelter with creosote. When this is dry, fit the window and hold it in position by pinning the previously cut pieces of wood into place.

2 Fit a 2½in (64mm) gate latch to secure the door. (*See* Chapter 5, page 34.)

3 Cover the roof with roofing felt (*see* Chapter 2, page 19) and secure it with a series of ½in (12mm) clout nails, fixed at approximately 2in (50mm) intervals around the edge (*see* Fig 22.21).

Fig 22.21
The completed shelter.

Assembly of the Completed Aviary

1 The modular design of the aviary means that it can be erected or taken down for transportation quite quickly. If there is a possibility that you will need to move it at some time, assemble it with bolts fitted with wing nuts. If it is going to be a permanent structure then wood screws are fine. Either way, the method of assembly is the same. Stand panel A up and screw panels C to it. Next, fit on panels B, followed by the end panel D and finally, the roof panel. If you are using wing nuts, drill the holes for the screws completely through both the panels that are being fixed together; if you are using wood screws, follow the method given in Chapter 2 (*see* page 12). Lift the shelter section into place and fix with screws.

Fig 22.22
Screwing together the side panels.

2 The aviary is now ready to be bolted down to a brick or concrete base or pegged down on the lawn (*see* Fig 22.23). To put a bolt in brick or concrete, use an expanding bolt. About six bolts should be enough to secure this aviary. Use plastic or metal tent pegs for pegging down onto lawn. The pegs should be approximately 8–10in (203–254mm) long.

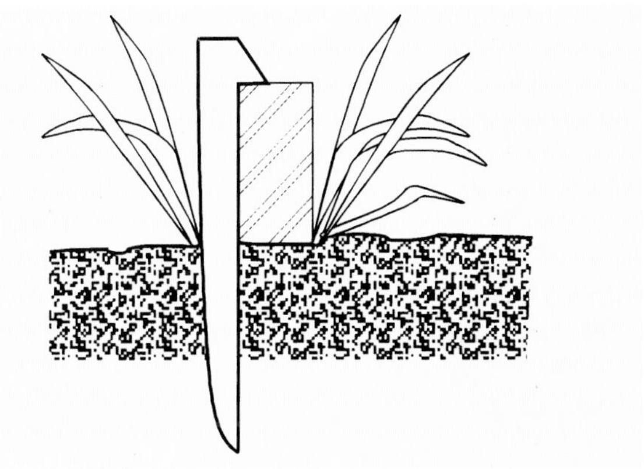

Fig 22.23
Pegging the base of the aviary to the lawn.

3 To finish, fit a couple of perches in the flight area (*see* Fig 22.24), and furnish with feeding and water facilities.

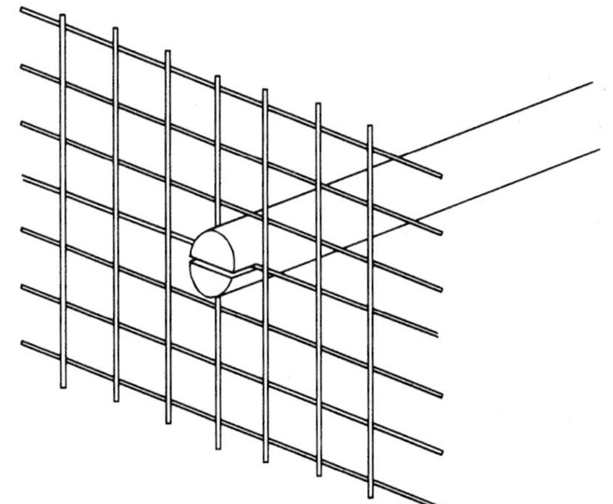

Fig 22.24
Method of fixing a perch to the mesh.

23

GUINEA-PIG HUTCH

Guinea-pigs are indigenous to the north of South America. They were domesticated in Peru around 2000BC, as a food source. While they are still eaten in a number of South American countries, today they are far more widely kept as pets.

This hutch is divided into two compartments, one for sleeping and the other, fitted with a mesh front, for daytime use. I recommend a supply of clean hay or wood shavings to keep the sleeping compartment warm, especially in the winter. Both compartments have a door so that they can be cleaned out.

The hutch is constructed mainly from various thicknesses of exterior quality plywood and finished with a water-resistant wood stain. It can be sited in a shed or garage or out in the open in a sheltered position.

CUTTING LIST

CARCASS

Base (1)	Plywood	34½ x 15¼ x ¾in (876 x 387 x 18mm)
Back (1)	Plywood	36 x 18⅜ x ¼in (914 x 467 x 6mm)
Roof panels (2)	Plywood	20½ x 17½ x ⅜in (521 x 450 x 9mm)
Sides (2)	Plywood	16 x 13½ x ¾in (406 x 343 x 18mm)
Dividing piece (1)	Plywood	17½ x 16 x ¾in (445 x 406 x 18mm)
Cross pieces for roof support (2)	Pine	36 x 1½ x ¾in (914 x 38 x 18mm)
Long roof supports (2)	Pine	21¾ x 1½ x ¾in (552 x 38 x 18mm)
Short roof supports (2)	Pine	18⅛ x 1½ x ¾in (460 x 38 x 18mm)
Roof support backing (1)	Plywood	34½ x 5⅝ x ¼in (876 x 143 x 6mm)
	ALSO REQUIRED:	
Roofing felt		36 x 18½in (914 x 470mm)

DOORS

Long pieces for mesh door (2)	Pine	17 11/16 x 1 x ¾in (449 x 25 x 18mm)
Short pieces for mesh door (2)	Pine	10 x 1 x ¾in (254 x 25 x 18mm)
Long pieces for ply door (2)	Pine	15 15/16 x 1 x ¾in (405 x 25 x 18mm)
Short pieces for ply door (2)	Pine	10 x 1 x ¾in (254 x 25 x 18mm)
Back for ply door (1)	Plywood	15 15/16 x 12 x ¼in (405 x 305 x 6mm)
Latch (1)	Pine	3 x ¾ x ½in (76 x 18 x 12mm)
	ALSO REQUIRED:	
Butt hinges (4)		1½in (38mm)
Wire mesh, ½in (12mm) square		17⅞ x 11½in (454 x 292mm)

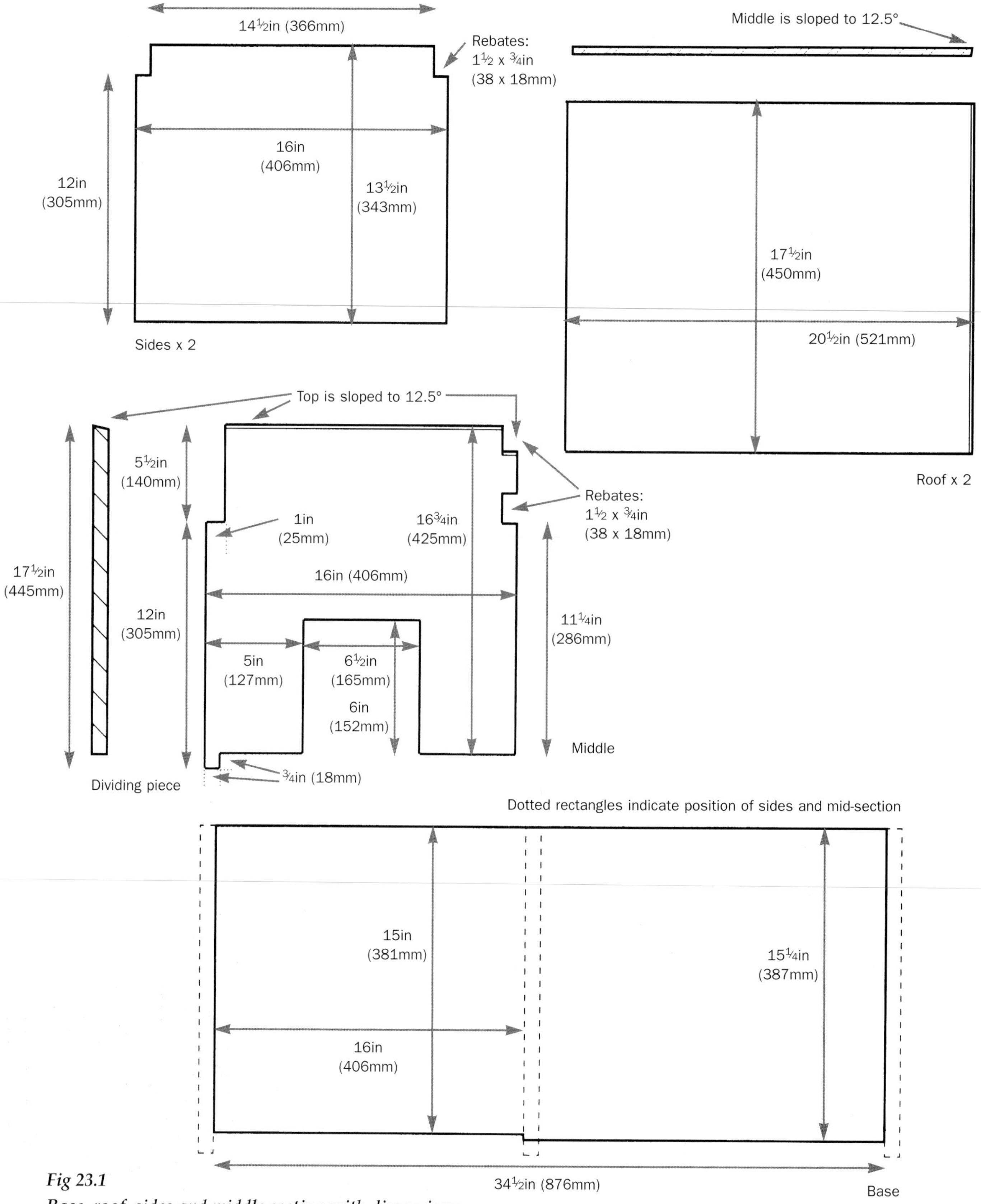

Fig 23.1
Base, roof, sides and middle section with dimensions.

CONSTRUCTION

CARCASS

1 On a suitably sized piece of ¾in (18mm) plywood, mark out the shape for the base using a pencil, rule and long straightedge. Make sure that it is square by getting both diagonals the same length. Cut it out with a panel saw and smooth the edges. Note that the floor of the sleeping section is narrower than the rest to accommodate the thicker door on that side.

2 The two sides and the central dividing wall are the next parts to be marked and cut out. Use a power saw to slope the top edge of the centre section set to 12.5°. Cut the rebates for the roof supports in all three sections, and the access hole in the central section using a tenon saw and a jigsaw. Nail and glue these three parts to the base (*see* Fig 23.3).

Fig 23.3
The base, sides and middle section.

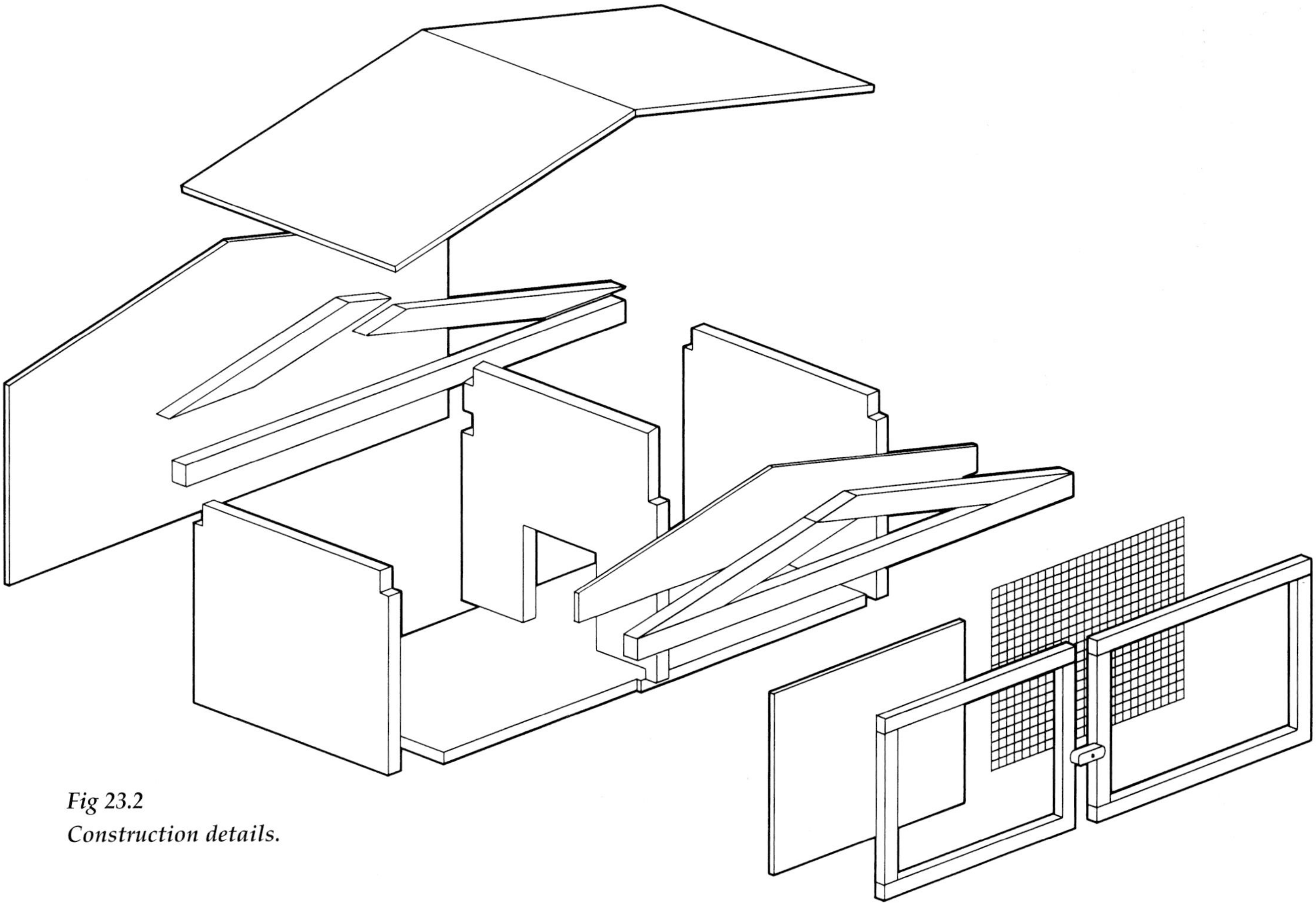

Fig 23.2
Construction details.

3 With a sliding bevel set to the correct angle, mark out and cut one of the sloping sections for the two roof supports. When this is done, use the angled ends as a template to mark out the rest of the sloping pieces and, together with the long horizontal pieces, cut them to size. Lay out the parts of the two roof supports in their correct positions to check that they butt together accurately (*see* Fig 23.5) and then join them permanently with nails and glue.

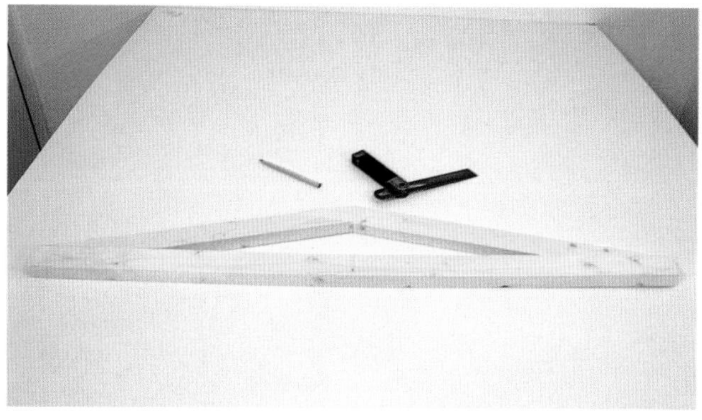

Fig 23.5
Testing the roof trusses for accuracy of fit.

***Fig 23.4** (below)*
Details of roof support and back.

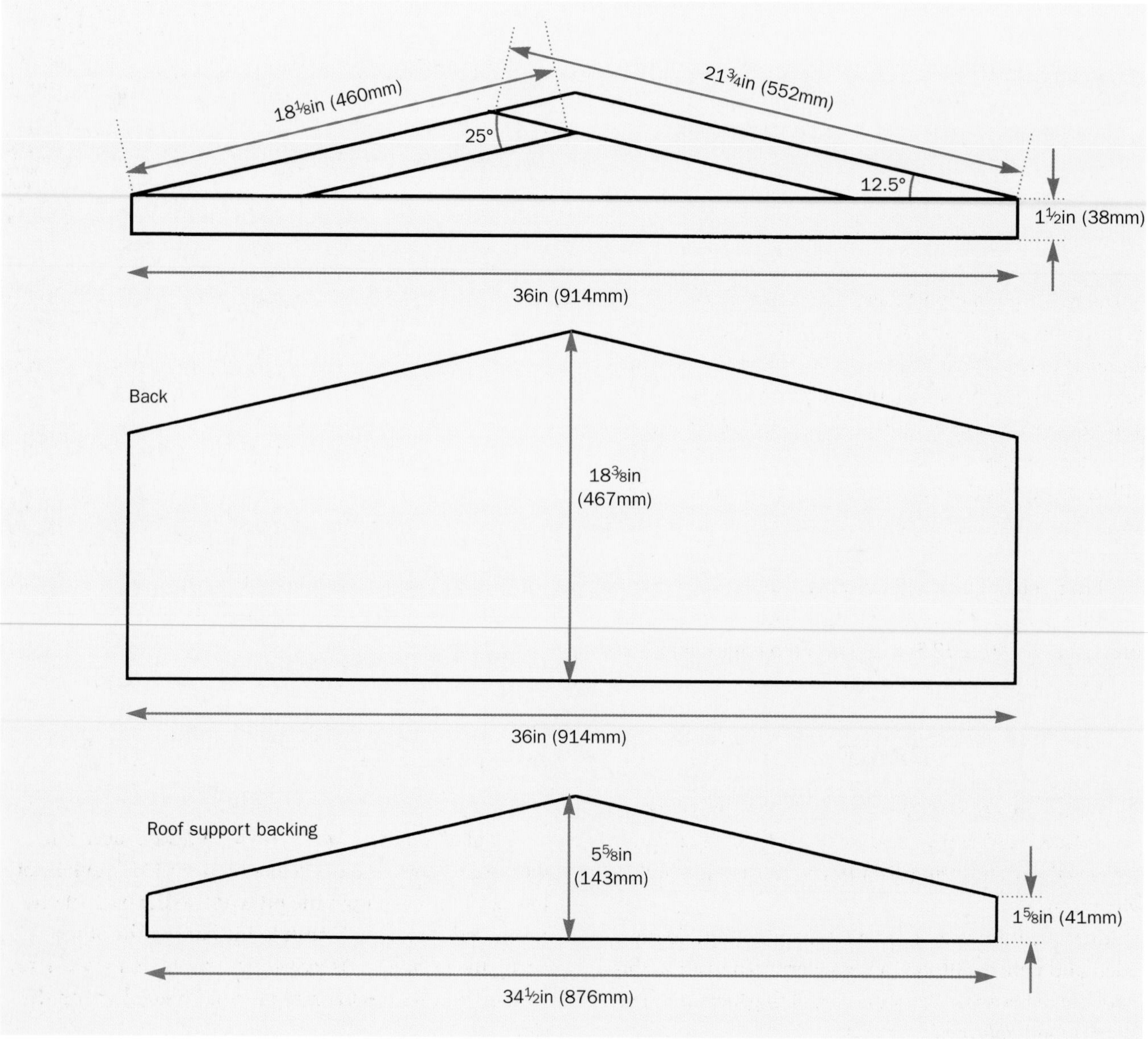

18⅛in (460mm)
21¾in (552mm)
25°
12.5°
1½in (38mm)
36in (914mm)
Back
18⅜in
(467mm)
36in (914mm)
Roof support backing
5⅝in
(143mm)
1⅝in (41mm)
34½in (876mm)

Fig 23.6
Fitting the roof trusses to the carcass.

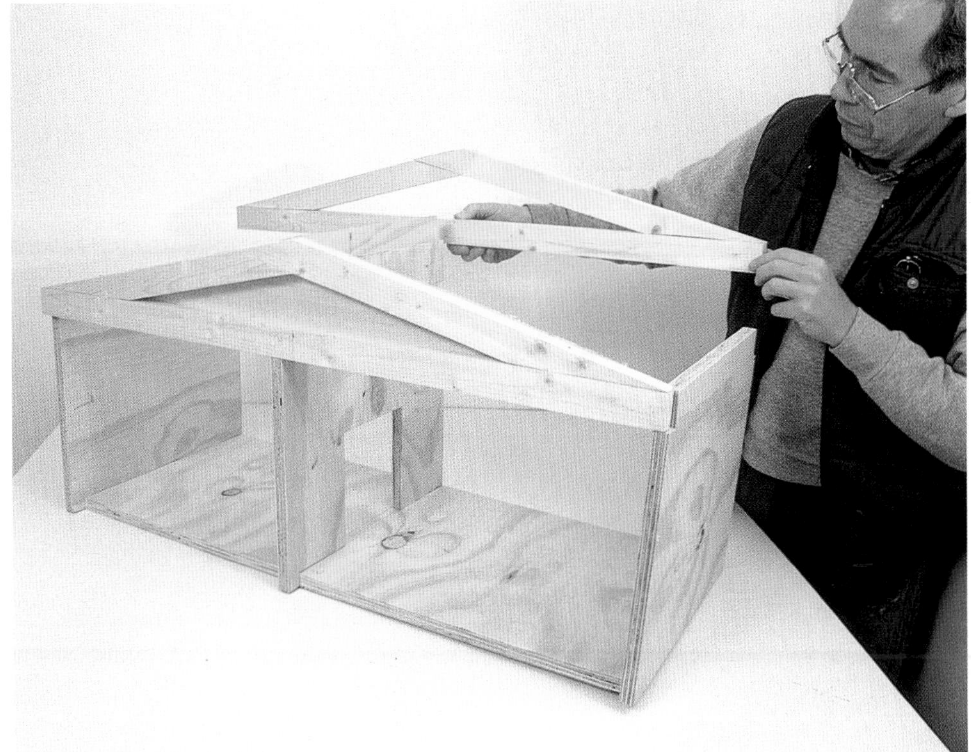

The front roof support has a back made from ¼in (6mm) plywood. To shape this lay one of the roof supports on a suitable piece of ply and draw around it before sawing it out. Note that the plywood stops ¾in (18mm) short where the roof support joins the sides. Pin and glue the plywood into place and trim the edges with a plane. Fix the two supports to the sides (*see* Fig 23.6).

4 From a piece of ⅜in (9mm) plywood cut the two roof panels. Where they butt together at the centre, form a slope with a 12.5° angle on both edges. Nail the roof onto the rest of the carcass.

Fig 23.7
The finished carcass.

DOORS

1 Both doors have pine frames. The left-hand frame is fitted with a plywood panel and the right-hand frame is filled with ½in (12mm), galvanized and welded wire mesh.

All of the frame corner joints are simple butt joints, glued and nailed. Although not a very strong joint, this is adequate because the frames are strengthened when the plywood and mesh are added.

Cut all the pieces for the frames to length and join them at the corners (*see* Chapter 2, page 14 for details of the joint). Glue and pin the plywood to the back of one frame and staple wire mesh to the back of the other. Using the technique described in Chapter 2, fit two 1½in (38mm) butt hinges to each door and hang them on the sides.

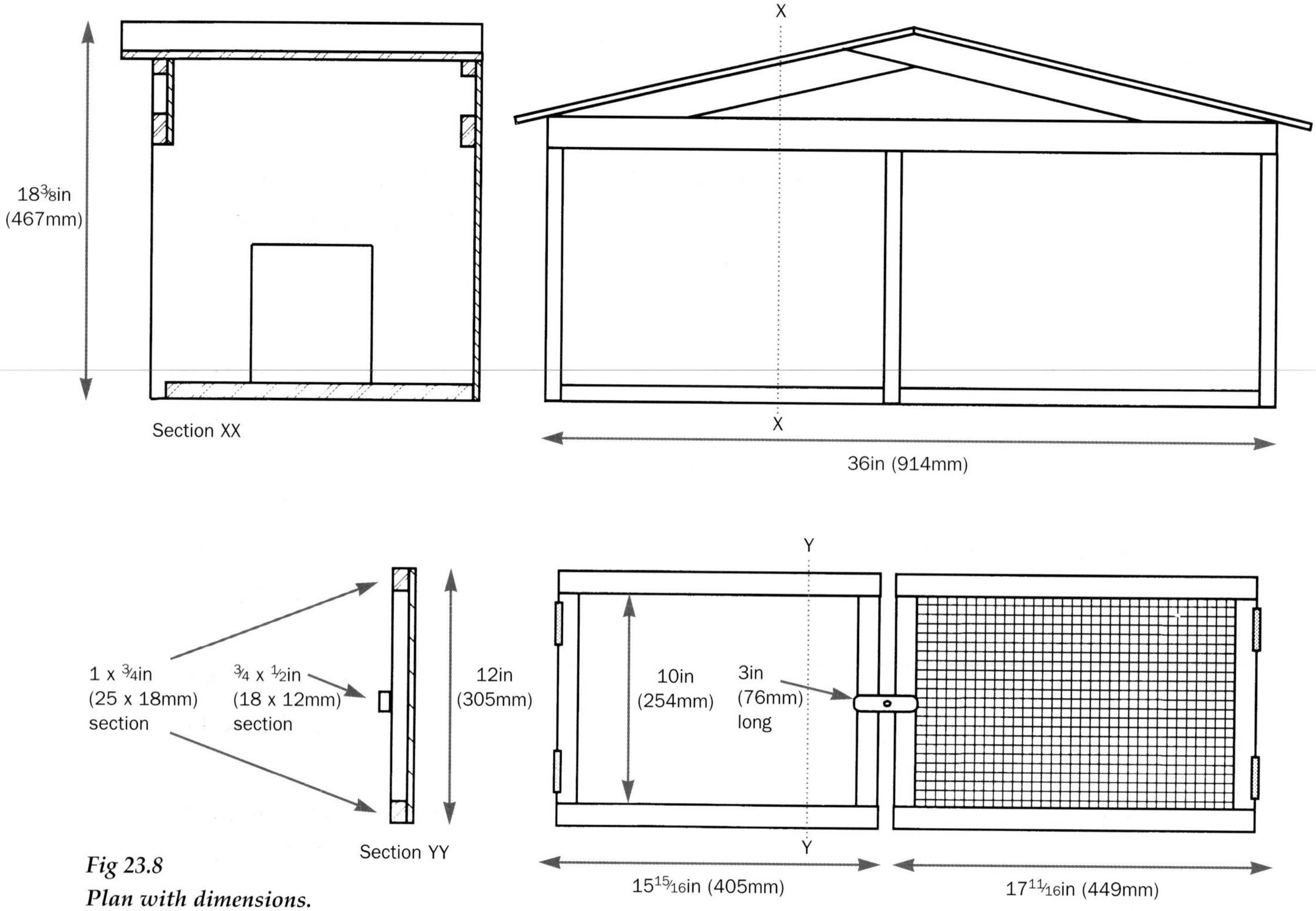

18⅜in (467mm)

Section XX

X

X

36in (914mm)

1 x ¾in (25 x 18mm) section

¾ x ½in (18 x 12mm) section

12in (305mm)

Section YY

Y

10in (254mm)

3in (76mm) long

Y

15$\frac{15}{16}$in (405mm)

17$\frac{11}{16}$in (449mm)

Fig 23.8
Plan with dimensions.

Fig 23.9
The finished doors.

FINISHING

1 Paint the entire hutch with water-resistant wood stain. If it is to be sited in the open air, cover the top with roofing felt (*see* Chapter 2, page 19) and fix it with ½in (12mm) clout nails.

SMALL MAMMALS

With the exception of grey squirrels, it is not as easy to get good views of the many small animals that come to our gardens as it is of the birds. This is because many of them are nocturnal, although they can often be seen at dawn and dusk.

With patience and care the more desirable visitors, such as hedgehogs and even badgers if you live in the right area, can be enticed to put in an appearance. The way to attract them is to leave out food on a regular basis. When they get used to calling in to get fed, a light can be put on to illuminate the garden so that they can be observed. The highlight of a visit to my friends, who have badgers that feed on their patio, is to watch them eating in the evening by the light of the patio window. In the summer the adults can be seen bringing their new cubs to show them where the free grub is.

Some gardens are lucky enough to get bats flitting around on warm summer evenings. As they only eat insects, which are not easy to supply on demand, the way to encourage them is to make available some desirable accommodation.

Some small animals are not so welcome, but will come anyway. Grey squirrels, mice, rats and rabbits fall into this category, although lots of people enjoy the antics of squirrels and rabbits. Mice and foxes will also use bird tables for the occasional snack. It is not uncommon for deer to visit gardens in the country, where they do a lot of damage to the shrubs and vegetables.

HEDGEHOG SHELTER

HEDGEHOG

LEISLER'S BAT

24

Bat Box

There are 14 different species of bat in the UK and many of them will use nest boxes for rearing their young. With luck, a bat can live for 20 years, and mature females will have one baby a year for most of their adult life. The most common, and one of the smallest bats in the UK, is the pipistrelle: although it weighs less than a two pence coin, it can eat several thousand insects in a single night. The noctule is the largest species and weighs about the same as three £1 coins. All the UK bats eat insects exclusively.

Bats like to live in old hollow trees, caves or lofts. The marked reduction in available roosting sites has been responsible for a decline in the bat population, so bat boxes are an essential extra to help bats and stop their numbers declining. Bats like their roosting places to be of a constant temperature year-round, hence their preference for caves and hollow trees. For this reason I made my box from thick softwood – 1½in (38mm). This will provide a well-insulated environment, that is waterproof and draught free. The wood used should be sawn and not planed, as bats require a rough surface to give them grip – they will land on the outside of the box and climb around until they reach the entrance.

To encourage bats to use a box, it should be situated high in a tree, in a sheltered position that gets exposure to the sun for part of the day. It is a good idea to fit two or three boxes on the same tree at the same height, but facing in different directions, to provide the optimum conditions for different times of the year.

The box is wedge-shaped to give extra room at the top where the bats roost, whilst having a smaller volume than a rectangular box so that there is less air to influence their body temperature. It might appear that the box is not very large, but a single pipistrelle can fit inside a match box.

There are laws against disturbing bats in any way, so the lid provided cannot be lifted for viewing. However, rather than fix it with nails and glue, I have fixed it with a screw so that it can be removed in the spring to enable cleaning.

CUTTING LIST

Back (1)	Pine	13 x 6¼ x 1½in (330 x 159 x 38mm)
Lid (1)	Pine	7½ x 7¼ x 1½in (191 x 184 x 38mm)
Front (1)	Pine	6¼ x 6¼ x 1½in (159 x 159 x 38mm)
Sides (2)	Pine	8 x 3¾ x 1½in (203 x 95 x 38mm)
Base (1)	Pine	3¼ x 2¼ x 1½in (83 x 57 x 38mm)

ALSO REQUIRED:

Self-adhesive, waterproof plastic flashing	1½ x 6¼in (38 x 159mm)

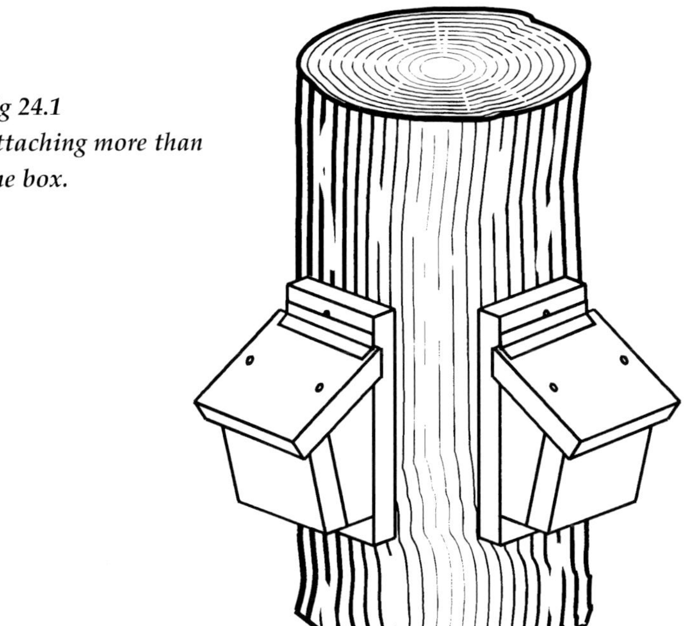

Fig 24.1
Attaching more than one box.

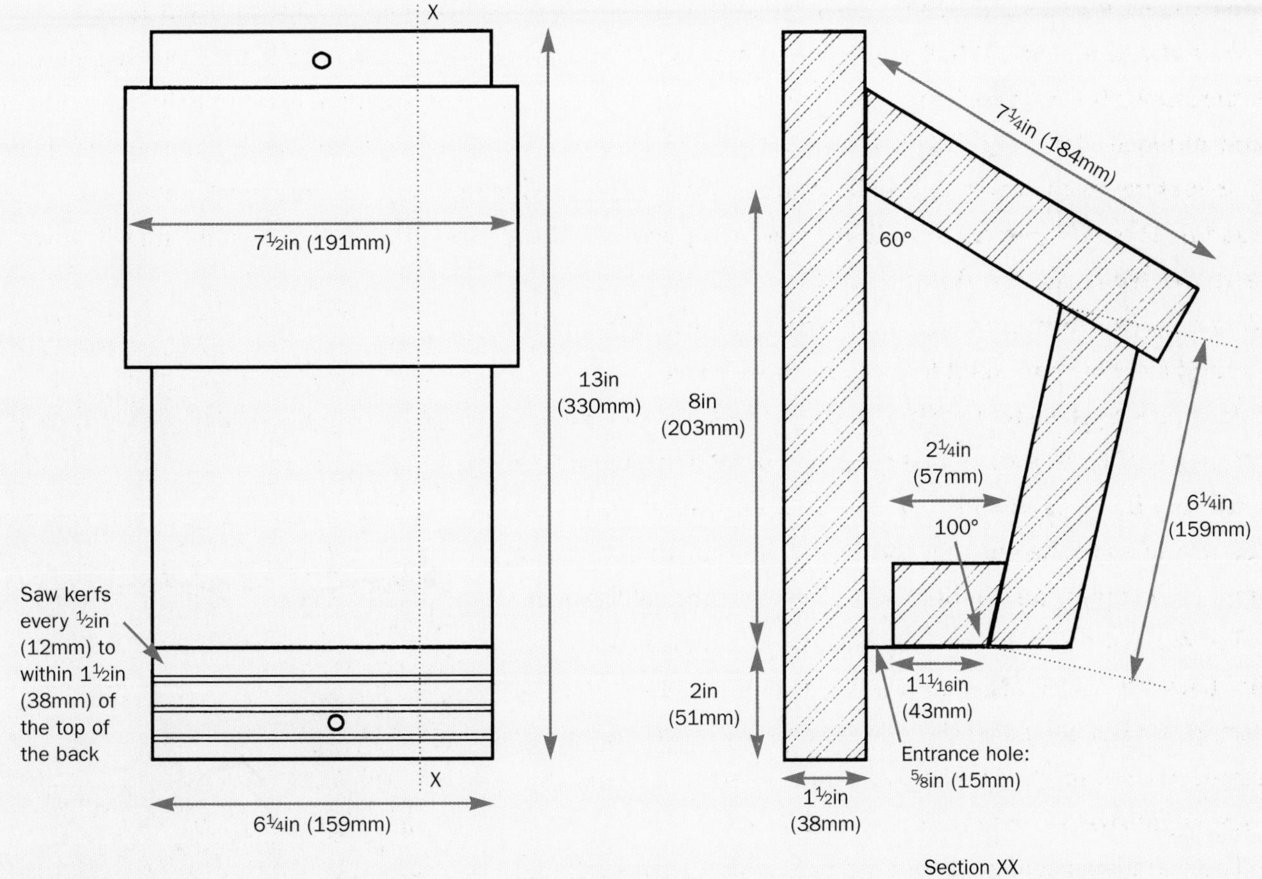

Fig 24.2
Plan and section with dimensions.

Fig 24.3
Construction details.

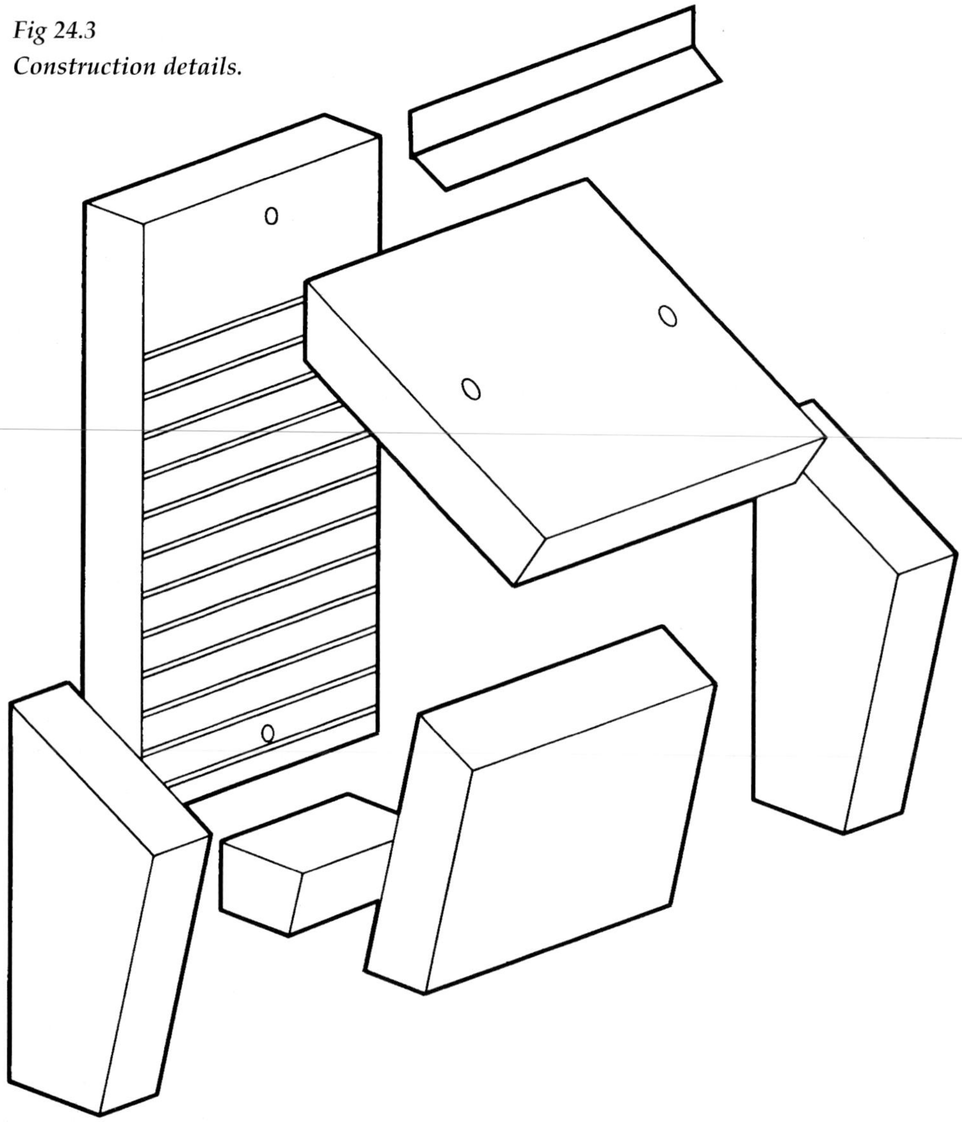

Construction

1 Cut the back to size and drill holes at the top and bottom to enable fixing to a tree when it is completed. On the inside face of the back, from the base to within 2in (50mm) of the top, roughen up the surface to make it easy for the bats to clamber up. I made a series of cuts with a saw (*see* Fig 24.4), but a rasp would do the job just as well.

***Fig 24.4** (right)*
Making the back rough with a saw.

2 Mark out one of the two sides using a sliding bevel and measurements from Figs 24.2 and 24.3 to saw the correct angles for the slopes. Then, use the first side as a template to mark out the second side, and cut both out with a panel saw.

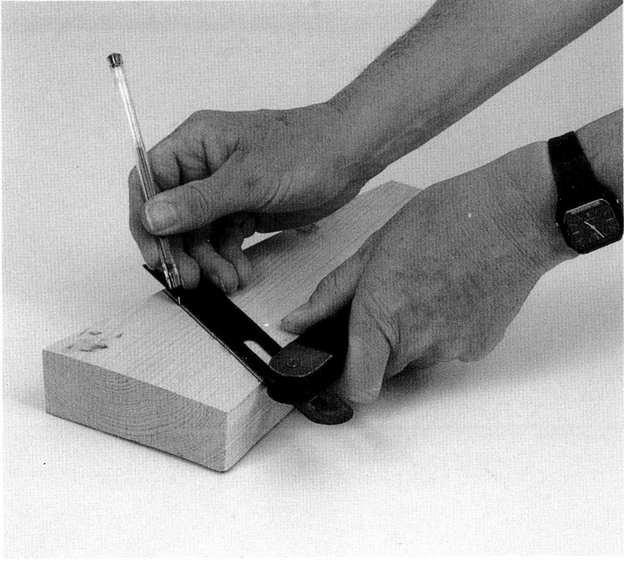

3 Use one of the sides to mark the correct angles for the top and bottom edges of the front, then cut the front out. Do the same for the lid.

4 Mark and cut out the base. The base joins the two sides and also limits the size of the entrance slot. Bats will enter through the base, climb up the back wall, and hang by their feet from the lid. The maximum size for the slot is ⅝in (15mm) which will give access to the biggest bats, but is small enough to prevent any birds from taking over.

Assembly

1 All the pieces are fixed together using water-resistant glue and 3in (75mm) round wire nails. To prevent the wood splitting, drill pilot holes for the nails. (*See* Chapter 2, page 11.)

Nail and glue the two sides to the back, glue the base into place without nailing (*see* Fig 24.6), and then fix the front to the sides using nails and glue.

***Fig 24.5** (above)*
Using a sliding bevel to mark the angle for the roof on the sides.

***Fig 24.6** (right)*
Gluing in the base.

2 Screw the lid to the two sides, and place a strip of self-adhesive waterproof flashing between the lid and the back to seal the gap and stop rain getting in.

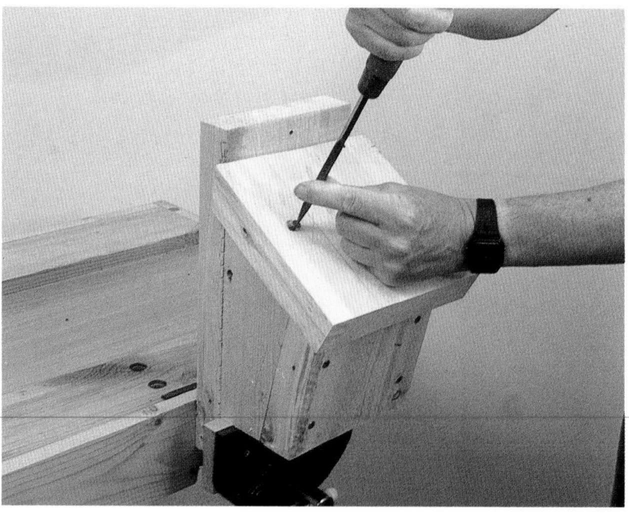

Finishing

1 I used second-hand timber which had a number of nail holes, so, in order to stop damp and insects getting in through these, I filled them, and any other gaps in the construction, with waterproof wood filler. The box should not be finished with paint or creosote as the smell will discourage them from using it. The wood is very thick and will last many years even if untreated.

Fig 24.7 (above)
Fixing the lid to the sides with screws.

Fig 24.8 (left)
Any holes are filled with water-resistant filler.

25

HEDGEHOG SHELTER

Hedgehogs are common in country and suburban gardens and, because they eat lots of pests, are generally welcome. Their natural diet comprises insects, slugs, snails and even mice, but they can be enticed out into the open on warm summer evenings by a bowl of cat food.

If there are hedgehogs in your garden, they will eventually find the box and take up residence. If you are fortunate, it will be used for nesting in June and July and for hibernation in the winter. It should be sited in a 'rough' part of the garden and covered with leaves and hedge clippings, leaving the entrance to the tunnel clear. This covering will help to keep the box warm in winter and cool in summer. The box should be positioned with the tunnel mouth slightly lower than the main chamber so that water does not run into the box when it rains. Using a brick or a block of wood to prop up the back of the main chamber will achieve this. Place some straw or wood shavings inside so that the hedgehogs can build a nest. The lid lifts off so that the box can be cleaned out in the spring.

Use water-resistant material for the box because it is not a good idea to treat it with creosote or paint – the smell will deter the hedgehogs. I used ½in (12mm) exterior quality plywood.

CUTTING LIST

Short side (1)	Plywood	13 x 11 x ½in (330 x 279 x 12mm)
Long side (1)	Plywood	19½ x 11 x ½in (495 x 279 x 12mm)
Base (1)	Plywood	19½ x 13 x ½in (495 x 330 x 12mm)
Back (1)	Plywood	14 x 11 x ½in (356 x 279 x 12mm)
Front (1)	Plywood	14 x 11 x ½in (356 x 279 x 12mm)
Top of tunnel (1)	Plywood	6 x 5 x ½in (152 x 127 x 12mm)
Side of tunnel (1)	Plywood	6 x 4½ x ½in (152 x 114 x 12mm)
Lid (1)	Plywood	15 x 15 x ½in (381 x 381 x 12mm)
Long lid strips (2)	Pine	13 x 1 x ¾in (330 x 25 x 18mm)
Short lid strips (2)	Pine	11 x 1 x ¾in (279 x 25 x 18mm)
ALSO REQUIRED:		
Roofing felt (1)		16½ x 16½in (419 x 419mm)
Copper tubing, ⅞in (22mm) (1)		18in (457mm)
Copper tubing 90° elbow, ⅞in (22mm) (1)		18in (457mm)

Fig 25.1
Overall dimensions.

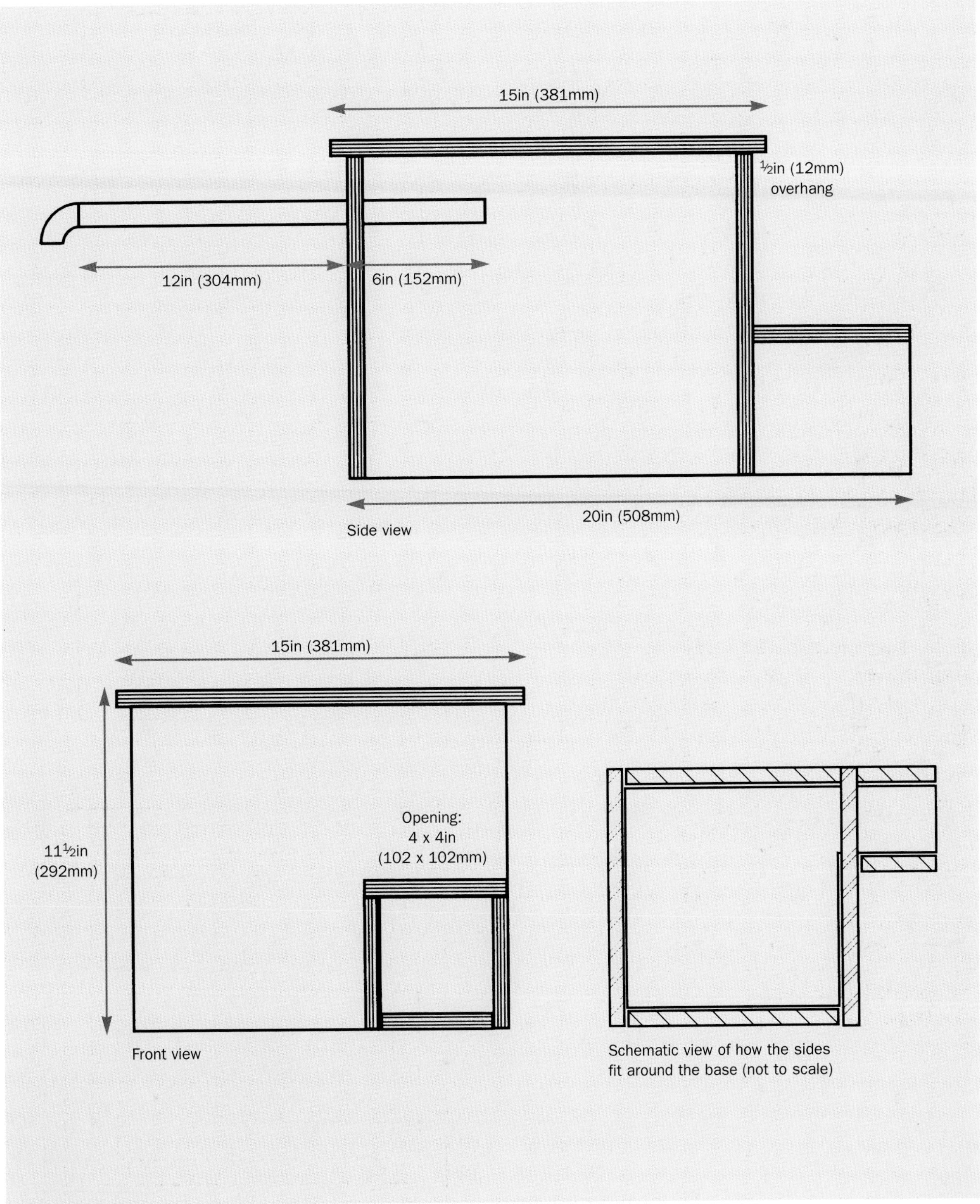

15in (381mm)

½in (12mm) overhang

12in (304mm)

6in (152mm)

20in (508mm)

Side view

15in (381mm)

11½in (292mm)

Opening:
4 x 4in
(102 x 102mm)

Front view

Schematic view of how the sides fit around the base (not to scale)

Fig 25.2
Front and side view with dimensions.

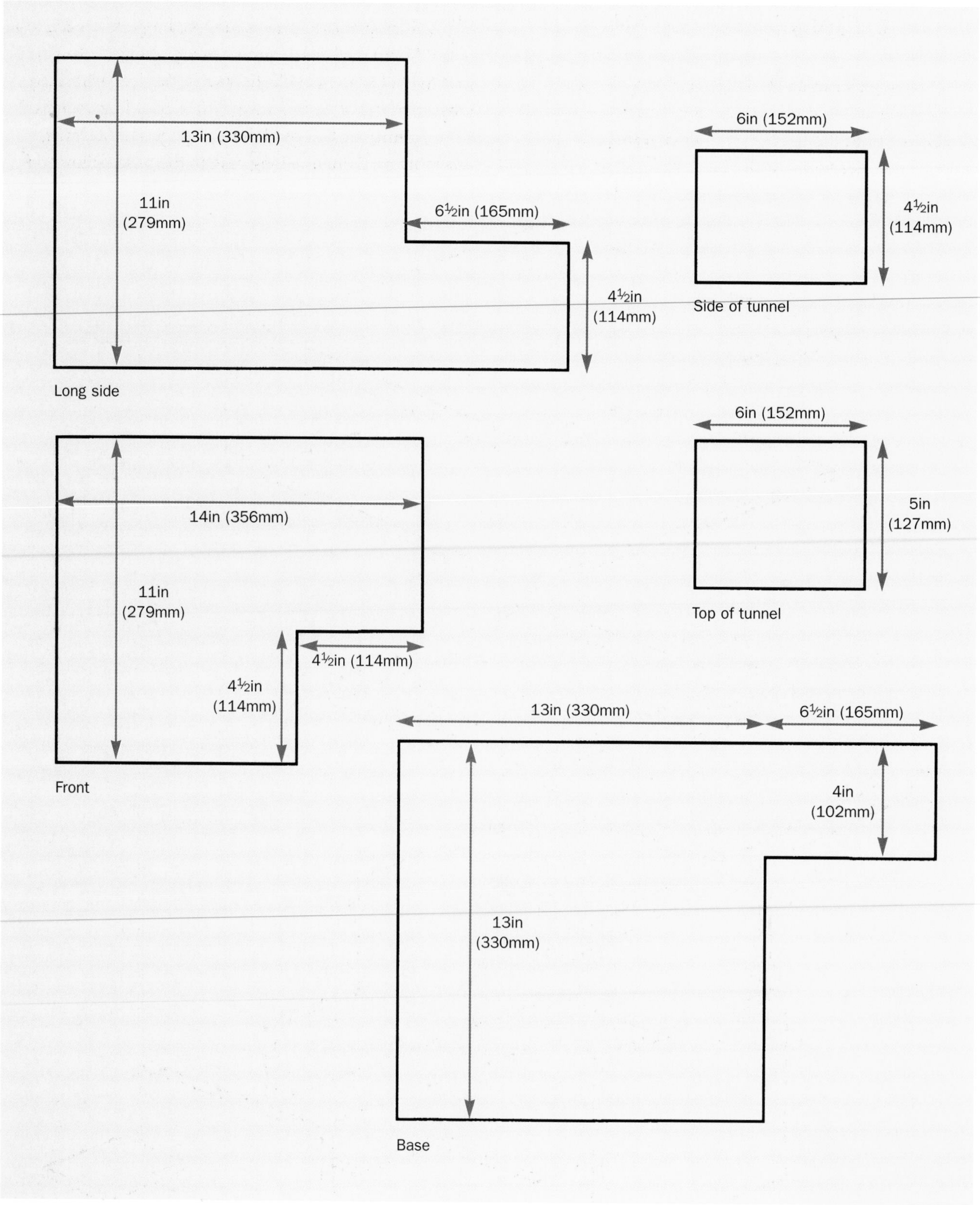

13in (330mm)
11in (279mm)
6½in (165mm)
4½in (114mm)
Long side

6in (152mm)
4½in (114mm)
Side of tunnel

14in (356mm)
11in (279mm)
4½in (114mm)
4½in (114mm)
Front

6in (152mm)
5in (127mm)
Top of tunnel

13in (330mm)
6½in (165mm)
4in (102mm)
13in (330mm)
Base

Fig 25.3
Some of the plywood parts with dimensions.

CONSTRUCTION

1 On a large sheet of plywood mark out all the components as economically and squarely as possible. Cut out the shapes with a panel saw and smooth the edges with a jack plane and glasspaper.

2 All the plywood panels are fixed together using 1in (25mm) oval brads and waterproof glue. To ensure that the holes do not split the layers of ply, particularly when they are close to an edge, drill pilot holes with a 1/16in (1.5mm) drill. (*See* Chapter 2, page 11.) Start the assembly by fixing the long side to the base, followed

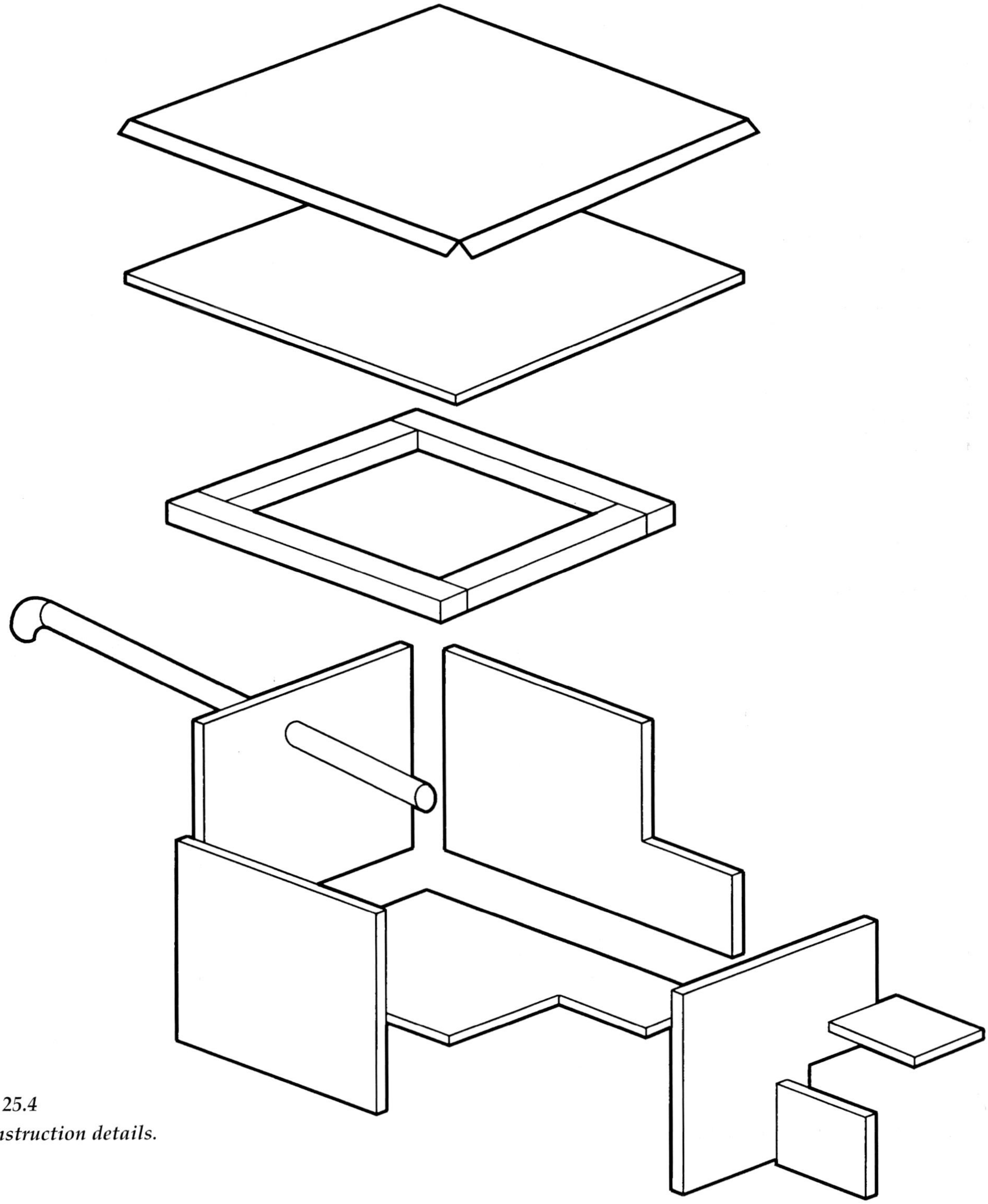

Fig 25.4
Construction details.

by the front panel, then the short side and the back (*see* Fig 25.5). Fix the side of the tunnel to the base and to the front panel by nailing from the inside. Treat the top of the tunnel in the same way (*see* Fig 25.6).

3 Cut four softwood battens to size and fix them to the underside of the lid (*see* Fig 25.7). They help to position it correctly when it is fitted. The lid is not fixed in place, but is removable, to allow cleaning.

Fig 25.5
Fitting the short side.

Fig 25.7
A view of the underside of the lid.

Fig 25.6
Applying glue before fitting the roof to the entrance.

4 To provide extra ventilation drill a ⅞in (22mm) hole in the top of the back panel, fit a ⅞in (22mm) copper pipe into this, and attach a 90° elbow to the protruding end. Both the tubing and the elbow are available from plumbers' suppliers. The tube should protrude from the leaves and twigs that cover the box after it is installed.

Fig 25.8
Fitting the ventilation pipe.

Fig 25.9
The shelter with roofing fitted.

Finishing

1 Cover the lid with waterproof roofing felt (*see* Chapter 2, page 19), using ½in (12mm) galvanized clout nails to hold it in place.

Fig 25.9
Cross section of box after installation.

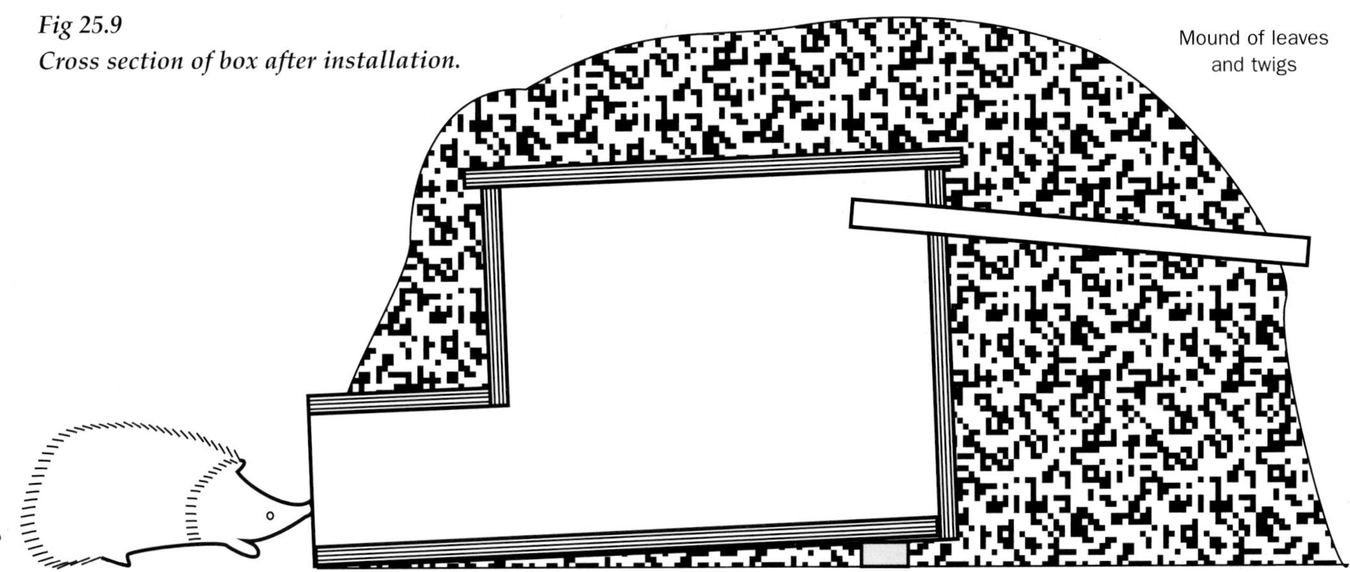

METRIC CONVERSION TABLE

INCHES TO MILLIMETRES AND CENTIMETRES

in	mm	cm	in	cm	in	cm
1/8	3	0.3	9	22.9	30	76.2
1/4	6	0.6	10	25.4	31	78.7
3/8	10	1.0	11	27.9	32	81.3
1/2	13	1.3	12	30.5	33	83.8
5/8	16	1.6	13	33.0	34	86.4
3/4	19	1.9	14	35.6	35	88.9
7/8	22	2.2	15	38.1	36	91.4
1	25	2.5	16	40.6	37	94.0
1 1/4	32	3.2	17	43.2	38	96.5
1 1/2	38	3.8	18	45.7	39	99.1
1 3/4	44	4.4	19	48.3	40	101.6
2	51	5.1	20	50.8	41	104.1
2 1/2	64	6.4	21	53.3	42	106.7
3	76	7.6	22	55.9	43	109.2
3 1/2	89	8.9	23	58.4	44	111.8
4	102	10.2	24	61.0	45	114.3
4 1/2	114	11.4	25	63.5	46	116.8
5	127	12.7	26	66.0	47	119.4
6	152	15.2	27	68.6	48	121.9
7	178	17.8	28	71.1	49	124.5
8	203	20.3	29	73.7	50	127.0

Conservation Organizations

The Royal Society for the Protection of Birds (RSPB)
The Lodge, Sandy, Bedfordshire SG19 2DL
Tel: 01767 680551

The British Hedgehog Preservation Society
Knowbury House, Knowbury, Ludlow,
Shropshire SY8 3LQ
Tel: 01584 890 801

The Bat Conservation Trust
45 Shelton Street, London WC2H 9HJ
Tel: 0171 240 0933

English Nature
Northminster House, Peterborough PE1 1UA
Tel: 01733 340345

Suppliers of Food for Wild Birds

CJ Wildbird Foods Ltd
The Rea, Upton Magna, Shrewsbury SY4 4UB
Tel: 01743 709545

John E Haith Ltd
Park Street, Cleethorpes, Humberside DN35 7NF
Tel: 01472 357515

BLACKBIRD

About the Author

Since giving up his day job in the electronics pre-press industry, Dave Mackenzie now divides his time between lecturing – on graphic design, DTP and magazine journalism – and woodworking.

This is his second book, following a couple of hundred magazine articles on woodworking and DIY published over the last 20 years, ranging from furniture design to kite making and much else in between. His first book, *Pine Furniture Projects*, is also published by Guild of Master Craftsman Publications.

Dave Mackenzie is married with two children and enjoys painting, walking and twitching.

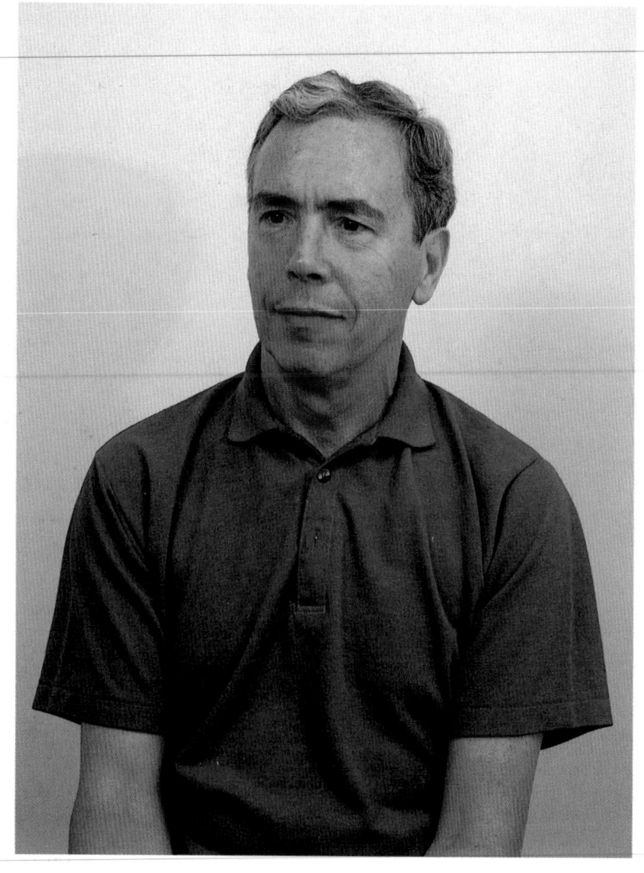

Index

TITLES AVAILABLE FROM
GMC Publications

BOOKS

WOODWORKING

40 More Woodworking Plans & Projects .... *GMC Publications*
Bird Boxes and Feeders for the Garden .... *Dave Mackenzie*
Complete Woodfinishing .... *Ian Hosker*
Electric Woodwork .... *Jeremy Broun*
Furniture & Cabinetmaking Projects .... *GMC Publications*
Furniture Projects .... *Rod Wales*
Furniture Restoration (Practical Crafts) .... *Kevin Jan Bonner*
Furniture Restoration and Repair for Beginners ..... *Kevin Jan Bonner*
Green Woodwork .... *Mike Abbott*
The Incredible Router .... *Jeremy Broun*
Making & Modifying Woodworking Tools .... *Jim Kingshott*
Making Chairs and Tables .... *GMC Publications*
Making Fine Furniture .... *Tom Darby*
Making Little Boxes from Wood .... *John Bennett*
Making Shaker Furniture .... *Barry Jackson*
Pine Furniture Projects for the Home .... *Dave Mackenzie*
Sharpening Pocket Reference Book .... *Jim Kingshott*
Sharpening: The Complete Guide .... *Jim Kingshott*
Stickmaking: A Complete Course .... *Andrew Jones & Clive George*
Woodfinishing Handbook (Practical Crafts) .... *Ian Hosker*
Woodworking Plans and Projects .... *GMC Publications*
The Workshop .... *Jim Kingshott*

WOODTURNING

Adventures in Woodturning .... *David Springett*
Bert Marsh: Woodturner .... *Bert Marsh*
Bill Jones' Notes from the Turning Shop .... *Bill Jones*
Bill Jones' Further Notes from the Turning Shop .... *Bill Jones*
Colouring Techniques for Woodturners .... *Jan Sanders*
Decorative Techniques for Woodturners .... *Hilary Bowen*
Essential Tips for Woodturners .... *GMC Publications*
Faceplate Turning .... *GMC Publications*
Fun at the Lathe .... *R.C. Bell*
Illustrated Woodturning Techniques .... *John Hunnex*
Intermediate Woodturning Projects .... *GMC Publications*
Keith Rowley's Woodturning Projects .... *Keith Rowley*
Make Money from Woodturning .... *Ann & Bob Phillips*
Multi-Centre Woodturning .... *Ray Hopper*
Pleasure and Profit from Woodturning .... *Reg Sherwin*
Practical Tips for Turners & Carvers .... *GMC Publications*
Practical Tips for Woodturners .... *GMC Publications*
Spindle Turning .... *GMC Publications*
Turning Miniatures in Wood .... *John Sainsbury*
Turning Wooden Toys .... *Terry Lawrence*
Understanding Woodturning .... *Ann & Bob Phillips*
Useful Techniques for Woodturners .... *GMC Publications*
Useful Woodturning Projects .... *GMC Publications*
Woodturning: A Foundation Course .... *Keith Rowley*
Woodturning: A Source Book of Shapes .... *John Hunnex*
Woodturning Jewellery .... *Hilary Bowen*
Woodturning Masterclass .... *Tony Boase*
Woodturning Techniques .... *GMC Publications*
Woodturning Test Reports .... *GMC Publications*
Woodturning Wizardry .... *David Springett*

The Art of the Woodcarver .... *GMC Publications*
Carving Birds & Beasts .... *GMC Publications*
Carving on Turning .... *Chris Pye*
Carving Realistic Birds .... *David Tippey*
Decorative Woodcarving .... *Jeremy Williams*
Essential Tips for Woodcarvers .... *GMC Publications*
Essential Woodcarving Techniques .... *Dick Onians*
Lettercarving in Wood: A Practical Course .... *Chris Pye*
Practical Tips for Turners & Carvers .... *GMC Publications*
Understanding Woodcarving .... *GMC Publications*
Useful Techniques for Woodcarvers .... *GMC Publications*
Wildfowl Carving - Volume 1 .... *Jim Pearce*
Wildfowl Carving - Volume 2 .... *Jim Pearce*
The Woodcarvers .... *GMC Publications*
Woodcarving: A Complete Course .... *Ron Butterfield*
Woodcarving: A Foundation Course .... *Zoë Gertner*
Woodcarving for Beginners .... *GMC Publications*
Woodcarving Test Reports .... *GMC Publications*
Woodcarving Tools, Materials & Equipment .... *Chris Pye*

UPHOLSTERY

Seat Weaving (Practical Crafts) .... *Ricky Holdstock*
Upholsterer's Pocket Reference Book .... *David James*
Upholstery: A Complete Course .... *David James*
Upholstery Restoration .... *David James*
Upholstery Techniques & Projects .... *David James*

Toymaking

Designing & Making Wooden Toys .... *Terry Kelly*
Fun to Make Wooden Toys & Games .... *Jeff & Jennie Loader*
Making Board, Peg & Dice Games .... *Jeff & Jennie Loader*
Making Wooden Toys & Games .... *Jeff & Jennie Loader*
Restoring Rocking Horses .... *Clive Green & Anthony Dew*

Dolls' Houses

Architecture for Dolls' Houses .... *Joyce Percival*
Beginners' Guide to the Dolls' House Hobby .... *Jean Nisbett*
The Complete Dolls' House Book .... *Jean Nisbett*
Dolls' House Bathrooms: Lots of Little Loos .... *Patricia King*
Easy to Make Dolls' House Accessories .... *Andrea Barham*
Make Your Own Dolls' House Furniture .... *Maurice Harper*
Making Dolls' House Furniture .... *Patricia King*
Making Georgian Dolls' Houses .... *Derek Rowbottom*
Making Miniature Oriental Rugs & Carpets ...... *Meik & Ian McNaughton*
Making Period Dolls' House Accessories .... *Andrea Barham*
Making Period Dolls' House Furniture ...... *Derek & Sheila Rowbottom*
Making Tudor Dolls' Houses .... *Derek Rowbottom*
Making Unusual Miniatures .... *Graham Spalding*
Making Victorian Dolls' House Furniture .... *Patricia King*
Miniature Needlepoint Carpets .... *Janet Granger*
The Secrets of the Dolls' House Makers .... *Jean Nisbett*

Crafts

Celtic Knotwork Designs .... *Sheila Sturrock*
Collage from Seeds, Leaves and Flowers .... *Joan Carver*
Complete Pyrography .... *Stephen Poole*
Creating Knitwear Designs .... *Pat Ashforth & Steve Plummer*
Cross Stitch Kitchen Projects .... *Janet Granger*
Cross Stitch on Colour .... *Sheena Rogers*
Embroidery Tips & Hints .... *Harold Hayes*
An Introduction to Crewel Embroidery .... *Mave Glenny*
Making Character Bears .... *Valerie Tyler*
Making Greetings Cards for Beginners .... *Pat Sutherland*
Making Knitwear Fit .... *Pat Ashforth & Steve Plummer*
Needlepoint: A Foundation Course .... *Sandra Hardy*
Pyrography Handbook (Practical Crafts) .... *Stephen Poole*
Tassel Making for Beginners .... *Enid Taylor*
Tatting Collage .... *Lindsay Rogers*
Temari: A Traditional Japanese
Embroidery Technique .... *Margaret Ludlow*

The Home

Home Ownership: Buying and Maintaining ..... *Nicholas Snelling*
Security for the Householder:
Fitting Locks and Other Devices .... *E. Phillips*

VIDEOS

Drop-in and Pinstuffed Seats .... *David James*
Stuffover Upholstery .... *David James*
Elliptical Turning .... *David Springett*
Woodturning Wizardry .... *David Springett*
Turning Between Centres: The Basics .... *Dennis White*
Turning Bowls .... *Dennis White*
Boxes, Goblets and Screw Threads .... *Dennis White*
Novelties and Projects .... *Dennis White*
Classic Profiles .... *Dennis White*
Twists and Advanced Turning .... *Dennis White*
Sharpening the Professional Way .... *Jim Kingshott*
Sharpening Turning & Carving Tools .... *Jim Kingshott*
Bowl Turning .... *John Jordan*
Hollow Turning .... *John Jordan*
Woodturning: A Foundation Course .... *Keith Rowley*
Carving a Figure: The Female Form .... *Ray Gonzalez*
The Router: A Beginner's Guide .... *Alan Goodsell*
The Scroll Saw: A Beginner's Guide .... *John Burke*

MAGAZINES

Woodturning ◆ Woodcarving ◆ Furniture & Cabinetmaking
The Router ◆ The Dolls' House Magazine
Creative Ideas for the Home ◆ BusinessMatters

◆

The above represents a full list of all titles currently published or scheduled to be published. All are available direct from the Publishers or through bookshops, newsagents and specialist retailers. To place an order, or to obtain a complete catalogue, contact:

GMC Publications,
166 High Street, Lewes, East Sussex BN7 1XU, United Kingdom
Tel: 01273 488005 Fax: 01273 478606

Orders by credit card are accepted